POLITICS AND FREEDOM

Human Will and Action
in the Thought of
Hannah Arendt

Gabriel Masooane Tlaba
Pius XII College

UNIVERSITY
PRESS OF
AMERICA

Lanham • New York • London

Copyright © 1987 by

University Press of America,® Inc.

4720 Boston Way
Lanham, MD 20706

3 Henrietta Street
London WC2E 8LU England

British Cataloging in Publication Information Available

Library of Congress Cataloging-in-Publication Data

Tlaba, Gabriel Masooane, 1948-
 Politics and freedom.

 Bibliography: p.
 1. Arendt, Hannah—Contributions in political
science. 2. Arendt, Hannah—Contributions in
liberty. I. Title.
JC251.A74T57 1987   320.5'092'4   87-13287
ISBN 0-8191-6468-2 (alk. paper)
ISBN 0-8191-6469-0 (pbk. : alk. paper)

All University Press of America books are produced on acid-free
paper which exceeds the minimum standards set by the National
Historical Publication and Records Commission.

To Ausi Mojabeng, Hlasoa, Seaja and 'Mope

TABLE OF CONTENTS

INTRODUCTION   xiv

CHAPTER I - FREEDOM AND ACTION   1
    Natality   2
    Motives and Goals   5
    On Homo Faber and Animal Laborans   7
    Principled Action   16
    Plurality   20
    The Disclosure of The Actor   21
    Appearance   27
    Conclusion   30
    Notes   33

CHAPTER II - FREEDOM AND POLITICS   36
    The Pre-philosophic Greek Polis   38
    The Roman Foundation of Order   42
    Revolution   48
    Freedom as Participation   55
    Councils   59
    Conclusion   61
    Notes   66

CHAPTER III - NON-POLITICAL ISSUES
    AND THE PUBLIC SPHERE   69
    Labor and Work   69
    Socio-economic Factors   76
    Force and Violence   82
    Liberation or Freedom?   87
    Critique   90
    Notes   93

CHAPTER IV - TOTALITARIANISM   95
    Totalitarian Organization   96
    Ideology and Terror   101
    Concentration Camps   104
    Totalitarianism and Modernity   108
    Critics   110
    Conclusion   120
    Notes   122

CHAPTER V - PHILOSOPHICAL FREEDOM   124
    Inner Freedom   125
    Thinking   126
    Willing   133
    The Faculty of Judgment   140
    Freedom and Necessity   146

TABLE OF CONTENTS

Conclusion   153
Notes   153

CHAPTER VI - CONTINUITY IN ARENDT'S THOUGHT   156
Apparent Shift in Arendt's Thought   156
Continuity in Arendt's Notion of Freedom   159
(i)   Appearing before others   161
(ii)   The connection between the role of
         intellect and the role of public   163
(iii)   Seventeenth and eighteenth century
         view of freedom as pre-political   167
General Problems with Arendt's Analysis   170
Conclusion   177
Notes   179

CONCLUSION   181

BIBLIOGRAPHY   188

ACKNOWLEDGMENTS

My sincere appreciation goes to professors Benoit Garceau and Hilliard Aronovitch, who have been the sensitive and insightful critics to the development of the structure and ideas of this book.

Thanks also should go to Fr. McComber, O.M.I., who has been instrumental in the preparation of the final manuscript.

INTRODUCTION

Each of Hannah Arendt's major works, at least prior to her last work,The Life of the Mind (1978), presented itself as an analysis of the situation of man with the purpose of exploring the nature of human freedom.1 Freedom has been the dominant theme of her work, and, as it has been observed, it is "her literary raison d'être; the very reason for her writing at all".2 Her investigation has been constantly guided by three basic presuppositions: that modern man has lost freedom as it was once experienced in the ancient Greek polis; that man's political life and its traditional values have been destroyed; and that to achieve a model of an order compatible with human freedom a return to the Greek notion of politics is absolutely essential.

Hannah Arendt's interest in freedom and her conviction that freedom is inseparable from a certain way of political life have gradually emerged from her own experiences and native disposition. First, she experienced some of the most convulsive political events of our time, the Nazi seizure of power and the beginning of the destruction of the Jews.3 Second, she had a lifelong affection for Hellenic politics, philosophy and culture. Finally, she received solid training in existentialist thought from the finest German philosophical minds of her time.

Born in Hanover, Germany, in 1906, Hannah Arendt was the only child of Jewish parents. From an early age she developed a spirit of independence and an attitude of pride in her identity as a Jew. At school she was tormented by anti-Semites as well as by other Jewish children. Later she became deeply involved with Jewish issues, which sparked her first work, Rahel Varnhagen: The Life of a Jewess, and influenced the rest. Even after leaving Germany in 1933 for Paris, France, she still dedicated herself to the Jewish cause through Zionist organizations.

At school, Hannah Arendt studied Greek and developed such a liking of Greek culture that, as a gymnasium student, she formed a group that read and translated Greek texts. In addition to taking courses on Greek political theory, she later often met with friends in her apartment to read Plato and other Greek classics. Thus, it was easy for her to trace the origin of Western ideas of culture and freedom to the classical ages of ancient Greece and Rome.

The life of the Aristotelian Greek polis constituted the heart of all her thought. For her, the time of the Greek polis was the most important period of political history, the period in which man "appeared" at his best. It represented the first historical appearance of political association, that is, it marked the beginning of the Western tradition of politics. The Greek polis determined both her definition and her system of politics. By emphasizing certain features of Greek political life, she put together a conceptual framework that gives us an idealized realm, a golden age for which she yearned.

From the Greek polis she also derived the dichotomies around which her thought revolved. In the Greek understanding of things, private life was the sphere in which household matters, such as happiness, economic security and material satisfaction, were taken care of. Public life was reserved for free speech and action. From this distinction between the private and the public life Hannah Arendt deduced the existence of two fundamental poles: necessity and freedom. She described the tension between these poles not only as the opposition between the public and the private, but also as the opposition between the political and the social, the city anf the household, the vita activa and the vita contemplativa.

The dichotomies formed the core of her notion of politics. Based upon them, for example, were her rejection of modernity and her condemnation of totalitarianism. In her major philosophical work, The Human Condition, she not only analyzed human action and its relationship to freedom, she also criticized past and present cultures because of their failure to provide the realm in which man can achieve freedom. She rejected the modern world because the social realm, which grew out of the private realm, eventually engulfed both public and private sectors and overshadowed traditional political concerns with pseudo-political economic concerns. She pointed out the destructive implications of the rise of the social realm and contrasted them with the political freedom of the polis. Referring to the same distinction between the private and the public, she attacked revolutions like the French Revolution and favoured others like the American Revolution. Likewise, she rejected liberalism's role in consolidating the triumph of economics over politics and Marx's economic theory.

Hannah Arendt became more convinced than ever of the destructive effects of deprivation of public space when her own public space was cut off by the rise of Hitler. She regarded totalitarianism as the antithesis of the polis because it destroyed the public realm and eliminated man's spontaneity and capacity for free action. All her works contain urgent pleas, heightened by her awareness of totalitarianism, for the revival of politics in terms of the polis, and reveal her passion for freedom.

While it is true that the reality of totalitarianism changed what was a philosophical mood into a committed political position, Hannah Arendt's political arguments never ceased to be guided by an existential outlook. Her German philosophical education as well as her philosophical concern with individual freedom   predated her work on totalitarianism.   At Marburg University she responded to the systematic form of existentialism taught there by Martin Heidegger.   She also studied with Heidegger's mentor, Edmund Husserl, at Freiburg before moving to Heidelberg where she studied under Karl Jaspers and received a Ph.D. in 1928 for her thesis Der Liebesbegriff bei Augustin.

From Heidegger Arendt learned to appreciate the need for essence and existence to coincide, an idea that later served as the inspiration for her theory of political action.   From Heidegger's conclusions she drew the metaphysical inferences necessary to support her view of political action as the arena that reveals who the individual is.

Although it is clear from many of her works that Arendt was indebted to Heidegger, it was Jaspers who had the most significant philosophical influence on her.   She found that Jaspers' philosophy of communication ensured the individual freedom in a world composed of others as neither Augustine's philosophy of free will nor Kant's theory of reason could do.   Arendt considered communication, which was for Jaspers a requisite to self-revelation, to be the sine qua non of politics and freedom.   It became the   core of her egalitarian existentialism.   She claimed:

> Speech corresponds to the fact of distinctness and is the
> actualization of the human condition of plurality, that is, of
> of living as a distinct and unique being among equals.4

Her concern was to extricate persons from whatever absorbs or destroys their basic human qualities of speech and action.   In On Revolution she showed, through her examination of the American and French revolutions, how political freedom becomes a reality when men are brought together for discussion, persuasion, decision and action.

While we can determine what Arendt inherited from both Heidegger and Jaspers, it is quite difficult to say what she derived from existentialism and such because it cannot be defined by means of a set of philosophical themes. However, the   existentialism   that influenced her in general involved both the analysis of the basic structures of existence and a call of individuals to an awareness of their existence in its essential freedom. But such freedom, as in the main tradition of Western political theory, was understood to mean either freedom of the will or inner freedom. It was not considered to be the worldly public phenomenon.

In summary, to understand Hannah Arendt's notion of freedom it is important to understand her as a German Jew who lived during the darkest time in the modern history of the Jewish people, as a scholar with a foundation in classics and German philosophy, and as someone who had studied under the great minds of her time.

The main thesis developed in Hannah Arendt't works prior to The Life of the Mind was that there is an essential link between freedom and politics. She considered freedom the raison d'être of politics, by which she meant that politics was the locus of freedom, the public realm in which action and full humandevelopment are possible. The link she made between freedom and politics was so strong that at times she seemed to be saying that freedom is an attribute of politics. She presented freedom neither as a mere condition nor simple consequence of politics, but as politics itself. Even when she talked about participation, she asserted that participation and action are part of freedom, in which case politics and freedom are virtually the same. At other times she simply claimed that wherever there is politics, there is freedom. While it is the purpose of this book to examine and determine what Arendt means by the statement "Freedom is the raison d'être of politics", it is quite clear that all her works prior to The Life of the Mind are pervaded by her emphasis on the relationship of freedom and politics.

As the "raison d'être of politics", freedom cannot be something private. Ever since Plato, the philosopher's abstention from the public realm (politics) was regarded as the highest and the freest way of life, the vita contemplativa. Philosophers made various attempts, both theoretical and practical, to escape from politics altogether.5 They thought they could attain immortality through contemplation rather than through action. They were concerned with eternal truths rather than with performing immortal deeds. They lived in mental solitude rather than in the public arena of men of action. Christians also, from at least the time of St. Augustine, have demanded to be absolved from the concerns of the public realm in order to be free. For them freedom has been regarded as an activity of the (inner) will and of thought, rather than as a characteristic of action. They took freedom to mean free choice. Arendt found Sartre andHeidegger to be excellent examples of genuine philosophic minds quite incapable of appreciating freedom as a worldly or political phenomenon.

Arendt observed that our notion of freedom is derived from these anti-political philosophical and Christian traditions. She reacted against these traditions; where they saw freedom as the possession of private individuals, she saw it as something enjoyed in public; where they thought of it as isolation, she saw it as an action among one's peers. Arendt advocated a type of freedom that was opposed to the "interiorization of life". She claimed that freedom as related to politics is not a phenomenon of mere will or choice (liberum arbitrium), but the freedom to call into being something that did not exist before.6 She therefore rejected any tendency to locate freedom in an inner domain of the mind. She focussed on freedom in political, not private, terms.

In 1962 the state of Israel brought Adolf Eichmann to trial. By virtue of this event, so carefully observed by Arendt as a reporter of the New Yorker, she was forced to recast her formulation of political freedom and return to a more basic premise concerning the cause of man's action. She began a kind of epistemological inquiry different from her exploration of the political freedom. Rather than exploring further the problem of political freedom, she began to consider the freedom of the mind's faculties and the relationship between intellectual freedom and political freedom. She did this in more detail in her work, The Life of the Mind, where she tried to reveal the nature of thinking, willing and judging.

Hence the problem with which this book is concerned: discontinuity versus continuity in the thought of Hannah Arendt. Her later work seems to deal with metaphysical issues rather than the political ones. Does she really change her earlier views in her later work?

I intend to demonstrate that, throughout her life, Arendt was preoccupied with establishing the primacy of political freedom over the inwardly philosophical, and that she consistently posited freedom in its true sense to be a political phenomenon. I will try to reveal the nexus between political and inner freedom in the formulation of her unique notion of freedom. I shall demonstrate that, for her, political freedom and the freedom of the will are complementary, although not concurrent.

The connection Arendt makes between political and philosophical freedom has not been given serious consideration, probably for fear of imposing a degree of cohesion on her work that she herself did not create. Many of those who have discussed her notion of political freedom have ignored her final concern with inner freedom, either because they wrote before the publication of her last work or simply because they did not find it relevant. Those who did mention her views on both political and inner freedom accused her of being inconsistent. I assume that there is a point of connection between her notion of political freedom and that of philosophical freedom without which her idea of freedom and her central concept of politics cannot be fully understood.

INTRODUCTION

The structure of this study is partly dictated by the logic of Arendt's views. Chapter I provides clarification of her theory of action. I will demonstrate how Arendt takes action as freedom's field of experience. Chapter II contains a description of historical models of political freedom. In Chapter III, I analyze her exclusion of socio--economic issues from public sphere. This analysis highlights a sharp distiction she makes between the political and the social realm: the latter involves necessity manifested in labor; the former involves freedom manifested in action. It underlines a distinction she makes between liberty and freedom.Chapter IV is on the collapse of freedom; in it I present totalitarianism as a symbol of the death of freedom. Chapter V is an assessment of her notion of philosophical freedom. Finally, in Chapter VI I test the internal consistency of her notion of freedom and suggest whether it needs to be revised.

INTRODUCTION

NOTES

1. By Arendt's major works I mean the following (listed chronologically):Der Liebesbegriff bei Augustin (1929). This is her doctoral dissertation, which she attempted to translate and clarify but gave up the idea because it was too much work. Rahel Varnhagen: The life of a Jewish Woman (1974). Her first involvement with Jewish issues is found in this work, which is a biography of a lady who is very much like Arendt herself. The Jew as Pariah (1978). This is a collection of essays on Jewish issues from 1942. The Origins of Totalitarianism (1951). This gives an analysis of anti-Semitism, imperialism and totalitarianism. Though one may legitimately doubt the historical accuracy of this work, one can find evidence of the dangers of mass culture. However, this work does not have much analysis of the human condition or of freedom. Men in Dark Times (1968). This work was written between 1955 and 1965. It is too much a narrative of too biographical and yet it provides illustration of the freedom of which men are capable as well as the stifling effects (dark times) of modern "society". Between Past and Future (1968). It contains eight essays written from 1957. She refers to those essays as "exercises in political thoughts" because that is where she deals with several topics like, tradition, history, authority, freedom, culture, education and truth in politics. The Human Condition (1958). This is her major philosophical work in which she analyzez the human action and its relation to freedom, and also criticizes history and modern cultures because of their failure to provide the realm in which man can act and achieve freedom. Eichmann in-Jerusalem (1963). It is in this work that we find Arendt's shift from exploring the problem of political freedom to considering the freedom of the mind's faculties and the relationship between the mental freedom and political freedom. This trend of thought is worked out in more details in her last work, The Life of the Mind, published posthumously in 1978. It is the two-volume work which we shall refer to, from now on, simply as Thinking and Willing. On Revolution (1965). In this work she examines the American Revolution and the French Revolution and shows how political freedom becomes a reality when men are brought together for discussion, persuasion, decision and action. For her, revolution's attempt to found a new body politic may lead to the rediscovery of freedom which once existed during the ancient Greek and Roman times. Crisis of the Republic (1972) is made up of several essays among which "On violence" provides us with Arendt's illumination of the distinction between power and violence and the role that power plays in maintaining the arena for action.

2.Wayne Francis Allen, "The Concept of Authority in the Thought of Hannah Arendt", unpublished dissertation (University of California Riverside, 1979), p. 198.

3 The details of Hannah Arendt's life can be found in her biography by Elisabeth Young-Bruehl, Hannah Arendt: For the Love of the World (New Haven and London: Yale University Press, 1982).

4 The Human Condition, p.178.

5 Ibid., p. 222.

6 Ibid., p. 165.

CHAPTER I

FREEDOM AND ACTION

Hannah Arendt has a tendency to define her key concepts in terms of other concepts. For example, the concept of labor is part of the definition of the concept of necessity and vice versa; and both labor and necessity are part of the definition of the private. She does the same thing with the concepts of freedom and action. She links them and claims that "action and politics among all the capabilities and potentialities of human life, are the only things which we could not even conceive without at least assuming that freedom exists".[1]

In this chapter I propose to explore some of the features of her conception of action. I hope to show why and how she asserts that freedom is synonymous with action. In order to achieve this goal it is essential to recognize that two facts about human condition, natality and plurality, serve as Arendt's starting point in her theory of the public-political realm. In these facts lies the basis of action and freedom. I will clarify what Arendt means by natality and by her claim that action is needed to actualize man's freedom, which is ontologically rooted in his birth. Then, I will examine the notion of plurality through her idea that only a man who abandons labor and work in order to engage in action can properly be described as human and truly free, and her idea that disclosure of the agent in speech and action is essential to freedom. Some of the topics dealt with in this chapter will, naturally, reappear in later chapters.

Of Arendt's works it is The Human Condition which bears most directly on the question of action and freedom.[2] In this work she expresses her concern for the loss of freedom in our time. She reverts to Greek political life to remind us of what freedom once meant. She also relates her conception of freedom to concepts of labor, work, action and thought as based in Greek and particularly Aristotelian thought. Aristotle considered that neither labor nor work possessed sufficient dignity to be termed a way of life (bios) at all, since they were not "autonomous and authentically human" activities. Arendt contends that "action", the highest form of activity for the Greeks, is less valued in the modern world than it was in the Ancient Greek polis. She recognizes the fact that during the Socratic era thought was more valued than action but labor was never considered more important than action. However, she complains that in the modern world labor has acquired a dignity which has placed it above all other activities and lifted it out of the oblivion of the private realm to which the Greeks consigned it. People are now preoccupied with the activity of laboring, that is, the activity keyed to the maintenance of life such as producing and consuming food.

Some philosophers, for example Kant in his Critique of Pure Reason, say that action is not essential to freedom, that man is free

1

whether he acts or not, that he is free so long as he can choose.3 For those philosophers who associate freedom with will or the faculty of choice, the connection of freedom to action is secondary. Arendt takes a different view of freedom. For her, man is potentially free by the mere fact of birth. This potential freedom is ontologically rooted in birth or what she calls the condition of "natality"; "natality" implies not just that we are mortal, but also that each of us represents something new and unique in the world and is capable of doing the unexpected and acting in ways that no role-prescriptions can foresee. So for her freedom cannot be manifest in "behavior", "role-playing", "doing a job", "belonging to a class" and the automatism of activities in the private realm, but instead in genuine speech and action.

Natality

Arendt discusses the Greek word archein, which she translates as "to begin", "to lead" and eventually "to rule", to set something in motion (which is the original meaning of the Latin agere).4 From this she comes to the conclusion that because they are initia, newcomers and beginners by virtue of birth, men can take initiative, are prompted into action.5

It is difficult to see why Arendt links action with natality and claims that "action as beginning corresponds to the fact of birth...it is the actualization of the human condition of natality".6 Action reflects the fact of human birth or natality because for Arendt action means to begin and innovate something that was not there, something unexpected and infinitely improbable. In the same way, with each birth something uniquely new comes into the world. Now to act freely, Arendt affirms, is precisely to take an intitiative, to start something new, to change things and to do or say something that could not have been foreseen or expected.

It is, however, quite difficult to grasp why Arendt concludes that man is capable of new, spontaneous beginnings just because through his birth he represents a new beginning in the world. She simply asserts that a man is capable of the unexpected and the infinitely improbable because each man is unique, each birth brings something uniquely new into the world.

It is also not apparent how, from the passive state of being born, one becomes a potential beginner. Arendt only tells us that one's natality is not fulfilled unless one acts. She asserts that it is only when one assumes responsibility for being a new beginning in the

2

world by deliberately beginning something new on one's own initiative that the condition of natality is fulfilled. According to her, action enables each man to fulfill his natality, his being something new by beginning something new. It thus enables men to "actualize the sheer passive givenness of their being...."7

Some clarification of Arendt's thinking comes from realizing that her initiative is derived in part from St.Augustine. She quotes St.Augustine: "Initium ergo ut esset, creatus est homo, ante quem nullus fuit /That there might be a beginning, man was created, before whom nobody was/."8 For Arendt, St.Augustine's supreme insight is that man, being created in the image of God, is radically free; like God, he is himself a creator who is unique and therefore capable of initiating something entirely new. She interprets the above quotation from St.Augustine thus:

> Here, man has not only the capacity of beginning, but is this beginning himself. If the creation of man coincides with the creation of a beginning in the universe (and what else does this mean but the creation of freedom?), then the birth of the individual men, being new beginnings, re-affirms the original character of man in such a way that origin can never become entirely a thing of the past; while, on the other hand, the very fact of the memorable continuity of these beginnings in the sequence of generations guarantees a history which can never end because it is the history of beings whose essence is beginning.9

Arendt describes "the original character of man" as the source of his unique capacity for beginning something which cannot be expected from whatever may have happened before. For her, it is in action that this capacity of beginning is manifested. Her notion of action lies at the basis of her claim that the unprecedented or new is possible in history and cannot be predicated by natural or historical laws.

Again, speaking of Augustine, she writes:

> According to him...God created man as a temporal creature, homo temporalis; time and man were created together, and this temporality was affirmed by the fact that each man owed his life not just to the multiplication of the species, but to birth, the entry of a novel creature who as something entirely new appears in the midst of the time continuum of the world. The purpose of the

3

creation was to make possible a beginning. "That there be a beginning man was created before whom nobody was."...The very capacity for beginning is rooted in natality, and by no means is creativity, not in a gift, but in the fact that human beings, new man, again and again appear in the world by virtue of birth.10

While this passage is found in Arendt's later writings, the point being made occurs also in her early writings:

With the creation of man, the principle of beginning came into the world itself, which of course, is only another way of saying that the principle of freedom was created when man was created.11

Arendt is saying that man's beginning as a radical creation gives him the analogous possibility to create himself anew radically in his actions. But then why does Aredt take over this view of Augustine? Why does she get involved in what is mainly a theologian's problem?

Arendt is interested in Augustine because of the distinction he made between, on the one hand, the creation of heaven and earth (principium), and, on the other, the creation of man (initium). Although she acknowledges that Augustine did not draw out as she herself does the consequences of the phrase "that there might be a beginning, man was created, before whom nobody was", she finds that Augustine made a significant distinction. The beginning of something but The beginning of man is not the same as the beginning of the world:"it is not the beginning of something but of somebody, who is a beginner himself".12 Arendt wants to show that for Augustine one's capacity for innovation is constituted by the nature of the self as a radical beginning. She also wants to rescue the meaningfulness of unique persons from the Immortal cycles of labor and life.

Mortality had always occupied the reflective mind, and it was always the centre of religious and philosophic thought. But natality has been curiously neglected in philosophical doctrine of man. For Arendt, natality is precisely that which defies and transcends the mortality of individual life and the natural cyclical processes which surround it. Each birth itself represents a new creation and new beginning with a potentially eternal significance. Action, because of its relationship to natality, is also a means of possessing immortality.

From the same interdependence of being a beginning and

4

beginning something new, Arendt derives her concept of what she calls the miraculous character of action. The miracle of the new and hence the miracle of action stem from the fact that "something new is started which cannot be expected from whatever may have happened before".13 She asserts that men are able to initiate the unexpected "only because each man is unique, so that with each birth something uniquely new comes into the world".14 This move predicates the unexpectedness of action on the new beginning which each person is by virtue of his uniqueness. Action is unpredictable because no person is absolutely like any other person; therefore, his action can never be indubitably predicted on the pattern of what other actors have done.

Since the capacity for action is founded on freedom, it is naturally "boundless".15 The range of possible actions can never be known or contained a priori. From this notion of unexpectedness in action Arendt goes on to assign an "infinite improbability" to action. By this she means that the novelty engendered by action resists calculation by statistical laws. Arendt distinguishes action both from behavior, which is the predictable and automatic obedience to norms, and from purely instrumental activity, which is merely putting into practice a preconceived plan.

It is clear that action's unpredictability, improbability and boundlessness constantly threaten the political order, because in its pursuit of newness action does not heed the counsel of restraint and moderation. Arendt impatiently dismisses order without freedom as sheer tyranny. Yet what is puzzling is that, because of action's incompatibility with control, the actor is rarely able to fulfill what he intended. What the actor began as a free being and on his own initiative, he can never control. The actor cannot deliberately conclude what he/she set out to do; the actor does not have the freedom to accomplish his/her intention since action is never determined by motive and goals. Let us look at these latter ideas more closely.

Motives and Goals

Free action always marks a new beginning, a beginning that is new even to the motives and goals of the action. Because of its unexpectedness it cannot be limited by motives and goals. This does not mean that it is unrelated to them; it only means that "it is able to transcend them".16 Here Arendt is not talking about action from the usual motivatinal point of view. For example, she is not concerned with analyzing whether or not a passerby who dashes into a burning building to save a child trapped there had in mind the principle

5

of excellence when he acted and how this principle is related to the action performed. Rather, she is concerned with what the action makes manifest to others. Excellence is revealed to others as the act is performed, whether or not the actor had this in mind from the start. As Arendt puts it, freedom is only a yearning of the human heart when it is not made manifest in public, in the company of other men.17 To put the same point differently, the meaning of action cannot be comprehended solely by reference to its motives and goals; and beginning has its source in action itself, not in the thinking about or planning of action. Action as beginning is "not bound into a reliable chain of cause and effect...it is as though the beginner had abolished the sequence of temporality itself".18

Arendt maintains that action, as the introduction of that which is genuinely novel into the world, must transcend all motives and goals of the individual actor and that it cannot be understood in a means-ends framework. If we think of it as undertaken for some specific, practical result, we might judge and regard it in utilitarian, expedient terms. And if we think of it as a product of any antecedent condition or intention, we might regard it as part of a causal chain and lose sight of its free nature.19 According to Arendt, action is its own end, not a means to other ends. By this assertion, Arendt is trying to distiguish action from both labor and work, which she thinks are inescapably part of a means-end series. For example, a worker must have a hammer, nails and wood. These are his means. His end is the finished table. Once this end is arrived at, that is, once the table is finished, it consequently becomes a means to something else. He can use it to write on, etc. In Arendt's view, the means-end chain never terminates unless man sets himself up as the final end, the end in itself. He can achieve this by revealing who he is in the company of other men. As George Kateb observes, Arendt considers action to be free from even emotions and passions such as love, goodness, conscience, compassion, pity and their opposites.20

Kirk Thompson, among others, regards as very inadequate Arendt's claim that action, to be free, must be free from motives, aims or goals, and that it cannot be understood in a means-end framework. For him, it reduces action to an existential life-process without any clarity of purpose.21 If Arendt's conception of action is to have any value, he suggests, it should include a clear specification of the instrumental nature of political action. Otherwise, he finds Arendt's politics as non-purposive. It is important at this point to clarify what Arendt means when she says that action is its own end and what it means to act from a motive, aim or goal.

On Homo Faber and Animal Laborans

Arendt's claim that action is its own end is derived from the distinction she makes between the private and the public, the realm of necessity and the realm of freedom. Through her separation of the realm of necessity from that of freedom she confines all economic matters to the realm of necessity and asserts that socio-economic matters cannot be the goal of action, because action belongs to the realm of freedom. In excluding economic matters from the public realm, she follows the ancient Greeks for whom economic matters belonged strictly to the private realm. Arendt complains that modern man, unlike the ancient Greeks, has lost the true notion of action and human agency because of an attitude of technical efficiency, the practical search for the best means to a pre-conceived end. She also rejects Marx's theory of labor for she thinks it has replaced action with labor. To establish that labor, work and socio-economic matters belong to the realm of necessity and action to that of freedom, Arendt returns to Aristotle and, further, to what informed his thinking--the pre-philosophical experiece of the Greeks.

In Greek antiquity, the private and the public were sharply distinguished. The public was the locus of freedom and action. Admission to the polis meant admission to a public "sphere of freedom", while the private sphere was governed by necessity--not just because of the domination of the master over the family and slaves, but also because the "necessities of life" would rule even the master if he did not have others to provide for him. The household, the private sphere, was considered the locus of economic life; it was the basic unit of production, as is suggested by the Greek word for household (oikia), which is the root of our word "economics". It was the proper place for labor, for activities "related to the maintenance of life", Arendt argues, just as the more direct necessities of bodily function and species reproduction are properly hidden away in privacy.22 For the Greeks, "no activity serving only the purpose of making a living, of sustaining only the life process, was permitted to enter the political realm".23 Anything "economic" was "non-political...by definition", for "everything merely necessary or useful" has to be "strictly excluded" from the bios politikos, the realm of freedom.24 Labor and production cut off man from genuine relations with other men. It chained him to the necessities of biological existence and subordinated him to the laws of nature. The aims of the household were narrowly utilitarian and privatistic. It was the division of labor within the household which produced the patriarchichal hierarchy of master and servant and thus provided the general model for despotic relations, while the concern with household management (oikonomia) later provided the prototype for impersonal bureaucratic administration. Arendt claims that in modern society, labor is the dominant mode of activity. It has been brought out of the private sphere where it once belonged and is now considered a public activity.

In Arendt's opinion, the definition of man in terms of his laboring amid the metabolic processes of life, in which man manifested his kinship with nature rather than the human world, was the worst debasement of the human image. Arendt claims that the modern age is characterized by the shift of allegiance from the life of contemplation (vita contemplativa), as it was understood and implemented by early Christians, to the life of action(vita activa), as understood by Hegel and Marx.25 Her logic of action is drawn from her examination of modern man's unreflective and perilous plunge into doing. This plunge was highlighted by the transformation from the autonomous "worker" (homo faber), who reigned after the initial reversal, to the sheer "laborer" (animal laborans) of the late nineteenth and twentieth centuries.

For Arendt, man as worker, in

> his instrumentalization of the world, his confidence in tools and in the productivity of the maker of artificial objects; his trust in the all-comprehensive range of the means-end category, his conviction that every issue can be solved and every human motivatin reduced to the principle of utility; his sovereignty, which regards everything given as material and thinks of the whole nature as of "an immense fabric from which we can cut out whatever we want to resew it however we like"26

viewed all nature as an instrument to his ends. This worker's attitude reduced the vita activa to sheer human doing. It relegated all things to some end. It also viewed all action as fabrication. Consequently, man's function in this process as the animal laborans came to dominate the vita activa, thereby turning upside down the classic vision of the human order in which the satisfaction of the necessary demands of life was deemed the lowest expression of the active life. All of the vita activa, its wordly institutions of government, of property, of nationhood, and even the technological world of the homo faber became subordinated to the facilitation of the life process. This consummate subordination translated all tasks and faculties into aspects of this process. Men became inured to the process and indeed complacently accepted as the fulfillment of the vita activa this perpetual labor to feed the species. The vita activa lost its connotation of a worldly yet enduring realm where individual actors were remembered for their distinct courses of action; instead, the constant rhythm of the devouring life process effaced the distinct image of men. When Hobbes, Locke and Hume tried to articulate a new vision from within the world view of man as a worker, they identified human action with making and fell victim to the deficiencies of homo faber.

Arendt in her consideration of Kant, Hegel and Marx explores the manner in which the mentality of homo faber and animal laborans became a dominant philosophy in the modern age. In the following passage we can see how she associates Kant with utilitarianism, the philosophy of homo faber:

> The anthropocentric utilitarianism of homo faber has found its greatest expression in the Kantian formula that no man must ever become a means to an end, that every human being is an end in himself...[I]t is only in Kant that the philosophy of the earlier stages of the modern age frees itself entirely of the common sense platitudes which we always find where homo faber rules the standards of society....His formula, however, can no more deny its origin in utilitarian thinking than his other famous and also inherently paradoxical interpretation of man's attitude toward the only objects that are not "for use," namely works of art, in which he said we take "pleasure without any interest."27

It is a bit difficult to see how Arendt links Kant's thought with utilitarianism because Kant's philosophy rests on the categorical imperative, which has nothing to do with consequences and proposed results. Utilitarianism, on the other hand, rests on what Kant calls the hypothetical imperative. For Arendt, they are similar in that they both involve the idea of seeing people as ends in themselves. For both Kant and utilitarianism, each individual is to regard himself and every other person as an end in himself/herself simply because he/she is a rational being and subject to moral laws.

Moreover, I do not think that Kant ever employs the model of homo faber, the model which Arendt is attacking. But this does not reduce the value of her argument against the homo faber mentality. This mentality, when applied to human affairs and actions, disposes men to see and treat each other as objects, means to private ends. It narrows their vision so that they forget their responsibility for the ends and the need to deliberate about ends with their fellow actors.

In the modern world, Arendt argues, it is man as laborer and consumer, the animal laborans, who has been permitted to occupy the public realm, the space reserved for action by the ancient Greeks. She blames Marx for this new development. According to her, Locke's society of property owners and Hobbes' society engaged in acquisition were precursors to Marx's society of producers or laborers. Marx, in valuing the laborers or "job-holders", influenced modern society to value labor's productivity. Both the Marxist and liberal (Adam Smith, John Locke and others) traditions were, in Arendt's view, glorifying what to the ancient Greeks was worthy only of slaves. For Arendt, the patterns of thought inappropriate to action are linked with economics and the social question, with the need for alternatives to both communist dictatorship and interest-group liberalism.

It is essential to explain Arendt's objection to and criticism of Marx in order to understand her view better. Before explaining her criticism of Marx we must remember that for her "work" is distinguished from "labor" by, first, the relative durability of its products, comparatively permanent "use objects", like monuments, against absolutely impermanent "consumer goods", like food; and second, the fact that it is

> performed under the guidance of a model in accordance with which the object is constructed./....an image beheld by the eye of the mind or a blueprint....28

She also distinguishes "labor" from "action" by asserting that it belongs to the realm of necessity while action is a vehicle of human freedom and creativity. Her main complaint against Marx is that

> in all stages of his work he defines man as an animal laborans and then leads him into a society in which this greatest and most human power is no longer necessary. We are left with the rather distressing alternative between productive slavery and unproductive freedom.29

The question is, then, whether Marx and Arendt mean the same thing by this term "labor". Marx discusses the "labor process" in the first volume of Das Kapital.30 Here his concept of labor coincides with Arendt's concept of work. He emphasizes that by labor he is not referring to the first animal-like and instinctive forms of labor, but labor in the form which is peculiar to man. He finds this peculiarity of human labor in the fact that the latter results in something which, at the beginning of the process, already existed as an idea in the worker's imagination. The human laborer not only effects (bewirkt) a change of form in natural objects, as animals and insects do, but at the time also realizes (verwirklicht) his own purpose in nature.31 This idea, as we have just seen, is one of Arendt's criteria of "work".

Furthermore, for Marx, the distinction between "consumer goods" and "use objects" does not constitute an essential demarcation Arendt makes between "labor" and "work". From the point of view of durability, products of labor do not last, whereas products of work, like table and chairs, last relatively longer. For Marx, such a distinction is highly relative and contingent.

In this sense it seems that Marx's labor has characteristics of both what Arendt calls "work" and "labor" in that it refers to providing for the survival of species. It also has some of the characteristics of Arendt's "action" because it is a fundamental form of human praxis. By means of it man creates not only the world but also himself. It is man's chief means to knowledge and development, since as man creates the world and himself, he also creates new social and political structures and new modes of perception and thought.

> The way in which men produce their means of sub-
> sistence...must not be considered simply as being the
> reproduction of the physical existence of the individuals.
> Rather it is...a definite mode of life on their part....As
> individuals express their life, so they are. What they are,
> therefore, coincides with their production, both with what
> they produce and with how they produce. The nature of
> individuals thus depends on the material conditions
> determining their production.

> This production only makes its appearance with the
> increase of population. In its turn this presupposes the
> intercourse (verkehr) of individuals with one another. The
> form of this intercourse is again determined by
> production.32

In trying to mold the objective world into forms which he holds in his imagination, man discovers the laws, independent of him, governing that world. At the same time, in trying to accomplish this transformation of the world he must call upon his own powers and, furthermore, develop them. Therefore, Marx's "labor", like Arendt's "action", raises man above the realm of necessity. Moreover, Marx's "labor" is rational and purposive activity. The objects it creates are not mere use-objects. In the objects he makes and the way he makes them, the laborer discloses himself. As we shall see, one of the chief characteristics of action, according to Arendt, is the disclosure of the agent. It is also important to remark that Marx draws heavily on Hegel's conception that man is the result of his labor.33

It is clear from the above that Marx's concept of labor is different from that of Arendt. For him labor includes Arendt's three basic activities, that is, labor, work and action. While Arendt neatly separates these activities, Marx views them as three different but interrelated dimensions of a single activity. It is from her criticism of Marx that it becomes clear that, in her rigid trichotomous division, labor belongs to the realm of necessity and action to that of freedom. Through her neat separation of the realm of necessity and freedom, we shall see how she manages to confine all economic matters to the realm of necessity. In that way, labor and work are performed for the attainment of socio-economic needs while action is its own end. Arendt concludes that to act, one must be liberated from socio--economic needs. Her exclusion of these socio-economic matters from the public realm is not just because the ancient Greeks confined such matters to the private realm, but also because this idea coincides with the unexpectedness of action.

We have so far seen how Arendt establishes that, because of its unexpectedness, action is an expression of human freedom. We shall now examine why she thinks action's infinite improbability, like its unexpectedness, makes it the highest expression of human freedom. She asserts that action "always happens against the overwhelming odds of statistical laws and their probability."34 She stresses this claim by adding that action is not merely some occurrence in the physical world or some behavioral event. This is similar to the idea found in analytic philosophy of action that "the types of explanations and description required to account for human action are categorically different from those used in the physical sciences...."35 It means we cannot perfect a science which has as its aim the prediction of human actions. I will try to link up Arendt's idea of the "infinite improbability" of action with the parallel concerns of the analytic philosophy of action.36

Arendt makes a sharp distinction between behavior and action, between routine or habit and the radically unpredictable. For her, action, as opposed to behavior and habit, is self-conscious and freely undertaken. It breaks through the bounds of the predictable pattern of natural and social life and begins something new. It is opposed to behavior because behavior is adhering to a routine, conducting oneself in a customary and predictable manner. Her view of behavior and automatic obedience to norms is clearly revealed in her reflection on what she calls "the social".

In the modern world, Arendt argues, the public and private realm have been blurred and largely supplanted by something she calls "society" or "the social", that is, a "relatively new phenomenon whose origin coincides with the emergence of the modern age".37 She regards society in the modern world as a kind of monstrous extension of the old household principle to the whole societal entity. All human activities in the modern world are related to laboring, to the maintenance of life, and the public itself has become a huge household, a social realm. Living in a society largely organized around economic processes means, according to Arendt, that our lives are governed on a grand scale by those motivations and attitudes which in ancient Greece were confined to the privacy of the household.

She claims that whereas in Greek antiquity the public realm was reserved for free action, in the modern world, since the public realm has been invaded by the social, action has been replaced by behavior. The social is a realm of uniformity rather than of individual distinction. It imposes "levelling demands", and conformism is inherent in it because in order to remain as a society its norms and rules have to be obeyed and its members have to conform to its customs. It contrasts with the plurality and distinctness once characteristic of public life. To confirm this she exaggerates:

> Society always demands that its members act as though they were members of one enormous family which has one opinion and one interest.38

She insists that an individual cannot act as he/she wants. Rather he/she has to conform to and behave in accordance with opinions and interests of society. In this way she concludes that society is the realm of behavior. She states this clearly in these words:

> It is decisive that society, on all its levels, excludes the possibility of action, which formerly was excluded from the household. Instead, society expects from each of its members a certain kind of behavior, imposing innumerable and various rules, all of which tend to "normalize" its members, to make them behave, to exclude spontaneous action or outstanding achievement.39

It is clear that Arendt prizes action and dislikes or rejects behavior and modern society for the same reason she rejects Marx's theory of labor. She sees the modern world with it is emphasis on norms as having replaced action with behavior; behavior, not action, is the dominant mode of modern activity.

But, firstly, the sharp distinction she makes between action and behavior is puzzling. It makes her overlook the fact that even customary and routinized acts involve some initiative and judgment. Habits can and are at times broken deliberately when people find them

13

useless or dangerous.   Habits are also developed and consciously cultivated when they are considered useful and fulfilling.   Therefore, at times, behavior and habit can be as self-conscious and freely undertaken as "action" in Arendt's sense.   Secondly, it is difficult to find a society without uniformities of behavior.   Finally, traditional societies, contrary to what Arendt is inclined to believe, are much more ruled by norms, customs, etc., than modern society.   We shall thus try further to see what Arendt has in mind when she says that the modern world with its emphasis on norms has made behavior, rather than action, the dominant mode of activity.   This will help us to understand her assertions about action as opposed to behavior.

Arendt has in mind Rousseau's reflections on contemporary society and the nature of man.   In his first two Discours, as well as in the Lettre à d'Alembert, Rousseau asserts that the artificial uniformity of behavior which society imposes on people causes them to ignore "the duties of man and the needs of nature", so that appearance and reality are constantly at variance in modern social life.
According to Rousseau, modern man lives outside himself; he bases his life on "opinion" rather than "nature", that is, on what others expect him to be rather than on what he really is. This disguising of the real self is the result of a "base and deceptive uniformity" which causes all men to be cast in the same mold.   Rousseau likens the life of contemporary man to the life of the salons and the theatre where people are only too anxious to forget themselves; they do not live in themselves but in others.

In this connection Arendt goes on to say that the sort of equality which existed in the polis of Greek antiquity has, in the modern world, been replaced by conformism, the modern mode of equality.

> This modern equality, based on the conformism inherent in society and possible only because behavior has replaced action as the foremost mode of human relationship, is in every respect different from equality in antiquity, and notably in the Greek city-states.   To belong to the few "equals" (homoioi) meant to be permitted to live among one's peers; but the public realm itself, the polis, was permeated by a fiercely agonal spirit, where everybody had constantly to distinguish himself from all others, to show through unique deeds or achievements that he was the best of all (aien aristeuein).   The public realm, in other words, was reserved for individuality....40

Arendt has both totalitarianism and Eichmann's character in mind as examples of this modern conformism. For her, totalitarianism is a system that is made up of people who cannot be distinguished by their responsible action. They make up the system by conforming to the orders of the leaders. This was the fate of the Jewish people in Europe since the beginning of the nineteenth century, which reached a climax during Hitler's regime. They were reduced to a sheer mass of peole who found themselves discarded or superfluous to the process of history.

Arendt finds that under totalitarianism human order degenerates into a mass society characterized by the monotonous abstract uniformity of millions of human beings who have lost their faith, interest and place in a common world. This mass assumes a strange self-centredness, not based on pride in achievement or even desire to promote the self in a calculating way; rather, the self-centredness is simply based on the biological exigencies of continued existence.

Arendt asserts that totalitarianism brings about robot-like behavior in people. It destroys "spontaneity, man's power to begin something new out of his own resources, something that cannot be explained on the basis of reactions to the environments and events".41 For Arendt, "spontaneity" does not mean that one is not responsible for what one does or that one's actions are the result of irrational forces either within or outside the self. By spontaneity she means cutting through biological processes so as to act independently and responsibly.

Her observation of the Eichmann trial convinced her that Eichmann was a clear example of what totalitarianism does to people. Eichmann regarded his own actions as unavoidable. He felt he had no choice, no opportunity for action, that he was merely obeying forces greater than his own will. He had lost his ability to act out of personal conviction. As a result, he did not dare to initiate anything; instead of acting, he behaved in accordance with the expectations of Hitler's regime. He did what he was told to do by those whose approval he wanted, and he obeyed the law of the land in doing so.

What we have seen so far is that Arendt's principal objection to the behavioralist attitude is precisely the fact that, in its search for uniformities in human behavior, it contributes to the making of a uniform man who knows how to behave efficiently but who does not know how to act responsibly. But there is definitely a connection between the capacity for efficiency and the capacity for responsibility, which Arendt overlooks. People are able to act more responsibly in a meeting, for example, by virtue of governing themselves by rules and knowing that others are doing so as well.

FREEDOM AND ACTION

Principled Action

I have shown what Arendt has in mind by "behavior", that is, expected and predictable activities. The unexpectedness and the unpredictability of action makes action appear arbitrary. But this seeming arbitrariness, Arendt argues, disappears once the true character of action is recognized.

Here is Arendt's key discovery into the grammar or logic of action: action connotes a new beginning only insofar as it perpetuates itself by calling forth other new beginnings, and it only does this by being what she calls "principled action". The main example Arendt gives is that of natality. We have already seen that for her every person is a beginning and that one's birth enables one to call forth other new beginnings when one acts. The potential new beginning signified by each person's entry into the world is fulfilled and confirmed by his initiative in starting a new beginning.

To describe the true nature of action, Arendt introduces the concept of acting from a principle, as distinguished from acting from a motive. She depicts free action as principled action. Borrowing from Montesquieu, she declares that an act is determined to be free, not by its metaphysical character, but by its power to call new things into being. From Kant's Critique of Judgment and Groundwork of the Metaphysics of Morals, she also gets the idea that free action is not undertaken or judged in terms of its adherence to principles. Its freedom is linked to its quality as principled action. For Arendt, the free actions of human beings acquire meaning through their inherent relationship with principles and not statistical norms. In fact, as we have seen, action is not merely some occurrence in the physical world, some behavioral event; it has a meaning. The principles that inspire actions and in terms of which they have their meaning are the same as actions. Actions and principles are coeval.

It is important at this point to try to clarify what it means to act from a principle and what a principle is, according to Arendt. To act from a principle is to act in an impersonal way, that is, not from inner determinations, whether these derive from the assertive will, the calculating intelligence, the impassioned heart or the urges of the body. A principle is not a moral principle in the usual sense. It is an idea or value, general in nature and universal in validity, which comes to one from outside and inspires "from without". It only appears when one acts from it: "the appearance of freedom, like the manifestation of principles, coincides with the performing act".42 Arendt gives these examples: honor, glory, love of equality, distinction, excellence, "but also fear or distrust or hatred". These principles of action can be repeated time and time again. They are made manifest in a free act and last only as long as the freedom is exercised. Though she refers to these principles only in the context of action, they can also be manifested in speech.

Another factor we can observe from the examples Arendt gives is that principles belong to the public realm. They display their validity each time they are acted upon, and their significance is inexhaustible and universal. Men are free, that is, they show something new only when they act on the inspiration of these principles. Only then is their object the action itself, rather than a motive or aim beyond it.

Recent analytic discussions of action may help to explain what Arendt means by principled action. Despite the apparent obscurity of her notion, I think Arendt is struggling with an idea that has become the dominant focus of much post-Wittgenstein philosophy.

Richard J. Bernstein remarks that in the past two decades "action" has come to signify a complex web of issues concerning "intention", "motive", "purpose", "reason", and "teleological explanation" that have dominated analytic investigations.43 The distinction Arendt makes between action and behavior is also an issue among analytic philosophers. The main concern of these philosophers is to show, on one hand, that there is something non-reducible and distinctive about the nature of human action such that it requires a conceptual framework which is radically different from the one which is used in the physical sciences. These "new teleologists"44 believe it is impossible to translate or reduce action concepts into a language restricted to the mechanical regularities of movements. On the other hand are the "reductive analysts", who insist that action concepts can be reduced or translated into an atomistic and mechanical framework or simply into the language of physical science.

What is particularly relevant for our concern is not the tendency of both sides to attempt to resolve the issue by a priori fiat--the reductionists claiming it must be possible to perform such reductions, the teleologists arguing it is logically or conceptually impossible to perform these reductions. Our concern is to find out what distinguishes actions from purposive and emotional activities.

Arendt's claim that principled action, as genuinely free human action, is distinguished from acting for a purpose or goal and is determined neither by intellect nor by will sounds very strange to us and to the new teleologists. We regard and appear to ourselves as beings who have intentions and motives, who at times act for reasons

17

and achieve goals. Our life is regulated by standards, norms, and ideals. Most of the time we give satisfactory explanations for our actions in terms of our purpose and goals. There does not seem to be anything controversial or startling in this. There are also actions which may not be done in order to achieve a goal or end. And there are some actions into which norms enter "and often entirely define the end".45 Arendt cannot possibly eliminate intentions, motive, purposes, goals, and norms from a genuinely human action.

Although there are sharp internal differences among many of the newteleologists, there is a consensus that intention distinguishes human action from non-action and movement or physical motion. Charles Taylor asserts:

> With action, we might say the behaviour occurs because of the corresponding intention or purpose; where this is not the case, we are not dealing with action.46

We can never specify an action exhaustively in terms of movements of the body. Similar movements of the body may mean totally different actions. A good example is given by Richard J. Bernstein:

> One might make the same movements, or the same types of movement and yet be performing very different actions. I may make the same type of movements when signing my name in two different instances, but in one case the act that I am performing is showing someone what a signature is, while in another situation, the same bodily movements may count as legally binding me to a contract.47

Therefore, while we can gain a scientific account of the movements involved in human action, we do not thereby explain human action.

Arendt might agree with the above contention because her point is not that action must have no goal but that it cannot be defined in terms of them. The particular ends of action are always transcended by the general principles which give them significance and meaning. In fact, she does not define action as free from motive, aim, or goal. She states explicitly that most actions concern specific purposes and interests. Her point is not that action must be free from these concerns but that it transcends and is not determined by them. Since the meaning of action transcends those motives and goals which inform it, action cannot be comprehended in a means-end framework.

To appreciate what Arendt means by human action we need to uncover what lurks behind these metaphors. What Arendt simply means is that intentions and goals are not causal antecedents of the action. They are causal antecedents of a predicted and controlled activity. An action, according to Arendt, is unpredictable. As for the goals, we have to understand what it means to say action is required for an end or goal. Charles Taylor states:

> [W]hen we say that an event occurs for the sake of an end, we are saying that it occurs because it is the type of event which brings about this end. This means that the condition of the event's occurring is that a state of affairs obtain such that it will bring about the end in question, or such that this event is required to bring about the end.48

According to Arendt, the outcome of genuine human action cannot be predetermined. She therefore insists that while intentions and goals may be understood as "inspiring" the action, they are related to it in a special non-causal manner.

Arendt further affirms the transcendence of action over intentions when she says that, insofar as action is free, it is determined neither by intellect nor will, even though it needs the "guidance of the intellect" and the "dictate of the will" for the "execution of any particular goal".49 The meaning of action is not fixed either by the intellect or by the will; rather, it is tied up with the principle manifested in that action.

Finally, Arendt tries to connect her notion of principled action with that of acting in public, which is the only genuine type of acting. She depicts principled action as an event taking place when men manifest their identities as innovators by acting on the basis of some principle outside themselves, which can be shared by others and again be taken up as the basis for new actions. Such principles invite other men to continue one's actions and confirm them as beginnings, but that does not contradict Arendt's notion of initiative as we shall soon see. It does, however, restrict principled actions to great men and to great movements of history. It is as if only great men who perform heroic acts are capable of principled action. It also appears as if only movements similar to the American Revolution, which she accepts as a new beginning in history, can be regarded as outcomes of principled action since men participated in human affairs according to its principles. But the actual fact is that whoever acts in public does the same principled actions.

Arendt is also not clear whether free action means establishing new principles. In this way it is quite difficult to comprehend the connection she makes between action and principles.

Plurality

We have been showing how Arendt links the notions of natality and action. It has so far appeared as if human freedom is a characteristic of isolated individuals. However, action for Arendt is not merely individuals doing certain things. It is a specific mode of human beings being together. Action requires the cooperation of one's fellows, and that cooperation must be freely given. "Plurality" as she calls it, like natality, is the sine qua non of action. It represents the basic condition of action, for in action men find themselves in concert with beings who are quite like them and yet distinguished from them on the very basic point of bodily appearance.

The miraculous character of the human being lies not only in the very existence of human beings as new beginnings (natality), but also in their public role as beginners of new actions. Arendt wants to hold together these two notions. In order to give a reason why slaves and women, as new beginnings, were excluded from the polis, she holds that human beings as new beginnings are only potentially significant and miraculous. It is as beginners of new public actions that their distinct identities are achieved and confirmed. This seemingly slight shift in the meaning of human beginnings bears much significance, for it means not every being possesses a distinctly personal existence, but only those who come to be defined in some way in terms of the world. This conclusion demands that human identity is confirmed only when one belongs to a community of expression, like the Greek polis. Human beginnings only arise by enlisting the aid of others, and this is possible only by a common reliance on certain conventions of a community:

> [I]t is only as a member of such a unit, that is, of a community, that men are ready for action. The manifoldness of these communities is evinced in a great many different forms and shapes, each obeying different laws, having different habits and customs, and cherishing different memories of its past....Montesquieu was probably right... that each such entity moved and acted according to a different inspiring principle, recognized as the ultimate standard for judging the community's deeds and misdeeds....50

One's appearance as an actor and therefore as the incipient initiator of a new series of actions only transpires when one's appearance conforms to and exemplifies these tacit standards of how one should appear.

It is clear that Arendt founds the miraculous capacity of action upon natality in the sense of the birth of each newcomer into the world. She also founds it on what she calls "second birth". She argues:

> With words and deeds we insert ourselves (individuals) to initiate, by their "words and deeds", new courses of action among their fellow men. One acts when one commits oneself to uttering those words and doing those deeds which give reality to one's stand in the eyes of one's fellow men.51

We shall now illustrate what Arendt means by this assertion.

The Disclosure of the Actor

The major criterion of action, according to Arendt, is the disclosure of the actor. Action, connected with speech, reveals man as an agent, the one who begins and rules (the Greek term <u>archein</u> meaning both), the one who initiates changes in the world. <u>Action</u> reveals the actor as subject, as a free being standing up in public. This leads us to Arendt's conception of the relationship between public space, the realm of freedom and the individual self. It is only in the public realm that action can take place. In the public realm "men can show who they really and inexchangeably" are.52 So action, in Arendt's sense, is a medium through which an agent can reveal his individuality. Showing what one stands for and doing it reveals who one is.

In no other activity can one disclose oneself, because in other activities men are burdened with other considerations of life. In labor man reveals his bodily needs; in work, his craftsmanship; in action he reveals himself, the totality of his unique being. According to Arendt, work and labor can only reveal <u>what</u> a man is, whereas action reveals who he is. From the perspective of labor and work, action creates nothing to be consumed and nothing merely useful. It is undertaken for the purpose of the revelation of the actor, as a virtuoso performer, as a beginner, as a person whose action calls attention to his inexchangeable and irreplaceable identity. The end of action remains the revelation of the actor himself.53

Here, Arendt is making an interesting distinction between "what" and "who" somebody is. She distinguishes <u>who</u> someone is from <u>what</u> he/she is in these words:

21

In acting and speaking, men show who they are, reveal actively their unique personal identities and thus make their appearance in the human world, while their physical identities appear without any activity of their own in the unique shape of the body and the sound of the voice. This disclosure of "who" in contradistinction to "what" somebody is--his qualities, gifts, talents and shortcomings, which he may display or hide--is implicit in everything somebody says and does.54

One discloses who one is when one acts and speaks. Both action and speech are needed to manifest one's uniqueness, which is implicit in all one's words and deeds. The only way one can get around revealing who one is is by remaining completely inactive and mute. The Greeks often use examples from the performing arts as analogies for political action: flute-playing, dancing, the practice of medicine, the profession of seafaring. For Arendt, examples from the creative arts only disclose what one is, one's qualities, traits, talents and the like. What one is can also be disclosed through one's bodily appearance and the sound of one's voice. For Arendt, action reveals the unique identity, not just the objectified essence, of the individual, not simply a composite of one's qualities, gifts, talents and shortcomings. Only through action can the uniqueness of the individual as subject, as an acting human being, be revealed to others.

Arendt also claims that the inner determinations of man, such as emotions, passions, volitions and thoughts, only reveal what man is rather than who he is. She contends that such psychological phenomena only manifest an unshareability and fall short of uniqueness. They are sheer private aspects of the human which though essential to the existence and appearance of the person cannot be marks of the deliberately expressed self, since at their best they exhibit a "monotonous sameness".55

In the same way she holds that bodily differentiation does not constitute a distinction between human persons even though different bodies initiate the sequence of events which distinguish each person and one's uniqueness is always bound up with one's appearance in the same body. She regards bodily appearance as a condition, but not the individuating principle, of human uniqueness. One's bodily appearance sets one off from others in the same way different animals species are set off from one another. This does not show the integral force of one's personal agency as the source of one's actions. Only one's speech and actions, including the movement and appearance of one's body in this world, constitute a true mark of who one is.

22

FREEDOM AND ACTION

Arendt's view is quite foreign to our common view of man. Both the classical and modern views of man as a unique being invariably posit certain qualities which mark him out. Human nature in its normative sense has always been identified with some qualities man possesses or ought to possess in his full development. Hence human status has been assigned on the basis of these qualities, moral or otherwise. In Arendt's view, such qualities tell us what man is or ought to be, but never who he is. The description of one's qualities just identifies one's character but not one's uniqueness: that is to say, "the moment we want to say who somebody is, our vocabulary leads us astray into saying what he is".56 Arendt's background may help us determine what she really means by this distinction between who and what somebody is.

When dealing with this distinction between who and what one is, Arenat refers to St.Augustine. She claims he "distinguishes between the questions of 'Who am I?' and 'What am I?' the first being directed by man at himself...and the second being addressed to God".57 She also adds that Augustine assigns to man himself the understanding and confirmation of who he is whereas God is the source of human knowledge about what man is in his essence or nature. This interpretation is plausible, especially within Augustine's philosophical anthropology.

As we can see, Augustine's understanding of who and what man is is theological rather than philosophical.58 Arendt is aware of this factor; hence, she argues that the sense of the distinction between who one is and what one is is of secular origin, not essentially indebted to the Christian focus of Augustine's work. 59 Therefore, Augustine's usage of who and what one is does not correspond to Arendt's distinction between who somebody is and what he is.

The real source of Arendt's theory is the Greek polis. The Greeks discerned that action is disclosed in an unnatural way:

> Before men began to act, a definite space had to be secured and a structure built where all subsequent actions could take place, the space being the public realm of the polis and its structure the law....60

It is in action in the polis that man shows who he is. His unique identity is expressed in his public conduct, which may or may not reveal all his personal qualities. In public action, then, man reveals who he is, in his words and deeds.

On the other hand, it is in the private realm that what someone is can be revealed. Arendt identifies what one is with such traits which can be "displayed or hidden" in the public realm without affecting the essence of who one is.

However, Arendt's comments on one's qualities, traits, and, in sum, one's character seem to belie this clear differentiation of the who and the what. For example, in her article on culture she declares that "by his manner of judging, the person discloses to an extent also himself, what kind of person he is..."61 Similarly, she describes the education of a child as the encouragement of "the free development of characteristic qualities and talents. This...is the uniqueness that distinguishes every human being from another...."62 Later on she identifies the uniqueness of individuals with the willful character or personality which emerges from one's consistent acts; this character or personality denotes,

> the conglomeration of a number of identifiable qualities gathered together into a comprehensible and reliably identifiable whole, and imprinted, as it were, on an unchangeable substratum of gifts and defects peculiar to our soul and body structure.63

So, Arendt here considers a consistently presented character, developed in the course of one's public appearance and based on one's naturally given qualities and traits, as an expression of the unique identity (the who) of the person. This is affirmed by her insistence that Eichmann's judgment was a human judgment. He was "a man of flesh and blood with an individual history, with an always unique set of qualities, peculiarities, behavior patterns, and circumstances".64

Ironically, Arendt falls into the same trap she warns us about:

> The moment we want to say who somebody is, our very vocabulary leads us astray into saying what he is; we get entangled in a description of qualities he necessarily shares with others like him; we begin to describe a type or a "character" in the old meaning of the word with the result that his specific uniqueness escapes us.65

Her own identification of the person's uniqueness with a particular set of qualities lapses into this failure. For example, the absolute uniqueness of Achilles, whom Arendt regards as a hero, is determined by a unique set of character traits--courage, fearsomeness, eagerness for competition, etc.--a great many of which were shared by many Greeks and by which he was distinguished only for possessing them in superlative degree. It is, therefore, difficult to comprehend how the sense of one's unique who can be revealed through such a process of classification. Either Arendt's statements are a simple contradiction or she intends to say that, because each person is a unique who, his traits and character exhibit an unshareable uniqueness as they appear in the story of life.

Another interesting point is found in her statement "the disclosure of the 'who' through speech, and the setting of a new beginning through action, always fall into an already existing web where their immediate consequences can be felt".66 This implies that although Arendt most definitely wants to hold action and speech together as a medium for personal revelation and freedom, she closely aligns speech with the revelation of the who and action with the new beginning. This will be clearer when we examine her notion of speech. However, we must not think Arendt divorces speech from action.

Without speech, action is held by Arendt to be a mute form of achievement--one way among others of producing things in the world. Only the joint presence of word and deed ensure that action is significantly personal, but it is especially speech which is affiliated with the disclosure of who one is. Since the uniqueness of the person renders all his acts unique and unshareably linked to "who he is", actions not accompanied by the actor's words disclosing who he is are without sense. Arendt expresses this factor in the following:

> The action he begins is humanly disclosed by the word, and though his deed can be perceived in its brute physical appearance without verbal accompaniment,it becomes relevant only through the spoken word in which he identifies himself as the actor, announcing what he does, has done, and intends to do.67

This sounds very strange because we all witness meaningful actions unaccompanied by words. But that fact can be explained through her notions of who and what one is. Who one is is disclosed by one's words, which are affiliated with one's deeds. Without speech, action could appear as nothing but the working out of pre-set rules in robot-like fashion.

Arendt is also aware of the shortcomings of speech. She admits, as we noted before, that we can never fully express in words who the actor is, because the moment we attempt to express in words who somebody is we end up describing what he is. Now this limitation on our ability to express in words who somebody is has an effect on the whole realm of human affairs. What Arendt is saying is that since we can never fully express in words who the actor is, this creates a problem in human affairs (action), the effect being that we never handle this realm as we handle the realm of work and labor. This is why she emphasizes the courage involved in action: because the actor can never know in advance the self he is manifesting or the principle that will emerge from his action.68 Action is such a gradual process that it can only be planned to be either a recreation centre or a prison before it is finished and is being used. The results of work can be planned and determined before the actual work takes place. Action, on the contrary, is highly unpredictable; we never really know the actor until he is dead.

Arendt does not mean we can never determine who the actor is or was. She claims that we can know who somebody is by knowing the story of which the actor is the hero, as story resulting from his words and deeds. Admiration for the hero takes the form, in her case, of an unqualified admiration for Achilles as the "doer of great deeds and speaker of great words". She holds that to get the full meaning of the story and thereby come to know who the actor is or was we have to wait until his life has come to an end. Since the essence of who somebody is "can come into being only when life departs, leaving behind a story", it follows that whoever consciously aims at leaving behind a story and an identity which will win immortal fame "must not only risk his life but expressly choose, as Achilles did, a short life and premature death".69

Arendt is here echoing the Greek maxim that we should call no man happy until he is dead. This can also be given existential connotations which might be in the back of Arendt's mind: that so long as the person is still alive, since he has no fixed human nature, he is constantly recreating himself in much the same way Sartre's actor is recreating himself through his choices and actions. This being the case, we can only get the full meaning and picture of who perceives and narrates the story. The actor cannot tell us who he is as accurately as the storyteller.

As we can see, there is a great amount of freedom in the fact that every individual can distinguish himself/herself by his/her actions and can begin a chain of new events by courageously acting and speaking. Since action and speech disclose and express what is unique, they are the medium of freedom. Freedom is the ability to take charge of events, to shape one's destiny.

FREEDOM AND ACTION

Appearance

For Arendt, who one is rests on actively appearing, on deliberately revealing oneself in the world in speech and deed. Sheer audibility and visibility are not enough. To establish one's uniqueness, one must do something in the common world: one must explicitly disclose oneself, in action and speech, to others. For this to be possible, a space of appearance, the public-political arena similar to the ancient Greek polis, is required.

What is crucial here is that speech and deeds enable one to demonstrate who one is for the minds and memories of one's fellows.Only through action and speech, in the company of men who relish the actor's performance, can the actor be said to have done well, to have appeared, to have established his "unchangeable identity".70

Arendt regards the public realm alone as the source of reality for men. She insists that reality or what must pass for reality in the human condition can only be found in the public realm:

> To be deprived of it means to be deprived of reality,
> which, humanly and politically speaking, is the same as
> appearance.71

We shall in the coming chapter determine what Arendt means by reality. At the moment it suffices to say that reality is whatever appears in the public realm and is judged so by the citizens. To Arendt, whatever "lacks this appearance" in the public space "is intimately and exclusively our own but without reality", that is, without significance to others.72 So, action yields reality, confirms personality, promises excellence and makes human life meaningful. Whether this reality can ever be "established beyond doubt" is not yet our concern. Anyhow, Arendt says:

> Without a space of appearance and without trusting in
> action and speech as a mode of being together, neither
> the reality of one's self, of one's identity, nor the reality
>   of the surrounding world can be established beyond
> doubt.73

What is interesting is that, outside the shared public space, the human hold on reality, individual identity, and excellence is uncertain.

Arendt regards the polis as this public space where free men deliberately decide to initiate a certain project, the undertaking of which has repercussions for the actors and for spectators within that realm. Thus, Arendt claims, action needs for its full appearance "the shining brightness we once called glory, and which is possible only in the public realm", because excellence and freedom "by definition require" the presence of others "as an audience, and not just casual, familiar presence of one's equals or inferiors", but necessarily the "formality of the public, constituted by one's peers".74 This implies that men cannot act in solitude.

In Arendt's view, action is inconceivable outside the realm of plurality: unlike labor and work, action is "entirely dependent upon the constant presence of others"75 In action man expresses his uniqueness, but he has to depend on other men. This is a paradox, since the most unique activity is the least independent. Nowhere else, declares Arendt, does man "appear to be less free" than in action, "whose very essence is freedom".76 Action is definitely independent of material necessities, which have to be taken care of before one can act. It is not autonomous even though in the public realm the actor can assert himself as a unique individual. In spite of the individualistic and singular origin of all action, it only becomes true action when one acts with others.

Action requires not mere plurality, not just the presence of some others, but the presence rather of one's peers, who are admitted to a public "sphere of freedom" without consideration of their background or talents but by virtue of their being human and free from necessities. It may appear strange that, for Arendt, action presupposes the existence of unequals, on one side and, on the other, the presence of peers, equal and equally free to act in the public realm.

Arendt borrows the notion of equality from the ancient Greeks. The equality men enjoy in community is a function of their citizenship, of their admission into the public sphere of politics. The Greek notion of equality had nothing to do with universal natural rights, nor parity in wealth, talent, ability or what we usually understand by this notion. Rather, it was equality of status as citizens. Citizenship in the polis meant admission to a public "sphere of freedom", while the private sphere was governed by necessity and depended on animal laborans and homo faber as we have seen. Each man was required to accept other members as equals, by virtue of their appearance and participation in the polis. This equality was not absolute, nor was it permanent: it lasted as long as men remained citizens participants in the polis. For Arendt, this is the only kind of equality possible for free men in the human condition of plurality: the equality of men as agents. Thus, "equality, far from being connected with justice, as in modern times, was the very essence of freedom" in ancienct Greece.77

In Arendt's view, men are not born equal but they can achieve equality by participating in the public realm. She argues:

> If men were not equal, they could neither understand
> each other and those who came before them nor plan for
> the future and foresee the needs of those who will come
> after them.78

Arendt is aware that equality does not elimate the differences which exist among peers. She points out not only the dimension of equality, but also that of distinction. She claims that if men were not distinct, they would not require the intricacies and risks of language and action to clarify themselves to others: "/S/igns and sounds to communicate immediate, identical needs and wants would be enough."79 While "signs and sounds" may be sufficient for animal species, man alone of all creatures needs speech to "communicate himself and not merely something--thirst or hunger, affection or hostility or fear."80 Arendt attributes the distinctions generated by plurality to the personal character of human expression.

Finally, both equality and human distinction presuppose freedom. Human freedom emerges only where individuals share a common status. The public realm is a space where all share a commitment to a mode of being together which recognizes and realizes the capacity for freedom in all individuals. Man's freedom as an individual is bound up with that of others. As he seeks his own identity in what he does, he reveals himself, which ensures the freedom of others and creates his own reality. It is therefore essential that action take place in public (a realm of equals), because the possibility of freedom is premised on a particular mode of being together.

From the above, we see that plurality is "the condition of human action".81 It is not in itself enough to produce action and certainly not free action. In order to produce action, human plurality has to be brought into a space of appearance or a public realm where men can freely engage in action in the presence of their peers. The space of appearance is the result of a particular kind which Arendt describes as action and freedom.

Thus, Arendt holds freedom to be the essential component of the public realm. But the question remains as to the substantive nature of freedom. In Arendt's view, freedom is synonymous with action. This means that freedom is public-political phenomenon. Yet, in the main tradition of Western theory the notion of freedom as a worldly public phenomenon has never been seriously considered.82 Rather, freedom has usually been understood to mean either freedom of the will or inner freedom.

Arendt's conception of freedom is also different from what we usually take freedom to be. When we speak of freedom we think of being left alone to do what we want. Some even recommend total withdrawal from a life of action and conveniently equate freedom with non-interference, while others insist that whoever wishes to act must remain in full control of his actions.

Arendt's main assertion is that genuine freedom was the one which men iof the ancient Greek polis enjoyed: the freedom "to move, to get away from home, to go out into the world and meet other people in deed and word".83 This was the freedom of the citizen, not of the slave who was unfree and remained a servant of "the necessities of life".84 We shall later see how liberation from necessity was, and is, the crucial condition of freedom.85

What is clear about this ancient Greek view, which Arendt follows, is that freedom is taken as an "outer manifestation", not as an "inner feeling".86 Freedom here is freedom because, like action, it is a public phenomenon. It is also enjoyed beyond the limited and limiting boundaries of the individuals, the private self. Arendt asserts:

> We first became aware of freedom or its opposite in our
> intercourse with others, not in the intercourse with
> ourselves.87

Freedom and action reside in the realm of the "many": they require the presence and active participation of others.

Conclusion

Thus far conceived, we see that for Arendt the birth of a human being marks the appearance of a unique being gifted with the capacity for freedom and capable of acting in an unpredictable manner. Through action man fulfills the promise inherent in his birth and "actualizes" his capacity to begin something new and realizes his uniqueness. Action is therefore a uniquely human activity.

Action has been presented as an interruption of what is going on and a beginning of something new. Freedom consists especially in breaking the recurrent cycles of necessity. In this sense action and freedom are equivalent. This is why Arendt argues that, since

FREEDOM AND ACTION

Aristotle failed to develop a theory of freedom and defined freedom merely as a choosing between given objects or alternatives rather than as forging a new beginning, he could not in turn develop a theory of action. Action is the medium by which man asserts and realizes his freedom; it is both an expression and a vehicle of freedom.

Arendt's distinction between labor, work and action seems to minimize the fact that products of work and labor, however trivial they may seem to her, loosen up the rigidity of life, generate a climate in which action becomes a daily occurrence, and create spaces within which freedom finds a wordly home. While she sets up a neat contrast between behavior and action, she also ignores the fact that even customary and routinized acts involve some initiative and judgment. This would have probably been made clear by an explanation of what counts as a new beginning, which she does not give. These deficiencies led Bikhu Parekh to conclude:

> Arendt's concept of action is so abstract that it does not connect with the world. For her, action represents man's capacity to transcend nature and necessity. Indeed, for her, action is not only a supranatural but a supernatural activity. In action man performs "miracles," creates the "extraordinary" and the "unpredictable," and "reveals" himself. Action appears from "nowhere" and cannot be causally explained.88

I do find Arendt's notion of action, besides being very complex, to be in a way paradoxical. Arendt regards a life without speech and action as literally dead to the world: "/i/t has ceased to be a human life because it is no longer lived among men."89 But, even those who choose the vita contemplativa, as we shall see, do so for the purpose of action. For Arendt, activity is the direct result of contemplation. Therefore, taking initiative is the act of individuals. But she insists that freedom does not exist until individuals act together, start new things and make a name for themselves. By this she means that freedom is a phenomenon of the public world. The plurality of mankind represents the basic condition of action. It is within the plural space of appearance that man's capacity to act, that is, his faculty of freedom, can be exercised. In this way, Arendt minimizes the role of individuals' ability to initiate something new by themselves, away from other men.

She is also aware of anther paradox, that when they act and speak in the human community men are most truly free yet least in control of their own destiny. When they exercise their capacity for initiative, the essence of their freedom, they help create a web of

31

human relationships which entangles them to the point that they seem more like helpless victims than the masters of what they do. Again Bikhu Parekh states it well in these words:

> To act is both to exercise freedom and to lose it, to assert oneself and to place oneself at the mercy of others whose responses may completely alter the character of the action and produce consequences opposite to those intended.90

It seems as if the actor forfeits his freedom at the very moment he avails himself of it, that human freedom exists only to lure men into necessity.

Arendt tries to solve this paradox through the use of the concepts of forgiveness and promise and also by insisting that the actor can develop into a full human being only in relationship with others. But this paradoxical character of action makes us doubt the very existence of freedom in the public realm; and we have become used to hearing about the discord between politics (life in the polis) and freedom. Yet Arendt insists:

> /F/reedom, which only seldom--in times of crisis or revolution--becomes the direct aim of political action, is actually the reason that men live together in political organization at all. Without it, political life as such would be meaningless. The raison d'être of politics is freedom....91

This claim must now be elaborated.

FREEDOM AND ACTION

NOTES

1 *Between Past and Future*, p. 146.
2 *The Human Condition* covers other major topics that appear in other works of Arendt.
3 Immanuel Kant, *The Critique of Pure Reason*, trans. by Norman Kemp Smith (New York: St.Martin's Press, 1965).
4 *The Human Condition*, p. 177.
5 *Ibid.*
6 *Ibid.*, p. 178.
7 *Ibid.*, p. 208.
8 *Ibid.*, p. 177, quoted from St.Augustine's *De Civitate Dei* xii. 20.
9 "Understanding and Politics", *Partisan Review*, 20 (July-August, 1953), 392.
10 *Willing*, pp. 216-17.
11 *The Human Condition*, p. 177.
12 *Ibid.*
13 *Ibid.*, pp. 177-78.
14 *Ibid.*
15 *Ibid.*, p. 169.
16 *Between Past and Future*, p. 151.
17 *Ibid.*, pp. 148-52.
18 *On Revolution*, p. 207.
19 *The Human Condition*, pp. 9-11, 177, 183, 233, 241.
20 George Kateb, "Freedom and Worldliness in the Thought of Hannah Arendt", *Political Theory* 5 May, 1977), 141-82.
21 Kirk Thompson, "Constitutional Theory and Political Action", *Journal of Politics* 31 (February, 1969), 659.
22 *The Human Condition*, p. 30.
23 *Ibid.*, p. 37.
24 *Ibid.*, p. 29.
25 *Ibid.*, pp. 301-2.
26 *Ibid.*, p. 305.
27 *Ibid.*, pp. 155-56.
28 *Ibid.*, p. 140.
29 *Ibid.*, p. 105.
30 Kark Marx, *Das Kapital*, Vol. I (Berlin, 1947), Ch. V, Sec. I., p. 183.
31 *Ibid.*, pp. 185-86.
32 Karl Marx and Friedrich Engels, *The German Ideology* (New York: International Publishers, 1947), p. 7.
33 *Ibid.*
34 *The Human Condition*, p. 178.
35 Richard J. Bernstein, *Praxis and Action: Contemporary Philosophies of Human Activity* (Philadelphia: University of Pennsylvania Press, 1971), p. 251.

36 Ibid, especially Part 4, pp. 230–304.
37 The Human Condition, p. 28.
38 Ibid., p. 39.
39 Ibid., p. 40.
40 Ibid., p. 41.
41 The Origins of Totalitarianism, p. 153.
42 Between Past and Future, pp. 152–53.
43 Bernstein, p. xii.
44 The term "New Teleologists" applies to a group of analytic philosophers who have been active during the past 20 years.
45 Richard S. Peters, The Concept of Motivation, 2nd ed. (London: Routledge and Kegan Paul, 1960), p. 5.
46 Charles Taylor, The Explanation of Behaviour (New York: HUmanities Press, 1964).
47 Bernstein, p. 256.
48 Taylor, p. 9.
49 Between Past and Future, p. 152.
50 Willing, p. 201.
51 The Human Condition, pp. 176–77.
52 Ibid., p. 38.
53 Ibid., pp. 207–8.
54 Ibid., p. 179.
55 Thinking, pp. 34–6.
56 The Human Condition, p. 81.
57 Ibid., p.10, cited from St.Augustine's Confessions.
58 However, it is not a fair interpretation of the Confessions as the
historical act of the person Augustine. In the light of the Confessions, Augustine's coming before God to find the answers to his "questio mihi factus sum [a question have I become for myself]" refers not to the question of his nature, but to the question of who he in fact is who has become an infirmity for himself. In order to find out who he is, Augustine tries to find what man is. He comes to the conclusion that a man is a person before God, who can only be confirmed in his personal standing before God. Augustine is trying to make sense of his seemingly desperate identification in the light of his claim to believe in God and his failure to back fully this claim in his words and deeds. If we take these two questions (who? and what?) within the context of the Confessions, Arendt's interpretation is altered so that it only refers to the greatness of God who alone can understand the failure of man.
59 The Human Condition, p.11.
60 Ibid., pp. 194–95.
61 Between Past and Future, p. 223.
62 Ibid., p. 189.
63 Thinking, p. 37; Willing, p. 195.

64 Eichmann in Jerusalem, p. 285.
65 The Human Condition, p. 181.
66 Ibid., p. 184.
67 Ibid., p.179.
68 Ibid., pp. 36, 186-87.
69 Ibid., p. 193.
70 Ibid.
71 Ibid., p. 199.
72 Ibid., pp. 196-99.
73 Ibid., p. 208.
74 Ibid., p. 180; and Between Past and Future, p. 169.
75 Ibid., p. 51.
76 Ibid., p. 234.
77 Ibid., pp. 31-2.
78 Ibid., p. 175.
79 Ibid., p. 176.
80 Ibid.
81 Ibid., p. 8.
82 Between Past and Future, p. 145.
83 Ibid., p. 148.
84 Ibid.
85 See Chapter III.
86 Between Past and Future, p. 146.
87 Ibid., p. 148.
88 Bikhu Parekh, "Hannah Arendt's Critique of Marx", in Hannah Arendt: The Recovery of the Public World, ed. Melvyn A Hill (New York: St. Martin's Press, 1979), 87.
89 The Human condition, p. 176.
90 Bikhu Parekh, Hannah Arendt and the Search for New Political Philosophy (London: The MacMillan Press Ltd., 1981), p. 117
91 Between Past and Future, p. 146.

CHAPTER II

FREEDOM AND POLITICS

The prime purpose of this chapter is to demonstrate the significance of "freedom" for Hannah Arendt's theory of politics. Hence, in what follows I will explicate her claim that freedom is the "raisond'être of politics".1 I will first establish what Arendt means by politics, although such an undertaking cannot be confined to a single chapter. Then I will consider how according to Arendt politics is the locus of freedom such that there can be no true freedom apart from political life. I will also provide a description of her historical models of political freedom.

Arendt's concern is lack of freedom in the modern age. According to her, modern politics is not authentic; it has in fact swallowed up genuine political possibilities and destroyed the true political realm, in which speech and action dominate. She attempts to rescue freedom and also political theory from political oblivion. She regards freedom as a political concept which can be preserved only in the context of political action. She claims that politics is impossible without the faculty of human freedom and that freedom is inconceivable outside the order which politics establishes. Freedom is "actually the reason that men live together in political organization".2 People organize themselves in authentic political community in order to have the daily actuality of freedom.

This assertion that freedom is attained in politics and the whole notion of an interdependence of freedom and politics stands in contradiction to common observation. To many people, both philosophers and laymen, freedom and politics are on bad terms; they live "always in tension and often in animosity" as Bernard Crick puts it.3 The well-known dictum that "the government that governs least governs best" expresses well the sense of opposition between freedom and politics.

Among traditional philosophers, Rousseau and Hobbes saw restricting elements in politics. It was Rousseau who observed: "Man is born free, but everywhere he is in chains." Arendt is aware of the views of these philosophers. She realizes also that modern political experience has cast doubt on the coincidence of politics and freedom. For example, she maintains that the rise of totalitarianism "makes us doubt not only the coincidence of politics and freedom but their very compatibility".4 Yet she insists on their compatibility and even interdependence.

Arendt is aware too that there have been so many scandals in political systems that politics is now easily associated with the perverse, the most inferior of human activities, rather than with noble human aspirations. This observation led Michael Oakeshott in his introduction to Hobbes' Leviathan to write:

> Politics, we know, is a second-rate form of human
> activity, neither an art nor a science, at once corrupting
> to the soul and fatiguing to the mind, the activity either
> of those who cannot live without the illusion of affairs or
> those so fearful of being ruled by others that they will
> pay away their lives to prevent it.[5]

Arendt's concern is, therefore, not only to defend politics against
totalitarianism and what we might call "modernism" but also to show
that freedom cannot be properly found in modern politics. It is,
therefore, essential for us to examine her concept of authentic politics
in order to determine whether or not it is the locus of freedom.

Arendt wants to recover the lost meaning of politics first by
analyzing its etymological origins in the political traditions of the
West. Leroy A. Cooper points out that such an attitude of paying
attention to the past linguistic usage of words in order to "understand
the significance of fundamental human activities that either have gone
unnoticed in the modern world or have become the prerogative of the
few...is supported by J.L. Austin, who remarks: '...a word never--well,
hardly ever-- shakes off its etymology and its formation. In spite of
all the changes in an extension of and additions to its meanings, and
indeed rather pervading and governing these, there will still persist the
old idea.'"[6] Arendt is greatly interested in researching what words
once meant in order to show the importance of what we have lost.

She finds the most illuminating models of politics in the
pre-philosophic Greek polis, in the Roman politics based on order, and
in certain aspects of modern revolutions. She is drawn to these
epochs and situations because they represent the times when men
experienced freedom and overcame their absorption into the process of
merely living.

I shall examine these paradigms of political life because they
embody the standards by which Arendt intends to prove that freedom
is the raison d'être of politics. Within these paradigms there is a
series of distinctions, which, according to her, clearly differentiate
political forms. For example, she distinguishes what she takes to be
political phenomena from social and economic phenomena. It is
through these distinctions that Arendt reveals the absence of freedom
in the modern world; they are the basis upon which she relies to
demonstrate that freedom is not possible outside the sphere of politics.

My concern will not be with Arendt's "political" reflections per se--with whether her interpretations of Western politics, including her views on particular revolutions, are valid; rather, my aim is to determine whether her delineation of the human condition supports her contention that an authentic political existence constitutes the essence of human freedom.

The Pre-philosophic Greek polis

Arendt draws our attention to the debt we owe the Greeks and Romans for our political theory. Hellenic thought is her starting place, and she continuously returns us to it so that we may remember that our political theory is derived from the Greek polis. She believes that we should retrieve the notions of political action and freedom found in the Greek polis as did the Romans who through respect for the sacred foundations of their society sought to renew the tradition behind it. Thus, Arendt is not seeking a sentimental revival of the classical tradition which would make us turn our backs on the modern world and its technology; rather, she is interested in the revival of the lost values of the past.

We saw in the preceding chapter that according to Arendt the political life of the Greeks in the polis depended upon exclusivity, upon sharply demarcating the public from the private realm and limiting the number and class of participants. The private realm comprised all activities which were necessary for the sake of survival. It therefore accommodated all those who were engaged in production, business, and commercial transaction; that is, women, artisans, craftsmen, slaves, and resident aliens. The public realm was enjoyed by men freed from necessary activities which belonged to the realm of privacy. Only a leisured class of citizens liberated from the activities of labor and work could devote themselves to politics. Of course, this leisured class was sustained by an economic system which belonged to the private realm. Aristotle stated that authentic politics depended upon a sharp separation betweeen equal citizens who engaged in politics and subordinate producers who, although their labor was necessary for securing the conditions of life, did not contribute directly to the actions that were the essence of politics.

The relationships of those who shared in the private life were governed by rules and conventions dictated by the necessities of life. In the public realm, where the necessities of life did not exist since they were already taken care of in the private realm, the relationships between the members were free and spontaneous. In the private realm, the master of the household or sometimes the chief slave ruled with despotic power while other members obeyed. There was no equality. In the public realm, men lived together and experienced freedom as equals. However, since the members of the polis were never economically equal, the richer members were more influential. Force and violence were tolerated in the private sphere, for sometimes it was necessary for a man to force his slaves to work or even to eliminate unproductive members of the household. In the private realm, man could use any means, even the most dishonorable ones, to attain the ultimate goal, that is, survival. However, the private realm was not all that negative because it was still the refuge for the attitudes of love, goodness, truth and compassion. In the public realm, no citizen was allowed to use violence, even though we shall see that coercion through word and action, which was acceptable in this realm, came very close to forcing or ordering other members. There was no ruler, tyrant or despot in this realm.

Arendt claims that she chooses the polis as the paradigm for political life because of a freedom experienced in the polis and which has "never again been articulated with the same classical clarity".7 For her, the polis embodies true freedom and shows us what politics is really about. Arendt is interested in the way that the polis provides the space in which men can find and experience freedom and identity. She firmly holds that the polis, the space that lies between men, is the original field of freedom; by contrast, in the mind we can only experience freedom of thought or freedom of the will.8 According to her, man first experienced freedom by sharing and living with others in the sphere where the necessities of life were not binding. Freedom was then understood as the status of any man liberated from the private realm. Thus, for Arendt, freedom is not a goal that lies beyond politics, and politics is not freedom's nemesis but its field of experience.

The polis, Arendt writes, "was permeated by a fierce agonal spirit, where everybody had constantly to distinguish himself from all others...through unique deeds or achievements".9 Yet, she also stresses that there was cooperation and equality in the polis. Unfortunately, it is not very clear how she thinks this combustible mixture of competition and cooperation was maintained.

Arendt also cherishes the polis for metaphysical reasons. To her the polis was the realm of free speech, without which there can be no free action. Through speech, the grandeur of the human enterprise can be salvaged from the futility of merely animal or natural existence. This means that in the polis human beings did not need to submit to the laws of necessity and of nature but could create their own laws. In the polis, man had a chance to emulate the immortality of nature's cycles, that is, the ever-recurring cycles of nourishment and consumption, life and death. Birth and death circumscribe the human condition, but from speech Arendt draws an antidote to despair. Through words and great actions one could achieve immortal fame. Arendt asserts that the polis was founded because of man's desire to achieve immortal fame:

> [T]he foundation of a body politic was brought about by man's need to overcome the mortality of human life and the futility of human deeds. Outside the body politic, man's life was not only and not even primarily insecure, i.e., exposed to the violence of others; it was without meaning and dignity because under no circumstances could it leave any traces behind it.10

Free political expression made the polis a forum for human appearance and an organized form of remembrance.

Silence ultimately meant oblivion. Arendt appreciates the contributions of the storyteller, the poet, the commemorators of the actions in the public realm. She argues that the polis was saved by those who, through the gift of tongues, commemorated the valor of free men and perpetuated their legacy. The polis guaranteed that men of action would not be forgotten. In short, the polis was the platform for launching acts that the community would always remember. It was a sphere where human achievements were endowed with significance, and spontaneity and freedom were assured of permanence.

The sharp dichotomy between the private and the public realm which Arendt presumes and her extreme praise of the Athenian polis suggest that her vision of the polis is not to be subjected to historical and empirical tests. The vision is a (deliberate) historical fiction, "like the state of nature or the primal horde or the laissez-faire state", as Stephen J. Whitfield suggests.11 Arendt ignores the historical material which shows that there was a considerable mixing of politics and economics of the public and the private sphere in the Athenian polis. Alfred Zimmern, among others, shows that the Greeks engaged in politics in order to gain and protect their wealth.12 Wealth might not have been the point or purpose of politics, but it certainly was a continuing issue in the political life of the free men. Even in Arendt's ideal polis, economics was involved for political stability. The free men got what they needed economically by forcibly excluding from the public realm whoever needed to bring up economic issues.

Some scholars suggest that Arendt refused to see the classical period "as it really was" because, like Walter Benjamin, she

40

believes that to articulate the past historically does not mean to recognize it "the way it really was" (Ranke). It means "to seize hold of a memory as it flashes up at the moment of danger", which is, for Arendt, the moment of obliteration of the memory of what genuine political life requires.13 Arendt refers to this idealized polis in the hope that we might learn what genuine politics is all about. Her invocation of antiquity is provoked by her wish to make history into a living science that can improve our political situation. Since this paradigm does not apply to the reality of the past or the present, it is hard to resit the conclusion that it is in fact an illusion. Arendt herself very rarely attempts to bring this model of politics to bear directly on contemporary issues, and she does not demonstrate how vision of the polis offers a constructive critique of the modern political life.

The function of Arendt's political model is to distinguish genuine political freedom from other kinds of political freedom discussed by philosophers. She also wants to draw a contrast between those governments where freedom of speech and action is present and those marked by totalitarianism:

> Totalitarian governments destroy the individual and his freedom by destroying his ability to act and speak. History and language cease to be meaningful in totalitarian regimes. The totalitarian state is therefore the antithesis of the polis.14

We shall later determine whether Arendt's notion of freedom is still plausible despite her disinclination to harmonize her ideal of the past with the needs of the present.   But there is no doubt that, for Arendt, the activity in the polis (politics) is the vehicle by which freedom is realized.

Is there, then, for Arendt, any hope for freedom in our modern world? She provides no means for regaining the lost freedom and so seems to become the victim of a concept of politics that is inapplicable to modern conditions. She at times presents an overly pure concept of politics, one purged of a fair amount of what we would usually attribute to politics. She finds very few examples of the genuinely political in modern times. Her politics seems to be just "politique pour la politique". It is therefore difficult to see how it can be the realm of freedom unless political freedom is nothing in reality.

But what of the other models of freedom she offers? Her references to the Roman foundation of order and to aspects of modern

41

revolutions closely tie in with those of the Greek <u>polis</u>. The importance of these models is summed up by the following premise:

> For if I am right in suspecting that the crisis of the present world is primarily political, and that the famous "decline of the West" consists primarily in the decline of the Roman trinity of religion, tradition, and authority, with the concomitant undermining of the specifically Roman foundations of the political realm, then the revolutions of the modern age appear like gigantic attempts to repair these foundations, to remew the broken thread of tradition, and to restore, through founding new political bodies, what for so many centuries had endowed the affairs of men with some measures of dignity and greatness.15

After elaborating upon this premise we shall examine the situations in which freedom has been realized, diminished or destroyed.

The Roman Foundation of Order

Arendt's efforts as so far explored have been to find room for and encourage individual freedom in a plurality. Now we are about to see why and how she anchors its permanence and durability in authority. For her, authority is not whatever makes people obey, hence a delimitation on their freedom. Rather, she defines it as the necessary condition for freedom's endurance, that is, as essential to give freedom a remembrance through history. Authority preserves and sustains freedom because it makes political communities possible. The relationship between authority and freedom is clearly described by her statement: "Authority implies an obedience in which men retain their freedom...."16

Arendt does not mean that authority is just like violence and coercion, for they are means of preserving freedom for those in power while others are forced into line. She argues that "[a]uthority precludes the use of external means of coercion; where force is used, authority itself has failed".17 Her concept of authority does not refer to leaders commanding and presiding over essentially helpless people. Authority, like power, is achieved through the concert of men who seek its confirmation. While some order is necessary for the maintenance and development of authority, there must also be room for individual spontaneity. Men who genuinely seek freedom in their daily lives as citizens come together to form authority.

In her view, the breakdown of authority leads to the invasion of the public realm, the sphere of freedom, by the private concerns of the household. The loss of authority also spells the loss of action and death of politics. This is because authority binds people together:

> [T]o live in a political realm with neither authority nor the concomitant awareness that the source of authority transcends power and those who are in power, means to be confronted anew...by the elementary problems of human living together.17

Since, for Arendt, freedom is experienced only in the public sphere where people act together, the loss of authority for that realm signals the loss of freedom. She finds no freedom in the modern world because "authority has vanished from the modern world".19 Even though, as she sometimes claims, "we are no longer in position to know what authority is",20 we can still understand what genuine authority was once like in the Hellenic-Roman past.

As we are about to see, Arendt's notion of authority is derived from both Greek philosophy and Roman history. She points out that while the word "authority" and its modern conception are etymologically Roman (derived from the Latin word auctoritas), the Romans themselves derived their understanding of authority from Greek theory.

We have seen that the Greek polis was a community of equals, who were in fact heads of household and masters to slaves. Arendt, borrowing from the Greeks, rejects tyranny, or rulership of heads of a household, as well as despotism. Tyranny and despotism were not tolerated in Greek public life because they were exclusive; the rule of one man precluded the public realm and turned politics over to personal whim. The Greeks had to look elsewhere for a source of authority "in which men retained their freedom". They sought for some relationship which precluded any form of coercion. Plato thought that law was the solution. He conceived that through the use of law tyranny and despotism could be prevented. He realized, however, that this was not a solution, and he claimed that "the law is the despot of the rulers, and the rulers are slaves of the law".21 This was affirmed by Aristotle and Arendt who realized that any form of rule might be grounds for
tyranny. For Arendt, it does not make any difference if the rule is exercised for the sake of the subject. The beneficience of the ruler is not what matters here. What she detests is the exclusion of the citizens from the decision-making process. Any rule that denies the citizens access to the public realm is grounds for tyranny since it

fosters a denial of human potentialities. Despite Plato's efforts to establish freedom by removing any element of coercion from the public realm and to salvage the political realm from the grip of tyranny, he endowed the public realm with a kind of authority which made freedom impossible.

In Book III of the Politics, Aristotle regarded ruling and being ruled as part of the definition of citizenship. "Rulership", which held political orders together, was for Aristotle not just a sheer authority. Arendt is aware of this fact. She realizes that it was a legitimate attempt on the part of man "to emancipate himself from life's necessity" and therefore allow him to take part in great deeds, political action, in the public realm.22 In this way rulership is closely connected with action or that which is done in freedom. However, Arendt finds both Aristotle's concept of rulership and Plato's conceptualization of authority as incomplete notions of authority. Thus the Greeks did not fully succeed in establishing the concept of authority: that remained for the Romans to do.

For Arendt, the root of the Western concept of authority is the Roman trinity of tradition, religion and authority. A loss of political authority in the West was always accompanied by a loss of tradition and a weakening of institutionalized religious beliefs. The power of the Roman trinity was defined by its intimate relation to the founding of Rome, which was taken as "the central, decisive, unrepeatable beginning of their whole history, a unique event".23 In fact, all political activity for the Romans was "to preserve the founding of the city of Rome", as Arendt puts it:

> At the heart of Roman politics, from the beginning of the republic until virtually the end of the imperial era, stands the sacredness of foundation, in the sense that once something has been founded it remains binding for all future generations.24

Thus, the essence of political activity for the Romans, was "to preserve the founding of the city of Rome".25

Tradition and religion gained their authoritative significance from the precedent-forming contest of founding. Authority depends on tradition to illuminate the past, so that one looks back to the beginning of the regime. Tradition became honored only when the past was acknowledged as a continuous binding process that joined the past, present and future generations. Then authority, depending on tradition, tells what can be legitimately done now and in the future. In the same way, religion, etymologically, symbolically and literally, was understood to mean "religare: to be tied back, obligated, to the enormous, almost superhuman and hence always legendary effort to lay the foundations, to build the cornerstone, to found for eternity".26 Religion endowed the Roman state with "durability, continuity, and permanence".

The sacredness of foundation is derived from the fact that the basis of Roman religion, itself past-oriented, was centred on the ideas of beginning and remembrance of that beginning. Arendt reminds us that

> the most deeply Roman divinities were Janus, the God of beginning, with whom, as it were, we still begin our year, and Minerva, the goddess of remembrance.27

This is illuminated by the fact that for the Romans, the patres, the elders or the senators, were respected not just because of their knowledge but because of their old age, which meant growth toward the beginning. Remembrace was also revered because it was the guiding principle for life through action which was directed toward the foundation.

Religion and respect for historical foundations were also to revitalize man's capacities to act. To act with authority meant to act with the weight of the past, which represented the archetypal and distinctly human act to which all other human acts were indebted and obligated. The capacity to act is also referred to by Cicero as the chance for the human spirit to unfold. In a quotation Arendt offers us, Cicero stated that

> /i/n no other realm does human excellence approach so closely the paths of gods (numen) as it does in the founding of new and in the preservation of already founded communities.28

From the above, Arendt concludes that the strength of the Roman trinity of religion, tradition, and authority as an authorizing basis for human action derived from the "binding force of an authoritative beginning to which 'religious' bonds tied man back through tradition".29

This is in short what authority was like in ancient Rome. It was built on the act of founding and was exercised by the senators who "represented or rather reincarnated, the ancestors" and who could just comment on the meaning of the beginning. The downfall of

45

authority, for Arendt, comes as a result of the crumbling of the two pillars: religion and tradition. Arendt strongly holds that if one of the pillars crumble, the whole trinitarian structure falls:

> Thus, it was Luther's error to think that his challenge of the temporal authority of the Church and his appeal to unguided individual judgement would leave tradition and religion intact. So it was the error of Hobbes and political theorists of the seventeenth century to hope that authority and religion could be saved without tradition. So, too, was it finally the error of the humanists to think it would be possible to remain within an unbroken tradition of Western civilization without religion and without authority.30

The breakdown of these principal ingredients of authority does not only reveal that the political order has lost its "absolute" quality, that is, its authority, but also that political freedom has vanished. Gordon Jackson Tolle claims:

> The down of authority, for Arendt, comes as the Roman-established parts break down. The progressive separation of church and state implies that the political order has lost its "absolute" quality and therefore its authority. The religious element had endowed the state with "durability, continuity, and permanence." The weakening of institutionalized religious beliefs was not all: the dignity of our tradition also declined. Without an awareness of the founding and what it meant, modern man had one more pillar removed. So that the contemporary distrust of political institutions is, for Arendt, largely the result of the crumbling of the earlier two pillars to authority: religion and tradition.31

We shall now examine why Arendt asserts that the breakdown of authority is tantamout to the disappearance of freedom.

Arendt points out several eras in which authority was fully practised. The first one is the time when the Roman Catholic Church took over the ideas of tradition and authority, combined them with religion, and set up what became a remarkably stable institution.32 In this institution, Arendt argues, "the miracle of permanence repeated itself once more". She adds that

> within the framework of our history the durability and continuity of the Church as a public institution can be

compared only with the thousand years of Roman history in antiquity.33

This era came to an end when Pope Gerasius I divided the world of authority between himself and Emperor Anastasius I, or, rather, into the realms of "the sacred authority of the popes and the royal power". For Arendt, this was not just the secularization of the political realm, which would be the "dignity of the classical period". Rather, this meant that

> the political had now, for the first time since the Romans, lost its authority and with it that element which, at least in Western history had endowed political structures with durability, continuity, and permanence.34

Following this era, there was a period in which the divine right of kings was used as a justification for absolute monarchy. In this era, religion and tradition were used to support the absolute authority of kings. After this period came a time in which absolute sovereignty passed from the king to the nation state. For Arendt, this was a last stronghold of authority. What happened after this period was a continuous breakdown of authority, tradition, and religion. Thus, Arendt concludes from her analysis of history that "authority has vanished from the modern world".35

For none of these eras does Arendt tell us how freedom was preserved. Since she regards authority as essential to genuine politics, we are to assume that wherever there was authority, in Arendt's sense of the concept, there was freedom. She believes that the decay of authority from the dawn of the nation-state to the present day created a realm in which it is impossible to have freedom.

It is apparent that a system based on authority, as in Rome, cannot preserve Arendt's kind of politics in which there is freedom in the same way as the Greek polis. The Greek polis provided a fuller freedom. The government based on authority allows inequality whereas the polis was founded on an equality of citizens. We have seen that in the polis there was no person ruling others or occupying a higher position than others. The government based on authority is characterized by hierarchical differences which Arendt presents thus:

> The pyramid is indeed a particularly fitting image for a governmental structure whose source of authority lies outside itself, but whose seat of power is located at the top, from which authority and power is filtered down to

the base in such a way that each successive layer possesses some authority, but less than the one above it, and where, precisely because of this careful filtering process, all layers from top to bottom are not only firmly intergrated into the whole but are interrelated like converging rays whose common focal point is the top of the pyramid as well as the transcending source of authority above it.36

Despite these differences between the different levels of a government based on authority, Arendt does not regard authority as a limitation on citizens' freedom. She sees authority as the necessary condition for the preservation of freedom. However, because of the differences between the polis and Roman government based on authority, I think the kind of freedom allowed under authority is not the same as freedom experienced in the polis. Whatever freedom there is in a system based on authority must be qualitatively inferior or very minimal as compared to the freedom found in the polis, since before there can be any authority, people must agree to act together and must accept the hierarchical order in which somebody has the preeminent position to lead and act. In this way, the individual does not have that much freedom to create on the political plane.

Although aware of the weaknesses of the realm based on authority, Arendt still sees possibilities for political freedom in it. She recognizes that within such a structure there are still possibilities for political participation and for performing memorable acts. Therefore, Rome as a system of government based on authority is considered by Arendt as a second paradigm of an authentic political body that guarantees freedom.

Revolution

Arendt's third model of authentic politics is revolution. For her, revolution is a deliberate action to found a new political sphere aimed at establishing freedom. It is the self-conscious attempt to erect a space where freedom might flourish. We have seen, when discussing Arendt's concept of action, that for her the capacity to begin something new is the truly human capacity and the manifestation of human freedom.

As usual, Arendt looks to the origins of a concept and recognizes that "revolution" was originally used in an astrological sense, referring to "the regular, lawfully revolving motion of the stars, which, since it was known to be beyond the influence of man and hence irresistible, was certainly characterized neither by newness nor by violence".37 In that sense, "the men of the first revolutions--that is, those who not only made a revolution but introduced the idea of revolutions into politics--" were not interested in creating new things.38 They wanted to return to a state they had once had in the past, as the Romans wanted to return to the foundations of their state. Arendt gives as a modern example the 1688 return of William and Mary to England for the restoration of the monarchy in what was termed the "Glorious Revolution".39 It was only in a later time that the term "revolution" took on the connotations of a new beginning, a starting over. So, for Arendt, revolution has the connotations of both new beginnings and of reestablishing authority and tradition.

As a new beginning, a revolution is "inextricably bound up with the notion that the course of history suddenly begins anew, that an entirely new story, a story never known or told before, is about to unfold...."40 It is a new attempt to establish a basis on which freedom might nurture and grow. The experience of freedom is "a new experience, not, to be sure, in the history of Western man-kind...but, with regard to the centuries which separate the downfall of the Roman Empire from the rise of the modern age".41 This newly recovered experience of freedom demonstrates man's faculty to begin something new:

> These two things together--a new experience which revealed man's capacity for novelty--are at the root of the enormous pathos which we find in both the American and the French Revolutions....Only where this pathos of novelty is present and where novelty is connected with the idea of freedom are we entitled to speak of revolution.42

This pathos is for Arendt the historically unprecedented quality of revolution itself. The incidents that looked like revolutions, which happened before both the American and the French revolutions, were begun by people who had no idea of the events and their own role in them. Thus,

> although there were enough words in premodern political language to describe the uprising of subjects against a ruler, there was none which would describe a change so radical that the subjects became rulers themselves.43

The idea that all could share in rule was a new one, and it provided the new context in which the pursuit of freedom became the heart of the revolutionary enterprise. What earlier revolutions sought was just to replace one ruler with another, and this was not novelty. For Arendt, revolution is not a mere replacement of one governing body by another or just a change in the personnel who supervise the economic matters. Neither does it establish full equality for all or guarantee freedom from governmental interference. It is, rather, a means to found a polity in which political participation is continuous and normal.

Arendt is convinced that the main impetus to revolution is the desire for freedom, a desire deeply rooted in the Greek polis. The true revolution is, for her, the one which establishes and secures freedom. As we shall see, she analyzes the problem of re-establishing and securing freedom in relation to both the American and French revolutions. While the French Revolution failed to re-establish freedom and ended up abdicating it, Arendt believes that the Americans adhered to the original purpose of revolution. They succeeded in establishing and securing freedom. The American Revolution is thus a third paradigm of authentic politics for Arendt.

She contrasts the American and French revolutions in the following passage:

> The direction of the American Revolution remained committed to the foundation of freedom and the establishment of lasting institutions and to those who acted in this direction nothing was permitted that would have been outside the range of civil law. The direction of the French Revolution was deflected almost from its beginning from this course of foundation through the immediacy of suffering; it was determined by the exigencies of liberation not from tyranny but from necessity; and it was actuated by the limitless immensity of both the people's misery and the pity this misery inspired.44

The difference between these two revolutions, according to Arendt, lies in the fact that while the American Revolution was aimed at freedom, the French Revolution was concerned with "liberation".

Liberation is freedom from biological necessity, a freedom which the poor and miserable sought so desperately in the French Revolution and which inspires many modern revolutions. Arendt takes liberation as an activity that precedes the "foundation of freedom" but is not itself freedom. It is, therefore, a negative notion of liberty, she argues; it is the quest to become "free from oppression".45 As we have seen, anybody who wanted to enter the polis had to be liberated from the most basic elements of human existence. So, liberation from

50

necessity was a prerequisite for the foundation of freedom in the polis sense. The liberation brought by the French Revolution was necessary for the poor, but it is not to be confused with the foundation of a political realm which in true political freedom is present. Liberation is the answer to the "social question", whereas the foundation of freedom is essentially bound up with the political realm. Arendt points out:

> It may be a truism to say that liberation and freedom are not the same; that liberation may be the condition of freedom but by no means leads automatically to it; that the notion of liberty implied in liberation can only be negative, and hence that even the intention of liberating is not identical with the desire for freedom. Yet if these truisms are frequently forgotten, it is because liberation has always loomed large and the foundation of freedom has always been uncertain, if not altogether futile.46

But she is also aware that

> since liberation, whose fruits are absence of restraint and the possession of the power of locomotion, is indeed a condition of freedom....it is frequently very difficult to say where the mere desire for liberation, to be free from oppression, ends, and the desire \for freedom as the political way of life begins.47

But a distinction between liberation and freedom must be made in order to understand that a true revolution is not just a deliverance from oppression; it is the establishment of freedom as the political way of life.

The revolutionaries who search for freedom from biological necessity are different from those who search for authentic freedom. While the former are just like the household heads in the ancient Greek polis, that is, just managers who ensure efficient operation within the social realm, the latter are true politicians, who operate in what Arendt would consider the realm of freedom. The revolutionaries of the French Revolution, like managers, functioned in a sphere of life whose principle was necessity. The American revolutionaries dealt with people rather than with satisfying socio-economic wants.

The French revolutionary model was concerned with the social question--with problems of exploitation, mass alienation and poverty. It was inspired by an idea of compassion. In her analysis of this model, Arendt emphasizes the irresistibility of the biological aspects of the social question and the Jacobins' response to the needs of the poor. The Girondins had tried to establish a government and did not succeed. The Jacobins tried too but became caught up in compassion for the poor. They also trusted that people's good will rather than institutions and a constitution would help in forming a stable government.48 Their hopes were shattered because shifting the emphasis from the rights of man to the rights of the poor was no way to save the revolution.

When their passion to relieve the poor from suffering was doomed to frustration, it then turned into rage. Terror became the expression of this explosive sentimentality. The result of their activity was violence, tyranny and revenge beneath which the original passion for freedom was submerged. Freedom totally ceased to be public and political and became restricted to the individual's private life. The French revolutionaries failed to establish not only the political realm but also the social one, for they did not succeed in alleviating any of the major problems which existed before the revolution.

George McKenna claims that Arendt is wrong in putting forth the determinist hypothesis that the emergence of desperate social needs into the realm of political life and revolutions necessarily leads to despotism as it did in the French Revolution. He points out situations in which the presence of the social question was not an obstacle to constitutional governments:

> Poverty existed in Cuba, but it has also existed in Puerto Rico; millions have starved in China, but they have also starved in India....[T]he lack of realism in thinking beyond the deterministic hypothesis becomes more apparent if one remembers that it is not the extremely poor who become des enragés but those whose wants have already been somewhat alleviated.49

McKenna would be right if Arendt's claim is that every attempt to solve the social question with political means leads to failure.

Certainly, Arendt is not saying that the emergence of desperate social needs in the realm of political life and revolutions will necessarily lead to despotism. She is not reporting what was the case in the French Revolution and other revolutions. She is not claiming that it is utterly inevitable that the social question leads to certain dire consequences. She says:

And although the whole record of past revolutions demonstrates beyond doubt that every attempt to solve the social question with political means leads into terror, and that it is terror which sends revolutions to their doom, it can hardly be denied that to avoid this fatal mistake is almost impossible when a revolution breaks out under conditions of mass poverty.50

Moreover, Arendt does not say that the plight of the poor should be overlooked. She is not insensitive to poverty's effects:

Poverty is more than deprivation, it is a state of constant want and acute misery whose ignominy consists in its dehumanizing force; poverty is abject because it puts men under the absolute dictate of their bodies, that is, under the absolute dictate of necessity as all men know it from their most intimate experience and outside all speculations.51

She also argues that the real impetus for introduction of the question of poverty into the public sphere was itself political, even if the consequences for politics were baleful. It is with regard to this issue that, for her, Marx's contribution to revolutionary theory is most significant. She claims that Marx's

most explosive and indeed most original contribution to the cause of revolution was that he interpreted the compelling needs of mass poverty in political terms as an uprising, not for the sake of bread or wealth, but for the sake of freedom as well....If Marx helped in liberating the poor, then it was not by telling them that they were the living embodiments of some historical or other necessity, but by persuading them that poverty itself is a political, not a natural phenomenon, the result of violence and violation rather than of scarcity.52

Arendt finds fault with Marx because she believes he later changed his view and argued that the "role of revolution was no longer to liberate men from the oppression of their fellow men, let alone to found freedom, but to liberate the life process of society from the fetters of scarcity so that it could swell into a stream of abundance."53 Since according to this argument, "[n]ot freedom but abundance became now the aim of revolution", Arendt's view was that freedom was surrendered to necessity.

53

But, as we have seen in the previous chapter, Arendt's arguments againstMarx on this issue are very shaky. She does not succeed in showing that when the poor are admitted to the public realm they generally opt for consumption rather than for virtue. She fails to prove that the poor are by nature unfit for political labor movement in the nineteenth century. What we can deduce from the above is that the main problem of Arendt's analysis of Marx's work as a whole is her failure to see that the phenomena of social realm could harbour the elements of plurality, as we shall see in the following chapter. In this context, the problem revolves around Arend's lack of clarity in dealing with Marx's claim that the presence of poverty was a political and not a natural phenomenon.

It is also not very clear how Arendt can deplore the intrusion of the social question into revolutionary politics on one hand, and on the other entertain the possibility of revolution cutting for men the bonds of necessity. She sometimes claims that political power could be used to liberate men from necessity in the interests of freedom and implies that such liberation is itself necessary and possible. We can at least say that Arendt does not dismiss liberation as inherently futile in its pursuit. As we shall see, this ambiguity arises again in Arendt's view of the role of the social question in the American Revolution. While she praises the American Revolution precisely because the social question was never a factor as it was in the French Revolution, she also claims that

> the absence of the social question from the American
> scene was, after all, quite deceptive and that abject and
> degrating misery was present everywhere in the form of
> slavery and Negro labour.54

At times it seems as if Arendt suggests that the social question should not be excluded from the revolutionary scene. This is affirmed by her analysis of totalitarianism, where she asserts that any community established on the exclusion of social question is a false one, whose existence would be purchased at the expense of large masses of people.

What is very clear, however, is Arendt's stern affirmation that freedom is not liberation and must not be cast in terms of liberation. She maintains that, while liberation is not freedom, freedom in fact requires liberation, and, as Marcuse, Habermas and others have often pointed out, the pursuit of liberation can be and must be shaped by the claims of freedom if political change is to be truly revolutionary.

We shall now turn to her model of the American Revolution to find out more about her concept of freedom. For Arendt, the American Revolution is the true model of authentic politics, unlike the French, Russian and many other modern revolutions. In the American Revolution, the foundation of political freedom took precedence over liberation, because Americans had already taken care of the necessities of life and their political background was more political than that of the French.

This does not mean that Arendt thinks that all Americans during the Revolution were middle class, prosperous, and solely interested in political freedom. After the time of the American Revolution there was genuine poverty and dehumanization for the slaves, but as in the Greek polis, slaves belonged to the private realm and had no role in the course of the Revolution except to help liberate the free citizens from the necessities of life.

The point which Arendt is making here is that American revolutionaries were much better prepared to start a true political revolution than were their French counterparts. They came from the British political system, which allowed for political participation by individual citizens, though for a very limited group. From the beginning, American government was based on covenants and mutual promises, such as the Mayflower Compact. These facts influenced the structure of the American Constitutional Convention, which was composed of delegates elected by smaller groups. The "founding fathers" realized that the process of constitution-making, which they started, was the key to the survival and stability of the republic. Their act of beginning provided the source of authority which in turn provided stability for the American republic.

Another advantage for the success of the American Revolution was that, at the time of the Revolution, labourers were poor but not miserable, not driven by want. So, the main issue of the Revolution was not the search for "liberation" in Arendt's sense, but for a space in which citizens would enjoy freedom. Finally, the most important feature of the American Revolution was that it gave the citizens the opportunity to participate directly in the operation of their political society. For Arendt, "the actual content of freedom...is participation in public affairs...."[55] We shall examine her notion of participation because it explains why she takes the "councils" as the fourth model of the sphere of freedom.

Freedom as Participation

In Arendt's view political freedom means the right to be a participant in government. Political freedom (political action) is, for her, direct participation in the public spheres of life, where society's crucial decisions are made and confirmed. Her insistence on participation implies a rejection of representation as a form of freedom.

Arendt opposes representation because, like Hegel, she holds that in order to be free the citizens must participate actively, continually and directly in politics. For her, representation cuts the individual off from debate and leads the representative to represent only interests, "neither...actions nor opinions". This is because for her the public realm, the space of freedom, can only be constructed by human action. And since all men are potentially doers and exerters of their human capacities, their direct action is essential for their freedom. She holds that actions and opinions cannot be represented; only interests, such as socio-economic affairs, which properly belong in the private realm, can. Therefore, action, which is the very essence of freedom, must be direct.

The gathering of free men, which Arendt calls "power", creates a sphere of opinions and discussion in which there is "the joy of discourse, of legislation, of transacting business, of persuading and being persuaded".56 While interests belong to groups, opinions adhere to individuals and cannot be transferred to anyone else. In this way, representation of political action is really not possible. Freedom can be experienced by individuals who participate directly in the public realm, which in turn is composed by direct participation of the self, the revelation of one's thoughts through speech and action. In fact, for Arendt, any individual who is represented has already renounced who he is. Therefore, authentic politics for Arendt is the self-made, self-directed arena of freedom, which is maintained by free individuals when they act and speak. She insists that political freedom is enjoyed and exercised in the company of other men and consists in the freedom to appear in the public realm.

Arendt inherited this idea of participation in politics from Aristotle who listed the bios politikos among the three ways of life worthy of a free man and stressed the importance of political participation. When the Greeks called themselves hoi eleutheroi, the free, they were actually referring to their participating in the community's decisions. Their freedom is the result of their constant participation in the polis where they shared in legislation and in executive and judicial activities.

The Romans were not much concerned with the freedom of the individual. Their concern was with the independence and freedom of the group. Roman citizens could therefore easily be asked to surrender their freedom of participation whenever the freedom of independence of the state was at stake. Whenever the group's independence was threatened, individual's opinions and interests were to be represented by someone, for example, an emperor. In our present democratic and representative governments, only those who are interested do actively participate in politics. When their participation interferes with personal preferences, they can withdraw and maybe recuperate for a new spurt of participation. Those who choose to take an active part in politics as representatives claim that their participation in public life is mainly to represent the citizens' interests. The majority of the citizens has thus accepted this type of politics in which popular access to public life is through groups or individuals who claim to speak for them.

When looking at this brief development of the notion of political participation, we are a bit perplexed to see that Arendt, despite her awareness that political philosophy, religion and modern politics diverted people's attention from what she calls authentic politics, still insists that political participation is an essential constituent of freedom and of a good life.

Arendt does not think that voting for representatives constitutes true participation. For her, the voter, the represented, can indeed exercise his will and influence over his representative, but only with regard to his interest or welfare; and since "interest is an essentially private matter, no genuine political freedom, can emerge". What the representative system fails above all to provide for, in her view, is the expression of opinion. True opinion can be formed only in a process of open discussion--a public realm where equals share their opinions. Since representative democratic government cannot provide a space for true opinions, she concludes that it is obsessed with economic interests. And economics is the enemy of politics. Therefore, apart from the fact that representation in itself is not compatible with participatory politics for all citizens, representative democracy is further removed from the politics in being based on interests, economic issues, which are not political. The economic issues have the effect of promoting an escape from politics and encouraging retreat into the social realm where the concerns of the private life dominate.

It is clear that Arendt thinks interests are private and cannot be brought in the public realm. However, it is not clear why someone who speaks for me on economic matters is not expressing my opinions. It is not clear whether Arendt rejects representation based on interests because my representative is expressing the issues that I should be expressing myself or because he is giving expression to issues that should not be expressed in the public realm because they are private by definition. Without explaining this enigma, Arendt just asserts that the revelation of the self through speech and action cannot be achieved through the representative. She declares that it must necessarily be realized by the self; otherwise, to be represented by someone else would mean an abdication of one's self--a renunciation of who one is. In this sense, only the participation of the self can make up participation in Arendt's public realm.

What is quite clear is that Arendt takes the establishment of representative government as distinct from participatory public freedom to be contradictory because representative government is formed to advance aims that are not compatible with the true aims of political action. The nature of representative government ensures that economic concerns will be advanced as the central issues. The success of such a government depends on the triumph of the private over the public sphere. But, as we have seen, Arendt rejects modern politics because of the tendency of the social to invade the public. In the same way, she is critical of representative government.

However, Arendt is aware that she cannot totally reject representation since revolution, while it gives freedom to people, somehow fails to provide a space where this freedom can be exercised. Also, in her affirmation of the American system of government she accepts representative democracy as a form of government that makes secure the structure of authority. She claims that the people concent, in the American republic, by electing representative to office in accordance with rules which have been mutually agreed upon so that power is transferred from people to the Congress and the Congress functions like a <u>polis</u> in the sense that each representative has an equal right to appear and participate in public.

But Arendt is not satisfied with the Congress as a public space. Even Thomas Jefferson was concerned that the Congress did not really symbolize or represent people's active participation in the government. What happened is that, after the War of Independence or what Arendt calls the American Revolution, "civil liberty" became more important than "public freedom". Representation, replaced participation. Arendt, like Thomas Jefferson, contends that civil rights are not the same as political freedom. The Congress was composed of representatives, who were elected by the people. This means that the citizens could not express their identity or their citizenship other than through the ballot box or infrequent trips t the polls. This, according to Arendt, minimized the individual's role as citizen by confining him to private life. She asserts:

/T/he danger was that all power had been given to the people in their private capacity, and that there was no space established for them in their capacity of being citizens.57

Arendt further claims that Benjamin Rush was also aware that the doctrine of participation through the ballot is dangerous because although "all power is derived from the people, they possess it only on the days of their elections. After this it is the property of their rulers."58 The failure of the American Revolution to provide space in which to exercise the freedom it had given to the people prompted Arendt to look somewhere else for examples of genuine political institutions that create and maintain the loci for participation. She came to the conclusion that "councils" or "soviets", the spontaneous creations of modern revolutions, are genuine "man-made public spaces" in which freedom can be exercised.

Councils

The "councils" to which Arendt is referring were spontaneously invented bodies. They were neither planned nor prepared. They were composed of people who in the course of a revolution spontaneously organized themselves outside all revolutionary parties and groups for the purpose of self-government. Arendt claims that they came about as a result of "a swift disintegration of the old power, the sudden loss of control over the means of violence, and, at the same time, the amazing formation of a new power structure which owed its existence to nothing but the organizational impulses of the people themselves".59 Unlike bodies organized by "the professional revolutionists", that is, those who study past revolutions and exert their "influence not in favour of new and the unexpected, but in favour of some action which remains in accordance with the past", the councils did not depend on any pre-revolutionary structures. The founding of these bodies was not based on any ideology or on an organized appeal but on personal trust.

They were not formed because of specific economic grievances. Their sole demand was for freedom.

Moreover, Arendt chooses the councils as spaces of freedom because they were organs of action. They were tailored to lay down the new order that was totally unpredictable and unprepared for. The members of the councils were interested in the direct participation of every citizen in the public affairs of the country. Arendt, citing the Austrian socialist Max Adler, claims:

59

[A]s long as they lasted, there is no doubt that "every individual found his own sphere of action and could behold, as it were, with his own eyes his own contribution to the events of the day".60

The councils were working "for a transformation of the state, for a new form of government that would permit every member of the modern egalitarian society to become a 'participant' in public affairs...."61 While these spontaneous creations of revolutionary fervor were being fought against by professional revolutionaries like Robespierre and Lenin whose programs of centralization and egalitarianism forbade anything but identical opinions, Arendt thinks that they are true models of participation in the public realm. She looks forward to the establishment of these bodies because she thinks that they are capable of creating an entirely new form of government, with a new public realm of freedom.

It is important to point out that Arendt derived most of her notions concerning the councils from her heroine Rosa Luxemburg. This factor is stressed by Margaret Canovan:

[M]uch of On Revolution is strongly remeniscent of the views of Rosa Luxemburg: the emphasis on the spontaneity of revolution as against theories of historical necessity or pressional planning; the exaltation of popular councils as a means of self-government, and the general concern for public freedom.62

From the 1905 Russian Revolution and the workers' councils that sprang up in it, Rosa Luxemburg learned the value of "spontaneity" and the principle that good organization does not precede action but is the product of it. She also abhors violence in revolution. These are matters on which Arendt agrees.

The councils to which Arendt is referring arose in Paris under the Prussian siege of 1870. They appeared again in the Paris Commune of 1891, in the Russian Revolution of 1905 and also the Revolution of 1917 until the Bolshevik coup, in Germany in 1918-1919, and in the 1956 Hungarian Revolution.

In actual fact, these councils were not as efficient as Arendt portrays them. While it is true that some councils created participatory politics, it is equally true that often they were concerned with things that Arendt regards as belonging to the private sphere. They failed to concretize freedom and action by being overly concerned with satisfying the necessities of life. Arendt is aware of this failure of the councils to form authentic politics. She also recognizes that their failure was due to the fact that they did not distinguish between participation and administration, because their business was economics not politics. Arendt argues:

> [T]he fatal mistake of the councils has always been that they themselves did not distinguish clearly between participation in public affairs and administration or management of things in the public interest.63

On this point the councils fell into the same trap as the revolutionary parties by holding that "the end of government was the welfare of the people, and the substance of politics was not action but administration".64 Their weakness is also disclosed by their failure to resist opposition. For example, the Bolsheviks easily overpowered the soviets, just as the Hungarian rebels were defeated in 1956. Thus she remarks that the councils, especially the soviets or workers' councils, failed because "they were incapable of organizing, or rather of rebuilding the economic system of the country", and "the chief reason for their failure was not any lawlessness of the people, but their political qualities".65

Conclusion

From the above, we realize that Arendt is mostly interested in the means by which public freedom can be achieved in the modern world. She thinks that these models, namely the polis, Rome, the Congress and the councils, embody true freedom and show us how the space of political phenomena is created, preserved, altered, abolished and destroyed. She regards these models as the spheres in which genuine freedom can be experienced. In these models we have seen how action, which she defines as political, takes place. What is outstanding in all these models is that whoever enjoys political freedom somehow participates in the public sphere.

We have also seen that her apparent preference for these models and the fervour with which she seems to embrace them does not make her oblivious to the weaknesses of these institutions. She realizes that they are representative bodies, and she maintains that even in the most healthy representative government only personal security and liberty are nurtured, not freedom. While representative government might obliterate oppression and promote a fair distribution of goods among the citizens, it does not provide the necessary basis for the direct participation that allows them to organize their common affairs. Arendt allows representative governments and "councils", as

61

we have seen above, only as far as they create some space in a field of discourse she calls the public realm, in which the speech of one becomes a discourse with others and where the action of one becomes participation with one's equals.

However, on many occasions Arendt seems to have lost hope that freedom can ever be gained in the modern age. She is aware that authentic politics has never been for everybody. She is convinced that politics has "never been and will never be the way of life of the many".66 It always depends "upon exclusivity, upon sharply demarcating the public from the private realm and narrowly limiting the number and class of citizen-participants". This fact means that in order to have a leisured class of citizens freed from the necessities of life so that they could devote themselves to politics, there must be a class of citizens totally engaged in production and in an economic system.

Rousseau also acknowledges that the ancient Greeks freely participated in politics because they had slaves to do the work for them. In this it appears as if only those who have been liberated from the demands of work and labor can freely participate in politics. But labor and work still have to be done in order to open possibilities of participation in the public realm. Usually workers and laborers are more than those who can do without work and labor. When looking at her brief development of the notion of political participation, we are a bit perplexed to see that despite her awareness that it is not the way of life of the many, she still insists that it is an essential constituent of freedom and of good life.

But, on the other hand, Arendt is critical of laboring and those who labor. She in fact encourages them to revolt against their conditions in order to be able to participate in the political realm. She acknowledges laborers' revolution as action:

> The incapacity of the animal laborans for distinction and hence for and
> for speech seems to be confirmed by the striking absence of serious slave rebellions in ancient and modern times. No less striking, however, is the sudden and frequently extraordinarily productive role which the labor movements have played in modern politics. From the revolutions of 1848 to the Hungarian revolution of 1956, the European working class, by virtue of being the only organized and hence the leading section of the people, has written one of the most glorious and probably the most promising chapter of recent history.67

If the masses succeed in participating in politics, then politics can no longer remain the preserve of the leisured class.

The inconsistency that everybody should directly participate in politics even though the "political way of life has never been and will never be the way of life of the many" is more prominent in Arendt's failure to take voting and people's will and consent seriously. While Hegel allows representation in government, Arendt strongly opposes it. On the other hand, she encourages the creation of "councils" and a congress. She seems to delight in the idea that some men should speak for the rest, especially if they are chosen to do so through the consent of the people, through the exercise of the power of the people. The power of the people can remain intact if every man has an equal right to vote for a representative.

It has been argued that Arendt's concept of "consent of the people" is similar to Rousseau's "general will".68 Rousseau's argument is that everybody participates in a political community since a community of citizens is unique and coeval with its members:

> Each of us puts his person and all his power in common
> under the supreme direction of the general will, and, in
> our corporate capacity we receive each member as an
> indivisible part of the whole.69

Leroy A. Cooper opposes the view that Arendt is similar to Rousseau in this:

> [T]he idea of a Rousseauan unity and perfect harmony of
> will, which has been attributed to Arendt, is actually
> quite foreign to her perspective.70

He asserts that the few similarities that exist between Arendt and Rousseau should not lead one to the conclusion that Arendt is only repeating what Rousseau said; there are differences between them. For example, Arendt considers constitutions as very important "written documents" that are indispensable for the running of the government, while Rousseau had no suggestion of how the "general will" should rule and how a despotism of the majority could be prevented. Arendt also makes a distinction between power and law, "power having its origin in the people and law having its locus in an objective, written constitution". Rousseau, on the other hand, attributes to sovereignty an indivisible and inalienable power to make law.

What is important for us is Arendt's realization that representative government, like the ancient polis, is an indication that politics has never been and will never be the way of life of many. This realization leads Arendt to a balanced conclusion that although all citizens should be provided with and encouraged to make full use of the advantages for political participation, they should not be expected to adopt the political way of life.71 The political life will always be left in the care of those who are "politically the best", that is, those who are distinguished by "political passions--courage, the pursuit of public happiness, the state of public freedom, an ambition that strives for excellence".72 However, since this idea leads Arendt to recommend that those who lack any inclination to pursue political life should be deprived of the suffrage, her desire to let men enjoy freedom through participation in public realm serves to intensify the inequality that she fights against.

The core of this argument is that since politics is the vehicle of freedom, freedom is not to be enjoyed by all. This echoes Rousseau's paradox:

What? Is freedom to be maintained only with the support of slavery? Perhaps. The two extremes meet. Everything outside nature has its disadvantages, civil society more than all the rest. There are some situations so unfortunate that one can preserve one's freedom only at the expense of someone else; and the citizen can be perfectly free only if the slave is absolutely a slave.73

However paradoxical and even sometimes contradictory the arguments on participation and representation might be, Arendt's claim that freedom can only be derived from authentic politics remains unshaken. What she considers to be essential for political freedom is participation in the public realm of life. She chooses the above historical models in order to show how the participants in the public realm enjoy true freedom while those who do not participate do not enjoy it, only have civil liberties, negative freedoms to be enforced against the state, and freedom from bother of politics.74

What really makes her claim that "that raison d'être of politics is freedom" appear coherent is her exclusion of some factors that we usually consider to be political from her concept of politics. It is therefore essential to show how socio-economic factors, which have become ideal for political life in our own times, are regarded by Arendt as essentially pre-political and, hence, allow for little political freedom. It is also necessary to elucidate how violence and terror, which we deem as fundamental for revolution, are for Arendt the reasons why revolutions fail to achieve political freedom. Finally, it is important to establish why Arendt uses totalitarianism as the paradigm of what she considers unpolitical. Through the careful examination of all these factors we shall see why Arendt claims that the only vehicle of freedom is political action, which means that freedom exists only when people engage in political action, which means that freedom exists only when people engage in political action. We shall survey how freedom is either diminished or totally destroyed by these pre-political and unpolitical circumstances.

NOTES

1 Between Past and Future, p. 146.

2 Ibid.

3 Bernard Crick, "Freedom as Politics", Philosophy, Politics and Society, ed., Peter Leslett and W. G. Runciman (Oxford: Basil Blackwell, 1967), p. 194.

4 Between Past and Future, p. 145.

5 Michael Oakeshott, ed., Leviathan (Oxford:Blackwell, 1960), p.xiv.

6 Leroy A. Cooper, "Hannah Arendt's Political Philosophy: An Interpretation", Review of Politics 38 (April 1976), 172.

7 Between Past and Future, p. 165.

8 Ibid., p. 145.

9 The Human Condition, p.41.

10 Between Past and Future, p. 71.

11 Stephen J. Whitfield, Into the Dark: Hannah Arendt and Totalitarianism (Philadelphia: Temple University Press, 1980), p. 136, citing McKenna's "Critic of Modernity", pp. 316-17.

12 Alfred Zimmern, The Greeks Commonwealth: Politics and Economics in Fifth Century Athens (London: Oxford Univerty Press, 1931), pp. 279-313.

13 James Miller, "The Pathos of Novelty: Hannah Arendt's Image of Freedom in the Modern World," Hannah Arendt, ed. Hill, pp. 181-83; Whitfield citing from Walter Benjamin, Illuminations, ed., Hannah Arendt (New York: Harcourt, Brace and World, 1968), pp. 257, 268.

14 The Origins of Totalitarianism, p. 466.

15 Between Past and Future, p. 145.

16 Ibid., p. 106.

17 Ibid., p. 93.

18 Ibid., p. 141.

19 Ibid., p. 91.

20 Ibid., p. 92.

21 Cited in Ibid., p. 106.

22 On Revolution, p.110 ; and Between Past and Future, pp. 119-120.

23 Between Past and Future, p. 121.

24 Ibid., p. 120.

25 Ibid.

26 Ibid., p. 121.

27 Ibid.

28 Ibid.

29 Ibid., p. 125.

30 Ibid., p. 128.

31 Gordon J. Tolle, Human Nature Under Fire: The Political Philosophy of Hannah Arendt (Washington D.C.: University Press of

America, 1982), p. 107.
32 Between Past and Future, p. 126.
33 Ibid., p. 127.
34 Ibid.
35 Ibid., p. 91.
36 Ibid., p. 98.
37 On Revolution, p. 35.
38 Ibid., p. 34.
39 Ibid., p. 36.
40 Ibid., p. 21.
41 Ibid., p. 27.
42 Ibid.
43 Ibid., p. 34.
44 Ibid., p. 87.
45 Ibid., p. 25.
46 Ibid., p. 22.
47 Ibid., p. 25.
48 Ibid., pp. 70, 94-100.
49 George N. McKenna, "A Critic of Modernity: The Political Thought of Hannah Arendt", unpublished dissertation (Fordam University, 1967), p. 263.
50 On Revolution, p.108.
51 Ibid., p. 54.
52 Ibid., pp. 56-7.
53 Ibid., p. 58.
54 Ibid., p. 65.
55 Ibid., p. 25.
56 Ibid., p. 229.
57 Ibid., p. 256.
58 Ibid., p. 239.
59 Ibid., p. 260.
60 Ibid., p. 267.
61 Ibid., p. 268.
62 Margaret Canovan, The Political Thought of Hannah Arendt (London: J. M. Dent and Sons, Ltd., 1974), p. 100.
63 On Revolution, pp. 277-78.
64 Ibid.
65 Ibid., p. 279.
66 Ibid., p. 275.
67 The Human Condition, p. 215.
68 This claim is made by O'Sullivan, Kariel and Deane in the works that Cooper cites at page 67.
69 Jean-Jacques Rousseau, The Social Contract, translated and with an introduction by Willmore Kendal (Chicago: Henry Regnery Co., 1954), p. vi.
70 Cooper, p. 167.

71 On Revolution, p. 283.
72 Ibid., p. 280.
73 Rousseau, p. 142.
74 On Revolution, p. 258-85.

CHAPTER III

NON-POLITICAL ISSUES AND THE PUBLIC SPHERE

We can gain further insight into Arendt's notion of political freedom by considering, in more detail than previously, the judgments she makes of some non-political things. Her praise of political freedom derives some of its energy from her radical evaluation of non-political things.

The distinction Arendt draws between non-political or pre-political things and political action or freedom is based on her distinction between the private realm and the public realm. Work and labor for her deal with biological and domestic necessities and so belong in the private realm and "should be hidden" from the public or political realm. These activities and economies as a whole are placed in the private realm since they concern mere survival of the species; they are pre-political affairs by definition. In ancient Greece, not only were these activities kept out of the polis, but so were those who engaged in them: women, slaves, and laborers. Arendt claims that all those who cannot participate in the public realm because of their being tied to a natural function cannot enjoy freedom. They are condemned to animal-like life. She asserts that the animal laborans' life is worldless and herdlike and therefore the animal laborans is "incapable of building or inhabiting a public, worldly realm".[1]

There was no equality among those in the private realm. The master ruled and the slaves and women obeyed. Force, violence, and coercion rather than persuasion were justified in this sphere because they were the means of mastering necessity. Mastery of the private realm was a condition of membership in the public realm.

While more can be said about the details of the distinction between the private and public realms, my present concern is just to explore why Arendt thinks that labor and work do not belong to the realm of freedom. Is she right to think that bringing economic issues into politics means surrendering freedom to necessity and that in the modern age we lack genuine politics and political freedom because economic matters have entered the public sphere? I shall show that Arendt, heavily influenced by Kant, sees the distinction between the realm of necessity and the realm of freedom,[2] and then explain why Arendt consistently eliminates violence and coercion from the realm of freedom.

Labor and Work

Arendt distinguishes between work and labor. She is aware that the distinction is unusual and that very few thinkers have made it. But she examines the etymology and the use of these words in both ancient and modern European languages and concludes that they are

69

"etymologically unrelated words".3

The human activity of labor specifically corresponds to what Arendt calls the condition of life. The labor process recreates and maintains the cyclical character of biological life in which the production and consumption of the means of life is the central feature. Labor ensures the life of the species. Animal laborans produces to consume and consumes to produce. Thus, labor possesses a certain futility. Man produces and consumes in a repetitive cycle. He devours the world, but he in turn is consumed by time. Also, labor cannot guarantee the existence of that stable, permanent world that serves as man's permanent habitation on earth because its products perish through consumption almost immediately following their production.

The ancient Greeks despised labor precisely because it served the "slavish" demands of necessity.4 The laborer was imprisoned in the ever-recurring cycle of the life process, that is, the natural process of growth and decay. Thus, necessity is a distinctive feature of labor. The labor process is wholly dictated by the urges and biological needs of life. Arendt realizes that no matter how necessary labor may be for maintenance of life, it must to some extent be mastered or escaped in order to enjoy freedom. We shall later examine how this is possible.

Unlike work, as we shall see, and action, as we have already seen, labor is essentially purposeless, with no definable beginning or end. Arendt further notes that the activity of laboring is painful and burdensome. Nothing "ejects one more radically from the world than exclusive concentration upon the body's life, a concentration forced upon man in slavery or in the extremity of unbearable pain".5 Moreover, labor is an activity that is not distinctively human; it is an activity that people share with other forms of life because human beings, like any other living organism, are forced to labor in order to keep themselves alive.

As Arendt sees it, labor alienates man from the public world or the human world because it lacks the expressive qualities (through word and deed) of action. The silence of the labor process means that labor is always and in every case a solitary activity, even when carried out by organized groups of men, for example, slaves or the laborers of modernity. However, we shall see that this is not true of all labor.

Arendt regards men who live exclusively private lives as

> deprived of things essential to truly human life...the reality that comes from being seen and heard by others...an "objective" relationship with them that comes from being related to and separated from them through the intermediary of a common world of things.6

She argues that whenever the concern for survival is allowed to dominate the other spheres of existence, alienation results; survival becomes more important than freedom. For Arendt, concern for the sphere of freedom means one must not be bound by concern for one's physical life. One must liberate oneself temporarily from the necessity of labor before one can engage in action.

The ancient Greeks despised laborers because of the solitariness of labor and its shamefulness. It had to be "hidden": it was not to be seen, heard or remembered, because of its futility. Arendt, like the Greeks, links the futile worldlessness of labor with the human sense of shame over our bodily functions, which are essential but which nonetheless seem to make us less than human. For the ancients and for Arendt, man's labor is literally the labor of his body.

Arendt is critical of modern politics because of the elevation of the laboring process to public status, to a position of primacy over work and action. Within an explicit reference of Marx, she argues that labor's rise to prominence is traceable to its enormous productivity beyond the point necessary for the laborer'ssubsistence. Such a surplus secures even the life processes of those who are not directly involved in the activity of labor itself: "/T/he labor of some suffices for the life of all."7 We might expect Arendt to welcome this, since in order to participate in the public realm one must be liberated from the bodily pain of toil in the service of necessity. However, Arendt considers the modern means of production a threat to the conditions required for a genuine politics. She argues that man is not in fact liberated from the private realm by the enormous productivity generated by the modern animal laborans. Modern society, by becoming a "laboring", or "consumer", society, has capitulated to the futility of labor and reduced life to "productive slavery".8 Man's apparent triumph over necessity has intensified necessity's hold on man and has as well created the possibility of greater social and political conflict. But Arendt asserts this rather than demonstrates the issue complicates it. How does triumph over necessity intensify necessity's hold on man. Arendt thus concedes that the key to human freedom is not in the elimination of necessity but in its rational mastery. She argues:

> Man cannot be free if he does not know that he is

subject to necessity because his freedom is always won in his never wholly successful attempts to liberate himself from necessity.9

But what is meant, then, by mastery of necessity? How does Arendt's laborer overcome necessity and enter into the public realm? We shall now examine her notion of work to find an answer to this question.

Unlike labor, whose products are immediately consumed by the living process, work's main features are durability and permanence of the products. In connection with the general conditions of natality and mortality, work and its products bestow a permanence and some durability on the futile and fleeting quality of life. This does not mean that the products of work last forever. They just enjoy a relatively permanent existence. They last longer than the products of labor, but they, too, ultimately disappear:

> The life process which permeates our whole being invades it, (the human artifact) too, and if we do not use the things of the world, they also will eventually decay, return into the over-all natural process from which they were drawn and against which they were erected. If left to itself or discarded from the human world, the chair will again become wood, and the wood will decay and return to the soil from which the tree sprang before it was cut off to become the material upon which to work and with which to build.10

To demonstrate the durability and permanence of the products of work, she refers to works of art. They have an outstanding permanence and durability. They withstand the corroding effects of nature because they are not used like other tools that are the products of work. Their durability is of a higher order for they can attain a permanence throughout the ages. The stability of the world becomes transparent in the permanence of the work of art. It is a premonition of immortality, "not the immortality of the soul or of life but of something immortal achieved by mortal hands".11

This durability and permanence is also characteristic of the tools used by laborers. These tools make the laborer's burden less difficult, but they do not do away with the burden altogether. Though Arendt may be overstating her own case, she does claim that the laborer overcomes his predicament with the help of the worker, who introduces tools to build a world. She argues

that the animal laborans could be redeemed from its

72

predicament of imprisonment in the ever-recurring cycle of the life process, of being forever subject to the necessity of labor and consumption, only through the mobilization of another human capacity, the capacity for making, fabricating, and producing of homo faber, who as a toolmaster not only eases the pain and troubles of laboring but erects a world of durability.12

It is clear that work, as Arendt understands it, is the way by which mortals become redeemed from the predicament of labor.

The activity of labor, as we saw, is geared to necessity, whereas the activity of work involves an element of freedom. The worker has far more freedom than the laborer in choosing means and ends. Moreover, the worker is free to undo what he has done. He is free to destroy what he has made.

Another important idea resulting from her conception of work is that products of work bestow some meaning on human existence, without which man's existence would not be distinguished from that of lower animals. However, Arendt realizes that the very tools and instruments, together with the network of means-end relations that help the worker bestow meaning on human labor also create problems. For the worker is not totally out of its predicament. He cannot truly find meaning because meaning is permanent and work produces an infinite regress of means and ends. He makes the tools as the means towards a certain end, which in turn becomes a means to another end, and so on. In Arendt's view, the means- end chain never terminates. For example, the worker makes a hammer and a chisel in order to cut stones, which he uses to build a house. His end is the finished house. But once the house is finished, it becomes a means to something else. The worker can break out of the unending means-end chain only by establishing himself as an end in himself. He "has to turn away from the objective world of use things and fall back upon the subjectivity of use itself".13

From the foregoing we can already see why Arendt rejects all forms of utilitarianism. She asserts that utilitarianism generates the futility of a means-end regress because it lacks an ultimate standard. She argues:

This perplexity, inherent in all consistent utilitarianism, the philosophy of homo faber par excellence, can be diagnosed theoretically as an innate incapacity to understand the distinction between utility and meaning-fulness, which we express linguistically by distinguishing

73

between "in order to" and "for the sake of." Thus the
ideal of usefulness permeating a society of craftmen...is
actually no longer a matter of utility but of meaning. It
is "for the sake of" usefulness in general that homo faber
judges and does everything in terms of "in order to." The
ideal of usefulness itself, like the ideals of other
societies, can no longer be conceived as something needed
in order to have something else; it simply defies
questioning about its own use....The perplexity of
utilitarianism is that it gets caught in the unending chain
of means and ends without ever arriving at some principle
which could justify the category of means and end, that
is, of utility itself. The "in order to" has become the
content of the "for the sake of"; in other words, utility
established as meaning generates meaninglessness.14

Arendt is quite clear on the issue that usefulness and utility simply
cannot be the ultimate standards for human life. The philosophy of
homo faber does run into difficulties in attempting to find an ultimate
standard by which to judge its activities; it gets caught in an infinite
regress of means-ends. Arendt, therefore, is critical of the activity of
homo faber because wherever it dominates, "value" seems to consist
solely in the exchange value of things as commodities.15 Thus, "work"
has just as much a negative consequence for human activity as does
"labor" when either is elevated to the highest of human actions.

Arendt insists that work does not belong to the political realm
because it is not rooted in the condition of plurality. Contrary to our
experience of modern factories, she insists that the worker typically
makes things in isolation. He does not necessarily need the presence of
others. He at times enters into relationship with others only by
entering the public market place and exchanging his products with
others. In this type of relationship the worker is defined by his
products, whereas for Arendt man should be defined by "words and
deeds". The market is a realm of politics that is merely "useful",
that serves only the ends of peace and security. This is not genuine
politics, which is manifested only when the actor freely speaks and
acts in the public realm. Unlike work, action is rooted in the
condition of plurality.

Arendt's discussion of works of art provides a bridge to her
delineation of action as distinct from labor and work. She characterizes works of art as the most intensely worldly of all things.16 These
works adorn the world through generations and endow men with a
home in the world. Their source is the human capacity for thought.
Their creation reflects the clear beginning and end in the thought and

the objectification of artist.

The role of thought in artistic creation has prompted some modern theorists to regard the work of art as a subjective expression of the artist's personality or emotions. Reacting against this modern theory, Arendt responds that the appearance of the art work, and not its creator, is the aim of the artistic process. The creation of objects of utility and beauty requires the initiative of the artisan and artist, but aims at the appearance of the worldly object itself. Arendt holds that only action and speech reveal the identities of personal actors.

Moreover, Arendt admits that speech and action are as futile as labor in that they leave no product after they are finished. They only leave the appearance of the personal agent himself/herself. Only the objectified expressions of artists, poets, historiographers--the various examples of homo faber in his highest capacity--can preserve the stories of the actors. Without homo faber, the story enacted and told by acting and speaking men would not survive at all.

We now see why Arendt holds that labor and work do not belong to the realm of freedom. From her discussion it cannot be said that she disdains repetitive toil or that she does not see the necessity for life-sustaining activities. What she objects to is the fact that life-cycles are sometimes seen as the sum total of life instead of necessities that are prerequisites for freedom. In the modern age, labor has become the only meaningful human capacity. Even work has ultimately given way to labor. The products of work are consumed at such a fast rate that the relative durability of work becomes transformed into the consumption of the labor process. The modern obsession with maintaining life (necessity) tends to reduce the sphere of concern for public freedom.

Labor and work both take place in the "private realm" of existence. For Arendt, as it was in Hellenic thought, only a man who abandons labor and work in order to engage in the public realms can properly be called human. Otherwise he is merely another of nature's creatures. Man must also abandon labor and work in order to be free to contemplate for the purpose of acting. Neither animal laborans nor homo faber have any freedom to act: "/T/he spare time of the animal laborans is never spent in anything but consumption, and the more time left to him, the greedier and more craving his appetites".17 Freedom can only be enjoyed by those who abandon labor and work.

Socio-economic Factors

Arendt rules out economic matters from the public realm. For her, these matters, like labor and work, are pre-political because of the connection to the process of life. She is critical of the modern "society" that makes possible the display of the socio-economic concern in the public. She concludes that the public realm has withered away because it has been superseded by the private, politics has given way to economics, so that what is now left is a bunch of "private activities displayed in the open".18 In this way, freedom is submerged by necessity. Politics, according to Arendt, should be about public matters.

Here, also, Arendt follows the ancient Greeks in their distinction between the public life and the household concerns. Economics belonged in the household, and, like all activities within the household, it was concerned with maintenance of life. As such it was an activity of necessity rather than of freedom. This is a reason why Arendt proposes a conception of politics devoid of economic concern. Free political life, both traditionally and in Arendt's view, presupposes the prior mastering of economic necessity; politics was precisely the realm from which "everything merely necessary or useful" was "strictly excluded", where "no activity that served only the purpose of making a living or sustaining only the life process, was permitted to enter".19

Thus, anyone who performed household activities was regarded as unfree. His endless physical labor and the pressure of physical need robbed him of the time to think and indulge in the high-minded life of free people. His urgent need was food rather than freedom, which he definitely did not have. Since his tastes were circumscribed by physical needs, happiness deriving from the satisfaction of his needs was his prime goal, rather than honor. His life by its very nature lacked the pursuit of public excellence. Being driven by needs of his body he was not in a good position to make genuine moral and political choices.20 Even if he were allowed to participate in the polis, his concern for the essentials of life would still haunt him and force him to change "politics" into the "accomplishment of mere physical welfare". For this reason Arendt states that such a person should not be allowed to intrude into the life of politics. She considers such a person a slave "imprisoned in the privacy of his own body, caught in the fulfillment of needs in which nobody can fully communicate".21 Thus, labor demoralizes and mutes; it has a biological but not a political dimension.

Some commentators are quite shocked by what they consider as

Arendt's harsh indictment of the animal laborans.22 They think Arendt unjustly condemns the laborers and labor unions, which play a significant role in politics and in building a better world, as "worldless"23 and "herdlike".24 They also claim that she contradicts herself by thinking that the exclusion of laborers from politics would make the world truly political and by asserting that "the use of servants" is indispensable for the life of the public realm while on the other hand praising the working class as leading the way in inventing new forms of political action and discovering the joys of public freedom.

However, Arendt does not contradict herself. Her indictment of animal laborans is the indictment of an activity, a human condition or a relationship to the world, but not of workers and laborers as human beings. Arendt is here referring to a "world whose chief values are dictated by labor, i.e., where all human activities have been transformed into laboring".25 Therefore, she is not saying that the exclusion of laborers from politics would make the world truly human. She just means that persons in their role as laborers, that is, the concerns of laborers qua laborers, should be excluded. She only accuses the modern age of surrendering freedom to necessity by bringing economic issues into politics.

Of course, at times it appears as if Arendt claims that since labor mutes, laborers lose one of the essential characteristics of human beings--speech.

> Men can very well live without laboring, they can force others to labor for them, and they can very well decide merely to use and enjoy the world of things without themselves adding a single useful object to it; the life of an exploiter or slaveholder and the life of a parasite may be unjust, but they certainly are human. A life without speech and without action, on the other hand--and this the only way of life that in earnest has renounced all appearance and all vanity in the biblical sense of the word--is literally dead to the world; it has ceased to be a human life because it is no longer lived among men.26

But what Arendt really affirms is that without action and speech, mere life can easily be elevated to the highest good; and that in the modern age, laboring, which sustains that life, has in fact become the dominant activity. What justifies human life for Arendt is that which defies and transcends the mortality of individual life and the natural cyclical processes that surround it. For her, freedom can only be fully enjoyed in a true public realm, not in a "world whose chief values are dictated by labor".

Arendt's argument, that once economic matters enter the public sphere political freedom is destroyed, is based on her view of the ever-expanding social realm. What she sees as the rise of the social realm is the destruction of the politics by consumerism. For her, this puts animal laborans and homo faber in a position of dominance. She attacks Marx directly as a symbol of the destruction of the Western politics. She argues that Marx exaggerated the importance of labor and made it the highest human activity.

We pointed out in the preceding chapter that Arendt failed to perceive the crucial distinction Marx made between animal laborans and homo faber and that her concept of labor is different from Marx's. Rather than championing animal laborans, Marx believed in the power of man as homo faber. Work, according to him, should take the place once occupied by those who participated in the polis. This was the revolution of labor, and he regarded it as a supreme political act. Marx directed his challenge against the classical conception of politics, which requires that the many labor to furnish the material conditions to enable the few to engage in political action. Marx could not accept the fact that the largest class of contributors (the proletariat) had no rightful claim to the civilized advantages that political society makes possible. Arendt, on the other hand, sees the participation of workers and laborers in the public realm as the "withering away" of the political realm and as the triumph of the social realm, which has in a relatively short time "transformed all modern communities into societies of laborers and jobholders" by allowing activities that by their nature are private to assume public significance.

For Arendt, the French Revolution is a good example of what happens when the multitude of the poor and oppressed, traditionally excluded from the public realm, begin to "doubt that poverty is inherent in the human condition" and to regard their needs as a political issue.27 The bursting of the poor into the public realm and their introducing into politics the very elements of physical appetite, of economic necessity, destroyed the French Revolution and disenabled it from founding political freedom. The failure of the French Revolution affirmed Arendt's claim that the goal of revolution should never be the elimination of economic injustice or liberation of people from poverty. Such matters she regards as "social" problems. So, for Arendt, all the issues of want and hunger are not political problems and cannot be solved by political means. They should be solved in the private realm where they belong.

NON-POLITICAL ISSUES AND THE PUBLIC SPHERE

In addition to denouncing the French Revolution as a means to achieve political freedom, she categorically states:

> Nothing, we might say today, could be more obsolete than to attempt to liberate mankind from poverty by political means; nothing could be more futile and more dangerous.28

If, then, mankind cannot be liberated from poverty by political means, Arendt indirectly admits the use of either pre-political or unpolitical means as a necessary instrument for the achievement of the political freedom, for one has to be liberated from poverty before one can enjoy political freedom. The distinction between what for Arendt falls into the public and what falls into the private domain does not apply in the way it once did in modern life. However, it is very difficult to determine what Arendt advocates since sometimes she appears to be saying that the existence of the pre-political sphere and the use of pre-political means are unavoidable if individuals are to be allowed to develop differences in character, which is a very important element for their appearance in the public realm. At other times, however, her remarks suggest that her attitude towards the pre-political sphere is predominantly hostile. Her sharp distinction between economic activity and political action is at times blurred by her admission that

> more than sheer economic activity is involved in exchange and that "economic man", when he makes his appearance on the market, is an acting being and neither exclusively a producer nor a trader and barterer.29

Her reduction of everything that bears on the maintenance of life to the "realm of necessity" obscures the close connection that exists between politics and economics in reality.

However, Arendt insists that economic issues are not political for they are conducted according to different principles from those of politics. The management of politics and economic affairs also needs "a different kind of talent". As Cooper points out, "this does not exclude the possibility that there would be governmental agencies for handling economic problems".30 But Arendt wonders whether

> the political principles of equality and self-rule can be applied to the economic sphere as well. It may be that ancient political theory, which held that economics, since it was bound up with the necessities of life, needed the rule of masters to function, was not so wrong after all.31

The failure of the councils as political bodies was precisely in their conducting both politics and economics in the same way. She contends:

> The fatal mistake of the councils has always been that they themselves did not distinguish clearly between participation in public affairs and administration or management of things in the public interest. In the form of workers' councils, they have again and again tried to take over the management of the factories, and all these attempts have ended in dismal failure.32

As we shall see later, the failure to distinguish between the economic and the political realms is the cause of modern totalitarian regimes, in which freedom is surrendered to necessity.

She suggests that in order to protect the political realm from being suffocated by economic issues, "the expropriation of the masses, which began with capitalism and was continued by socialism, must be halted and reversed".33   She assumes that once the masses "regain" sufficient property, they will be free for political action.   In fact, she believes a form of private property, although property belongs to the private realm, is absolutely required if there is to be a meaningful political realm at all.

Yet Arendt also makes a distinction between the private property essential for entrance into the political realm and the private property that modern government seeks to maintain.   What is now commonly called private property is in reality wealth.   This distinction between private property and wealth prompts Arendt to argue that the present potentially wealthy societies are ironically becoming increasingly property-less.   Finding out what she means will help us understand why she excludes socio-economic issues from the realm of politics.

Historically (in both ancient Greece and Rome), of all private concerns, private property had the greatest relevance for the public realm because it served as the chief condition for admission to the political realm.   Arendt asserts:

> Originally, property meant no more or less than to leave one's location in a particular part of the world and therefore to belong to the body politic, that is, to be head of one of the families which together constituted the public realm.34

Property helped the owners to meet physical necessity.   It also offered

Property helped the owners to meet physical necessity. It also offered "the only reliable hiding place" from common affairs, a refuge required because a "life spent entirely in public, in the presence of others becomes...shallow".35 Private property was thus a necessary element of privacy, which was important for the development of certain distinctively human attributes--"the passions of the heart, the thoughts of the mind, the delights of the senses"36 that constitute the sphere of intimacy.

However, at the beginning of the modern age, when "the emergence of society--the rise of housekeeping, its activities, problems, and organizational devices--from the shadow interior of the household into the light of the public sphere" began to take place, "the private care for private property became a public concern". Arendt claims:

> Society, when it first entered the public realm, assumed the disguise of an organization of property owners who, instead of claiming access to the public realm because of their wealth, demanded protection from it for the accumulation of more wealth.37

However, what is happening in the modern age is that economic security is no more a prerequisite for entrance into the public realm but has become the goal the modern government is to achieve for all citizens. The work of the household has become everyone's concern, and self-interest has entered the public realm. More and more individuals demand from government protection and stability for the accumulation of private wealth. Today it is hard to imagine economic transactions taking place without government intervention at one level or another.38

Wealth, as Arendt thinks of it, bears some relation to property. Wealth, like property, concerns the means by which one draws a livelihood. It also has political significance because it can make freedom possible by organizing the realm of necessity within walls of the household such that one can leave it and enter political life. Since public life is possible "only after the much more urgent needs of life itself" are met, to possess wealth means "to be master over one's own necessities of life and therefore potentially to be a free person, free to transcend his own life and enter the world all have in common".39

On the other hand, wealth lacks the durability and stability of property. It is a continuous flow of material utilities. It is capable of expansion, that is, it can be accumulated. It is accumulation that lures property owners. But, in antiquity, the property owner who "chose to enlarge his property (wealth) instead of using it up in leading a political life...willingly sacrificed his freedom and became voluntarily what the slave was against his own will, a servant of necessity".40

Arendt regards the continuous accumulation of property (wealth) as destructive of property in the proper sense. Property is sacrificed to the demands of accumulation. She attacks modern government for failing to defend property as such and for encouraging the unhampered pursuit of more property.

Thus far conceived, Arendt's analysis of wealth and property is a distinction between property as a stable basis for free activity and property as capital. This distinction simply affirms Arendt's assertion that politics is concerned with freedom rather than with material utilities that belong to the private realm. Before deciding whether this assertion and distinction is possible in practice, we shall examine the last factors that Arendt claims should be excluded from the realm of freedom.

Force and Violence

Arendt further claims that the introduction of economic issues into the public realm is a source of force and violence, which have no role in the establishment of political freedom. Her views on the role of force and violence, as on the character and function of private property, grow out of an analysis of the central elements of the private realm and the nature of labor. In Arendt's view, force and violence are to be excluded from the public sphere because they are implicit in the performance of the household function. She concludes that the slave in antiquity and the worker under capitalism are not free because they are subjected, at least potentially, to the exercise of force by the master or the market. The master-slave or capitalist-worker relationship implies the condition of ruling and being ruled, which is necessarily coercive.

Arendt agrees that force and violence may be necessary in the private realm because man cannot completely escape the pull of necessity. Given the demands of necessity and the private realm,

> force and violence are justified in this sphere because
> they are the only means to master necessity--for
> instance, by ruling over slaves--and become free. Because
> all human beings are subject to necessity, they are

82

entitled to violence towards others; violence is a prepolitical act of liberating oneself from the necessity of life for the freedom of the world....To be poor or to be in ill health meant to be subject to physical necessity, and to be a slave meant to be subject, in addition, to man-made violence.41

She sees force and violence as the main instruments of control in the realm of necessity. She recognizes that man's relation to physical nature is antagonistic and that violence does help men to unleash this sublimated force against man. But this does not mean that violence becomes political. It is still pre-political because, before he can construct a genuine political realm, man must first master necessity or somehow extricate himself from it.

Sometimes the use of violence might be necessary for the maintenance of a state's independence from other states. But, as Francis Wayne Allen remarks, "this only points up the absence of politics in international relations".42 It may be used in world affairs, but it "cannot be used domestically without undermining politics altogether". In domestic affairs, "violence functions as the last resort of power against criminals or rebels...that is, against single individuals who, as it were, refuse to be overpowered by the consensus of the majority".43 This sort of violence is just for the maintenance of power, especially when those who act violently refuse to accept the consensus of power.

However, Arendt's rejection of violence is directed against Machiavelli's claim that violence is necessary for the new building up of the world; Marx's claim that violence is a necessary part of a society's revolutionary birth pains; Sorel's claim that violence is essentially creative and therefore the proper mode for society's producers, the working class, as opposed to society's consumers; and Sartre's claim that violence is essential to man's creation, in "man recreating himself".44 It is from Arendt's arguments against these justifications of violence that we find her notion of violence and force and the reasons why she thinks they must be excluded from the public realm.

Her rejection of violence in the political sphere is primarily found in her romantic reconstruction of the polis model. Even though she does not tell us how the government in the polis worked, she tells us that free men, who were neither rulers nor ruled, were the core of the polis. Laws and formal structures were not the heart of the polis. In this way Arendt's model for political life is different from our usual understanding of politics in which sovereignty and power over the play a major role. Since in the polis each individual acted spontaneously, it was unheard of that one person held power by which he ruled others. The existence of such a power would involve the right to command or to coerce by force or violence; hence, it would be totally incompatible with the polis idea of political freedom.

It is important to recognize that Arendt makes a distinction between "force" as coercion and "power", which is closely related to authority that preserves political freedom. She clearly states that power creates the stability necessary for endurance of the public realm. The strength of an authentic political body does not lie in violence, force or coercion; it is based on free agreement among participants. This consent of the participants is "power":

> /P/ower corresponds to the human ability not just to act, but to act in consent. Power is never the property of an individual; it belongs to a group and remains in existence only so long as the group keeps together. When we say of somebody that he is "in power" we actually refer to his being empowered by a certain number of people to act in their name.45

Acting in consent implies some respect for human freedom. On the other hand, force can only be exercised by one side against the other, or as Arendt puts it, force is "one against all".46

Many revolutions, in Arendt's view, failed to establish a realm of freedom because the leaders did not distinguish between "violence" and "power".47 They ignored people's opinions and kept everybody in a state of perfect obedience and even sacrificed others "to their 'principles' or to the course of history or to the cause of revolution as such".48 They used force in order to realize some goals rather than rely on the mutual assistance and loyalty of the people. They assumed that violence would produce power. But power is always formed by a group of people who deliberately bind themselves together, and it belongs to this group and remains in existence only as long as this political group empowers the public space and makes it legitimate.

Revolutions failed whenever revolutionaries acted like tyrants, even though tyrants have sometimes been "successful" in ruling by "blood and iron". Tyranny is not power, but its diminution and the breakdown of politics. Montesquieu pointed out that tyranny relies not on power but isolation, "on the isolation of the tyrant from his subjects and the isolation of the subjects from each other through mutual fear and suspicion".49 This brings Arendt to the following conclusion:

> Tyranny prevents the development of power, not only in a
> particular segment of the public realm but in its entirety;
> it generates, in other words, importance as naturally as
> bodies politic generate power.50

Tyranny comes into the picture only when power breaks down.

What is clear from the above is that, according to Arendt,
"power" is political whereas violence and force are not. They may
appear at the same time with power. In that case, power remains the
dominant element because it allows people to think and act together.
When power begins to diminish, violence at times comes into play as
means of keeping control. But violence hardly leads to a new space
empowered by the people. Thus, violence does not enter the realm of
freedom; it destroys it. Then, "to speak of non-violent power is
actually redundant. Violence can destroy power; it is utterly incapable
of creating it."51

Furthermore, Arendt finds that the mistake of including violence
in the political realm is the result of considering violence as action.
There has been a tendency to equate violence with action because the
beginning of something new "must be intimately connected with
violence...."52 Like action, which is the beginning of something new,
in the violent exercises of the revolutions we find the initial
intimations that a new order, a new beginning, is imminent. For
revolutionaries, this new order was a tearing down and building up of
the world. Arendt claims that Machiavelli first intuited the necessity
of violence in this building:

> Like the Romans, Machiavelli and Robespierre felt
> founding was the central political action, the one great
> deed that established the public-political realm and made
> politics possible; but unlike the Romans, to whom this
> was an event of the past, they felt that for this supreme
> "end" all "means", chiefly the means of violence, were
> justified. They understood the act of founding entirely in
> the image of making....It is ...because of his rediscovery
> of the foundation experience and his reinterpretation of it
> in terms of the justification of (violent) means for a
> supreme end, that Machiavelli may be regarded as the
> ancestor of modern revolutions....53

Later on, however, Arendt recognized that even the Roman
experience of foundation indicates the affinity between beginnings and

85

violence.   The violent element during the foundation of Rome is expressed in the legend of Romulus's slaying of Remus.54

Martin Jay suggests that Arendt accepts violence as a necessary element in the foundation of a stable society. He argues that Arendt makes a clear affinity between beginnings and violence, and he concludes that "such an affinity serves to muddy her distinction between violence and politics...and that her distinction between politics and violence is less than convincing...."55 Nonetheless, Arendt insists that the violent activity, which Machiavelli and Robespierre regard as necessary for building up the world, is a sheer fabrication and therefore cannot be included in the public realm, where only action has a role. She also observes that the foundation of Rome was not a result of the affinity between beginnings and violence:

> It was perhaps because of the inner affinity between the arbitrariness inherent in all beginnings, and human potentialities for crime that the Romans decided to derive their descendance not from Romulus, who had slain Remus, but from Aeneas.56

Arendt's point here is that politics, as an orderly process, is the opposite of violent upheaval. Violence makes impossible genuine action and speech. It cannot create the grounds for endurance of freedom. So, Arendt eliminates violence from the political realm because it isolates those who have guns from those who must follow the course of the revolution. It isolates the subjects from each other through mutual fear and suspicion.

She also excludes violence from the political realm because it is not the characteristic political relationship among the members of the public realm. Unlike speech and action, it is mute; it destroys the space of freedom between persons because it is an attempt to destroy some of the persons themselves. It cannot reveal who one is. Thus, violence does not enter the realm of freedom; it destroys it.

Finally, Arendt excludes violence from the political realm because of its instrumental character. Violence is not an end itself but a means to some end. It is instrumental, and it is always done for the sake of something. Arendt argues the following:

> The very substance of violent action is ruled by the means-end category, whose chief characteristic, if applied to human affairs, has always been that the end is in danger of being overwhelmed by the means which it justifies and which are needed to reach it.57

Violence can never be accepted in the political realm where actions of political men are never predictable.

The difficulty we face here is that Arendt does not show us how violence can be excluded from the political realm. I do not mean that politics is a perpetually violent upheaval as opposed to an orderly process. The problem is that Arendt does not tell us how this orderly and genuine political situation can ever be restored once it is destroyed, for example, by the tyrant who substitutes violence for power. If people rise up against him, Arendt says they are just a mob who can only substitute one form of violence for another and never attain true power. She takes their rebellion as a sheer reflection of social activity rather than political action. She does not consider them as acting politically since they usually act without principles and since their uprising does not spring from a desire for freedom but from a condition of oppression, which is similar to that of poverty. Their activity is just for liberty, that is, liberation from oppression rather than for freedom. In the same way, she concludes that the French Revolution failed because the poverty of the masses became a public issue and therefore introduced rage and compassion that led to the demand "for swift and direct action, that is, for action with means of violence".58 But it is not true, as Gene Sharp remarks, that the struggle of the poor "inevitably produces terror. Compassion and rage do not always lead to violence. And swift direct action can be nonviolent."59

Liberation or Freedom?

Arendt distinguishes sharply between "liberation" and "political freedom". While for us freedom and liberation from oppression is the same thing, Arendt holds that liberation from oppression is just liberty and not freedom. She claims that in the modern age freedom is wrongly confused with the ending of possibly tyrannous actions and is identified with "the more or less free range of non-political activities which a given body politic will permit and guarantee to those who constitute it".60 These "non-political activities" are socio-economic and moral issues. These activities are insufficient and marginal to freedom, though far from irrelevant. They render political life, in Arendt's understanding, sterile.

Political freedom for Arendt is something positive. It is an opportunity to participate directly in public discussion and actions of one's political society. The actual content of freedom is participation in the public affairs.61 Freedom is not simply a "liberation", that is, the casting off of the old tyranny and getting the civil and non-political liberties. The eighteenth-century revolutions were aimed at these liberties. They wished to claim civil rights that would eliminate any tyrannous action. In Arendt's view, they wished to liberate people from the oppressive affairs. They also wanted freedom in the sense of general participation in public affairs or general admission to the public realm. Thus, the revolutionary spirit has included both the desire to liberate and the desire "to build a new house where freedom" could dwell.62 This attempt both to end tyranny and to build freedom was, in Arendt's view, unprecedented and unequalled. It has not, however, always been successful. In America, this effort reached fruition in the work of the founding fathers; in France it was killed by the more desperate ambitions of the Jacobins.

It is mainly in her reasons why the American and French revolutions failed to establish political freedom that we find the differences between "liberation" and the foundation of political freedom. Liberation is the answer to the "social question", whereas the foundation of freedom is essentially bound up with the political realm. Arendt declares:

> It may be a truism to say that liberation and freedom are not the same; that liberation may be the condition of freedom but by no means leads automatically to it; that the notion of liberty implied in liberation can only be negative, and hence, that even the intention of liberating is not identical with the desire for freedom. Yet if these truisms are frequently forgotten, it is because liberation has always loomed large and the foundation of freedom has always been uncertain, if not altogether futile.63

The very process of conquest of poverty "liberation" as the basic revolutionary end defeats the foundation of political freedom. The advent of the poor as a political force and poverty as the prime social evil directed the French Revolution's emotions into different channels from political ones. Pride, like one of the participants in the Greek polis, gave way to compassion; the desire to be heard in the public arena gave way to the desire to alleviate those sufferings of men that stem from material necessity. Thus, the objective of the French Revolution became not freedom but happiness, not creation of public space in which men could act but the safeguarding of their private welfare.

Arendt holds that compassion and happiness, by their very nature, are not political. She affirms that "pity, taken as the spring of virtue, has proved to possess a greater capacity for cruelty than cruelty itself".64 In her view, the public self cannot be happy, nor should it seek after happiness. The happiness she is talking about is the satisfaction that results from a life lived with some satisfaction, which results from a life lived with some measure of pleasure in family and material things and some measure of certainty about the future. This happiness, like the "warmth of the hearth", can only be experienced in the privacy of the home, not in the public realm. It is also the ideal of animal laborans because it is intimately associated with the natural "rhythms" of social or bodily life. To the contrary, the man of action does many things that necessarily cause him to suffer from the consequences of his action, for "to do and suffer are like opposite sides of the same coin".65 This image of the man of action is a familiar one in ancient Greek tragedy.

Liberty is also concerned with socio-economic justice. This type of justice is the quest for approximate material equality. Thus, it is necessarily tied to life and its expanding needs. In this way, the demand for justice is interminable since the collective needs of men are insatiable.66 Arendt insists that freedom is not concerned with securing justice of this kind, even if such justice were deemed to be a desirable goal. Like the ancient Greeks, Arendt holds that such justice is a private "household" affair, which has no business in the public realm. The sphere of freedom is for the sake of "good" life, whereas the satisfaction of human needs and wants is not part of the political equation at all.

Another way of looking at the difference between liberation and freedom is to see it as a question of management against politics in Arendt's sense. Liberation is an involvement in quasi-political activities like legislation of laws and the administration of legal justice. Those who are managers or administrators function in a sphere of life whose principle is necessity; their duty and their aim is to ensure efficient operation within the social realm. Those who are politicians, in Arendt's sense, are supposed to operate in the field of human relations. They deal with people rather than with satisfying wants; they operate in what Arendt would consider the realm of freedom.67

Arendt's theory is radically different from the modern view, which identifies the political and the social, or the political and the moral, or some combination of both. Thus, the modern view of politics does not distinguish between liberation and freedom. Although Arendt's conception of the political is purged of a fair amount of what modern opinion would attribute to politics, she does not regard the socio-economic and moral issues themselves as irrelevant to politics. Therefore, according to Arendt, "liberation" from material necessity precedes the "foundation of freedom" but is not identical with it. Even Aristotle recognized material necessity as the origin, though not an end, of politics. Liberation from necessity was p-rerequisite for entrance into the polis. Arendt insists that it is also a necessary condition for the foundation of freedom in the polis sense. Liberation is necessary for those who are in need of material necessities, but liberation in the sense of socio-economic stability is not to be confused with the foundation of a sphere where public-minded men encounter one another--to be more precise, a sphere in which true political freedom is present. Liberation can occur under monarchical (although not under tyrannical or despotic) rule, but freedom, in Arendt's view, needs the constitution of a republic.

It is therefore clear that while freedom and liberation from oppression is the same thing for us, for Arendt, liberation from oppression is just liberty and not freedom. Those who try to liberate themselves from oppression are not free because they act from necessity. They cannot found and maintain a public realm. On this point Arendt is really being consistent with what she considers to be an authentic political action. Therefore, for her, violence is pre-political and can be used as coercion in the private realm. It does not belong to the public realm.

Critique

We have just seen that Arendt insists on a split between politics and economic issues so that true political activity must be free from all economic interests or must be devoid of instrumental concerns. She claims that even violence must be excluded from the political realm because it is the result of the introduction of the economic matters into the public realm. I shall then determine whether Arendt really advocates an absolute split between politics and economic concerns as some critics claim,68 and whether her views are possible in the modern world.

Some critics of Arendt's views on politics and socio-economic concerns maintain that in asserting the primacy of the political realm Arendt fails to see how politics is a function of socio-economic forces. They conclude that her sharp distinction between political and economic concerns is unreal in the modern world. Jurgen Habermas states this conclusion in these words:

> I want only to indicate the curious perspective that
> Hannah Arendt adopts: a state which is relieved of the
> administrative processing of social problems; a politics

which is cleansed of socio-economic issues; an
institutionalization of public liberty which is independent
of the organization of public wealth; a radical democracy
which inhibits its liberating efficacy just at the
boundaries where political oppression ceases and social
repression begins--this path is unimaginable for any
modern society.69

Such critics further point out that Arendt's relegation of everything
that bears on the maintenance of life to the "realm of necessity"
obscures the close connection that exists between politics and
economics in any advanced society. They complain that with one
stroke Arendt cuts out most of the stuff of modern political discussion
and stamps it as the invasion by modern society of politics.

The critics' main contention is that politics cannot be free from
socio-economic concerns. Martin Jay asserts:

Both conceptually and historically, her view of politics as
performing art utterly uncorrupted by extraneous
considerations is without foundation.70

However, some agree that at one time in history it was possible to
separate politics from economic concerns.   But there is a consensus
that regardless of what happened in the polis, our modern political
situation demands whoever enters the political realm to be somehow
involved in the economic affairs.   Arendt fails to convince her critics
that such an involvement is totally incompatible with excellence in
words and deeds. George Kateb firmly asserts that economic issues
show "signs and traces" of real political action.71   The competi-
tiveness or the wish to excel, which is a characteristic of the
economic issues, is also one of the characteristics of political action.
In short, Arendt's critics regard the involvement in economic issues as
necessary, given the modern age's situation.

Like James T. Knauer, I think that this criticism is based on a
misinterpretation of Arendt's position on the relationship between
politics and socio-economic concerns.   Arendt does not view politics as
unhampered by socio-economic concerns but as not determined by
them. This is what I meant when I insisted that her point is not that
politics is free from these concerns but that it transcends and is not
determined by them.   This means that, for Arendt, economic issues
are neither the cause, nor the effect, nor the purpose of politics.
What is suggested here is that the meaning of politics is not fixed by
economic concerns; rather, it is tied up with the principle manifested
in politics itself.   What these critics fail to understand is that

Arendt's contention is not that politics must be devoid of the socio-economic issues, but that it cannot be defined in terms of them. Its meaning cannot be explained in terms of socio-economic matters. For example, it would be missing what politics is to claim that it is essentially for fair distribution of wealth.

Arendt does not advocate the absolute purity of the political. She is aware that today it is quite hard to imagine economic transactions taking place without government intervention at one level or another or to find a government that is not involved in both economic and political matters. She wants to remind the modern world that the essence of politics is the foundation of freedom and not the settlement of socio-economic issues. She makes a sharp distinction between politics and socio-economic concerns in order to show us their relevant differences and also to help us locate ourselves in history, since this distinction is based on an analysis of history. All her favorite models involve pre-industrial conditions.

If Arendt's intention is to show us how we can apply the sharp distinction between political and economic issues in our modern age's situation, she definitely fails to do so. She never adequately comes to terms with the realities of our modern large-scale economic development. The polis model does not accommodate that great variety of possible modes of economic organizations and their different political implications. Her emphasis on the negative impact of economic concerns on the political realm would also minimize the importance of certain modes of economic organization. In short, it is quite difficult to apply a strict separation of politics and economics to concrete political decisions in the modern age. It is also too much to claim that politics has nothing to do with economic issues such as the distribution of wealth. Arendt's sharp distinction between politics and the issues that belong to the private realm serves to remind us of the autonomy of politics. She affirms that the strictness of this division enables one to understand the rationale behind the primacy of politics.

NOTES

1 The Human Condition, p. 140.
2 Arendt's division of these two realms is analogous to Kant's dualistic separation of the noumena and the phenomena.
3 The Human Condition, p. 80.
4 Ibid., p. 80-84.
5 Ibid., pp. 112.
6 Ibid., p. 58.
7 Ibid., p. 88.
8 Ibid., p. 106.
9 Ibid., p. 121.
10 Ibid., pp. 136-37.
11 Ibid., p. 168.
12 Ibid., p. 236.
13 Ibid., p. 155.
14 Ibid., p. 154.
15 Ibid., pp. 163-64.
16 Ibid., p. 167.
17 Ibid., p. 115.
18 Ibid.
19 Ibid., pp. 25, 29, 34.
20 On Revolution, p. 54.
21 The Human Condition, p. 102.
22 Margaret Canovan and George Kateb.
23 The Human Condition, p. 102.
24 Ibid., pp. 190-99.
25 The Origins of Totalitarianism, p. 475.
26 The Human Condition, p. 176.
27 On Revolution, p. 54.
28 Ibid., p. 110.
29 The Human Condition, p. 185.
30 Leroy A.Cooper, "Hannah Arendt's Political Philosophy: An Interpretation", Review of Politics 38 (April 1976), 174.
31 The Origins of Totalitarianism,p. 198.
32 On Revolution,pp. 277-78.
33 This idea is clearly expressed in her interview found in the Crisis of the Republic (New York: Harcourt Brace Jovanovitch, Inc., 1972).
34 The Human Condition, p. 61; the same idea is found in On Revolution, p. 180
35 Ibid., p. 71.
36 Ibid., p. 50.
37 Ibid., p. 68.
38 Ibid., pp. 31, 43.
39 Ibid., p. 65.
40 Ibid.

41 Ibid., p. 31.
42 Wayne Francis Allen, The Concept of Authority in the Thought of Hannah Arendt, unpublished dissertation (University of California, Riverside, 1979), p. 88.
43 On Violence, pp. 50-51.
44 Elisabeth Young-Bruehl, Hannah Arendt: For Love of the World (New Haven: Yale University Press, 1982), p. 414.
45 On Violence, p. 44.
46 Hannah Arendt, in Hannah Arendt: The Recovery of the Public World, ed. Melvyn A. Hill (New York: St. Martin's Press, 1979), p. 332.
47 On Revolution, p. 134.
48 Ibid., p. 85.
49 On Violence, p. 41.
50 The Human Condition, p. 202.
51 On Violence, p. 56.
52 On Revolution, p. 10.
53 Between Past and Future, p. 73.
54 On Revolution, p. 10.
55 Martin Jay, "Hannah Arendt: Opposing Views", Partisan Review 45/3 (October 1978), 360.
56 On Revolution, p. 210.
57 On Violence, p. 4.
58 On Revolution, p. 82.
59 Gene Sharp, Social Power and Political Freedom (Boston: Porter Sargent Publishers, Inc., 1980), p. 148.
60 On Revolution, p. 22.
61 Ibid., p. 25.
62 Ibid., p. 28.
63 Ibid., p.22.
64 Ibid., p. 136.
65 The Human Condition, p. 169.
66 Ibid., pp. 292-94.
67 On Revolution, p. 270.
68 The outstanding critics of Hannah Arendt on this issue are Kirk Thompson. "Constitutional Theory and Political Action", Journal of Politics 31 (1969), pp. 655-81; Jurgen Habermas, "Hannah Arendt's Communications Concept of Power", Social Research 44, 3-24; Martin Jay, "Hannah Arendt: Opposing Views", Partisan Review 45/3 (October 1978), 348-67.
69 Habermas, p. 15.
70 Jay, p. 363.
71 George Kateb, "Arendt and Representative Democracy", Salmagundi, 60, 29.

CHAPTER IV

TOTALITARIANISM

Arendt's concept of totalitarianism arose from her confrontation with the Nazi regime. She also uses this concept to refer to Bolshevism. However, she insists that totalitarianism cannot be explained by reference to historical analogies and precedents "because its very actions constitute a break with all our traditions".1 She regards it as an unprecedented event and as a phenomenon unique in the history of the world.

Nonetheless, she thinks that something could be understood about it since the "road to totalitarian domination leads through many intermediate stages for which we can find numerous analogies and precedents".2 The Origins of Totalitarianism is the result of her effort to comprehend the event of totalitarianism. She herself says:

> What I did...was to discover the chief elements of totalitarianism and to analyse them in historical terms, tracing these elements back in history as far as I deemed proper and necessary. That is, I did not write a history of totalitarianism but an analysis in terms of history....3

She also thinks it is worthy of study because it affects both individual and political freedom:

> In other words, the success of totalitarianism is identical with a much more radical liquidation of freedom as a political and as a human reality than anything we have ever witnessed before.4

Arendt deems this historical phenomenon a paradigm of the destruction of freedom. It is important to point out that her notion of the human condition, freedom and politics grew out of her meditation on and investigation of totalitarianism. She realized that the totalitarian regime was the antithesis of the polis way of life. Although she nowhere claims that the polis is totally opposed to totalitarianism, a careful reading of her works reveals that for her the polis represented man at his political best, while totalitarianism represents him at his worst. Therefore, totalitarianism cannot be anything but a symbol of the collapse and death of freedom.

Does the structure of totalitarianism, as Arendt understands it, leave no room for freedom and individuality? I shall examine whether a totalitarian sphere is a place of total dominion, where there is neither community of equals as in the polis, nor equality with a council as characteristic of an authoritarian government. Arendt also regards it as the realm of oblivion, in which no witnesses exist to

95

remember those who have disappeared, in which speech and action are meaningless, and in which there is no room for human beings to disclose "who they are and what they can do". Secondly, I will show that since totalitarianism is dominated by an ideology enforced by manipulation and violence, it cannot be the realm of free exchange of opinions through persuasion and debate. Finally, I will demonstrate that Arendt's analysis of totalitarianism is consistent with her claim that political freedom can only be experienced in the public realm.

Totalitarian Organization

A short sketch of what Arendt considers a totalitarian regime will clarify why she thinks totalitarianism is a destruction of both human and political freedom. Arendt compares the totalitarian government's structure to that of an onion. This type of government is composed of series of facades and distortions of the traditional lines of authority. She describes this image as follows:

> All the extraodinarily manifold parts of the movement: the front organizations, the various professional societies, the party membership, the party bureaucracy, the elite formations and police groups, are related in such a way that each forms the facade in one direction and the center in the other, that is, plays the role of normal outside world for one layer and the role of radical extremism for another.[5]

Each layer of the onion is composed of people who conceal the reality from themselves by pretending that they have a deeper and more radical insight into the truth than the more "normal" layer outside it. All members of different layers harbour the false feeling that they are not at all out of touch with reality. For Arendt, those closer to the centre actually move in a world largely dominated by their own illusions, even though they can conceal this fact from themselves.

The leader occupies the centre, a sort of an empty space within which he operates. He does not operate from above. Arendt proposes Hitler as the perfect example of a leader who operates with such a structure. While the idea of a leader operating from within and not from above might sound like the ideal for a genuine political organization, in the totalitarian regime he does not operate in collaboration with the people. He isolates himself at the centre of the onion so that he alone understands and knows the workings of the various facades and the principle that keeps them going. He alone acts and "claims personal responsibility for every action, deed, or

96

misdeed committed by any member or functionary in his official capacity".6 In this case, he deprives everyone else of the right to act and to be responsible for his own actions.

Since everyone presents a facade, the leader showing one face to one group of people and different faces to other groups, the members also showing one face to the public and another in their private affairs, Arendt concludes that totalitarianism is a monstrous lie. It creates a totally fictitious world in which no one appears as he or she is. While the same thing might be said about the members of the polis, that they show different faces in different spheres (the private and the public spheres), the Greek distinction between private and public life is not maintained under the totalitarian regimes. The totalitarian regimes assimilate all aspects of life into the onion-like structure so that both private and public life, as they were conceived in antiquity, cease to exist. In the polis, individuals appeared in the public space as free agents, and when they resigned to their private spheres, they acted like fathers, husbands, and masters of their households. In the totalitarian regime, people neither appear as free agents in public nor masters in the private realm. No one appears as he is; no one appears unambiguously:

> Nobody ever experiences a situation in which he has to be responsible for his own actions or can explain the reasons for them.7

In Arendt's view this peculiar onion-like structure of totalitarianism negates both authority and freedom. She makes a distinction between dictatorship and totalitarianism and demonstrates that, unlike totalitarianism, dictatorship involves a hierarchical structure that presupposes authority and obedience at its various levels. Within this structure, freedom may be limited or restricted, but it is not abolished.

According to Arendt, the totalitarian structure obliterates freedom because it obscures "the space of appearances". She continuously points out that true political freedom is dependent on a political space in which men can speak and act freely. Any system that prohibits and destroys their freedom of speech cannot be the realm of authentic political freedom. One of the most important elements of authentic politics is the preservation of participants' words and deeds. The political space of the polis made possible this preservation of words and deeds so that they could be remembered as part of the public space. In the polis, the citizens were able to allow the words and deeds of the participants to come out in the open and be appreciated in their full significance.

TOTALITARIANISM

Totalitarian regimes do their best to destroy the memory of words and actions and intimidate anyone who tries to speak the truth in public. Words and deeds, in the totalitarian state, become meaningless since one can no longer say what one means, or know that the words one uses are meaningful to anybody. People under such regimes usually pretend that everything is all right and quickly try to forget what happened rather than risk their lives by speaking the truth.

People's silence ultimately means oblivion. The destruction of memory is the destruction of a major part of what Arendt considers to be authentic politics.
The political space of the polis was saved and preserved by the poets and the storytellers. Through the gift of tongues they guaranteed the living-on-in-memory of the activity of politics, because the organization of the polis was a kind of "organized remembrance". It is therefore clear that, for Arendt, polis and totalitarianism represent opposite meanings.

While in totalitarianism the grandeur of the human enterprise is hidden and destroyed behind the layers of the onion to the extent that man is reduced to the futility of a mere animal or natural existence, in the polis, the citizens, through their words and deeds, were able to come out in the open and be appreciated in their full significance. To Arendt, free discussion and free action (that is, free political expression) makes everything else possible. This possibility is what Arendt calls freedom. So, the destruction of memory is the destruction of one of the elements Arendt considers essential for authentic politics. Since the destruction of memory is also the destruction of the ability to act and speak publicly (that is, the destruction of political realm), it is, therefore, the destruction of freedom.

When men lose the ability to communicate, they become more and more isolated. Arendt suggests that freedom "as an inner capacity of man is identical with the capacity to begin, just as freedom as a political reality is identical with a space of movement between men".8 So, the insulated structure of the totalitarian regime, by isolating men from one another, destroys the public realm and political freedom.

This isolation of men from one another not only destroys the public person and the public space, it also destroys all aspects of the private person, including his uniqueness and his freedom to act. Man loses the ability to call attention to himself and to others and fails to notice the distinctions in their qualities. Uniqueness signifies that

only man can express this distinction and distinguish
himself, and only he can communicate himself and not
merely something....Speech and action reveal this unique
distinctness. Through them, men distinguish themselves
instead of being merely distinct; they are the modes in
which human beings appear to each other, not indeed as
physical objects, but qua men.9

Man needs others to confirm him. Without the confirmation of
other men, "man loses trust in himself as the partner of his thoughts
and that elementary confidence in the world which is necessary to
make experience at all".10   It is plurality, according to Arendt, that
represents the condition of the most human activities--personal action.
We have seen that the polis, where actors show themselves, is
inhabited by a plurality of men and is constituted as a space of
appearances. The plurality of this order signifies that the actors
within are deemed equal by their participation in this realm but are
also unique individuals who freely and deliberately pursue their own
courses of action. The polis
perpetuates a space of appearances, a public realm of actors and
spectators who share a common world, which makes possible the
meaningfulness of human speech and action.

Totalitarianism isolates men from one another. In this way it
demolishes the plurality of the public realm that thrives on the words
and deeds of unique persons, who distinguish themselves not just by
reference to their distinct qualities but by self-reference to the
"someone" they are. In the totalitarian state, an individual is lost.
There are no voices from outside to arouse his conscience since if he
is an outsider he only comes into contact with symphizers, and if he is
a real militant he is surrounded by a world of less extreme party
members who represent "normality" to him. There is nobody to turn
to for guidance. When Pastor Grueber was asked by the court directly
whether he had tried to influence Eichmann, when asked, "Did you, as
a clergyman, try to appeal to his feelings, preach to him and tell him
that his conduct was contrary to morality?", he had to answer that he
had not, because "words would have been useless".

Individuals are so atomized by this kind of regime that they
suffer from radical loneliness or radical loss of a world. Loneliness is
a severe removal of individuals from the world. It is based on a sense
of not belonging to a world at all. It entails the loss of meaning of a
common world. Sometimes it may involve being in the presence of
other men but not sharing a common sense of reality with other men.
This loss vitiates the entire concept of a world, for a world emerges
only with the faith in one's common sense being shared by others as

they move and are confirmed in the common world. Loneliness, therefore, undermines the coherence and meaning of existence and disparages one's own integrity as a capable, reliable individual. It is the personal experience of world-alienation. Arendt asserts:

> What makes loneliness so unbearable is the loss of one's own self which can be realized in solitude, but confirmed in its identity only by the trusting and trustworthy company of my equals. In this situation, man loses trust in himself as the partner of his thoughts and that elementary confidence in the world which is necessary to make experience at all. Self and world, capacity for thought and experience are lost at the same time.11

What is important here is that, according to Arendt, loneliness, which she regards as an essential element of totalitarianism, divorces individuals not necessarily from sense experience but, with just as significant effects, from experience they can make sense of.

Within this sphere of the atomized individual, masses of people are made to feel superfluous in the world, having no reason for their existence. When they are convinced of their own helplessness and unimportance, they devote themselves to any organization that gives them a place in the world a reason for existing. Into this ambiance of disorientation, totalitarianism appeared with its claim to understand the deeper significance of the vast mysterious processes and to be able to turn these processes in novel forms on man himself. The central assumption of totalitarianism was its belief that "everything is possible".12 This is why Arendt regards totalitarianism as a lie so monstrous that it leads to the creation of an entirely fictitious world.

The difficulty here, however, is that Arendt does not tell us what "reality" is. She merely distinguishes between attempts to describe factual reality, that is, attempts to tell the truth, and attempts to distort factual reality, that is, attempts to lie. It is therefore difficult to establish why Arendt thinks that totalitarianism as a "big lie" actually eradicates the very ground required for the pursuit of politics. We also do not know what telling the truth involves, according to Arendt. We only know that truth is needed for the establishment of a commonly recognizable world, that is, a "space of appearances", the realm required for the conduct of politics.

Ideology and Terror

Arendt totally rejects two other features of totalitarianism because of their failure to allow room for freedom or novelty:

[First], an ideology which, when thought through to its logical conclusions, makes the outrages of totalitarianism inevitable; and second, the bureaucratization of terror in particular and political power in general, which gives political power and efficiency it did not have before.13

For her, totalitarian ideology supplants the need for an inspirational principle of action within the community. It stamps out the very bases of human creativity, the human activity to begin anew, which is the human capacity for freedom. Arendt emphasizes this point:

No ideology which aims at the explanation of all historical events of the past and at mapping out the course of all events of the future can bear the unpredictability which springs from the fact that men are creative, that they can bring forward something so new that nobody ever forsaw it.14

It also allows no room for the individual to take any initiative in word and deed. A careful analysis of Arendt's notion of ideology will show us clearly why she finds it unacceptable:

An ideology is quite literally what its name indicates: it is the logic of an idea. Its subject matter is history, to which the "idea" is applied; the result of this application is not a body of statements about something that is, but the unfolding of a process which is in constant change. The ideology treats the course of events as though it followed the same "law" as the logical exposition of its "idea." Ideologies pretend to know the mysteries of the whole historical process--the secrets of the past, the intricacies of the present, the uncertainties of the future--because of the logic inherent in their respective ideas.15

This definition is hostile to Arendt's conception of political freedom and man's own existence. Ideology assaults man's freedom to act. It destroys "a principle of action" from which, in Arendt's scheme of political freedom, the individual takes direction. One of the principal ways in which Arendt sees political freedom destroyed by totalitarianism is through the appropriation of an ideology as a logically consistent explanation for everything that happens. There is an underlying affinity of ideology with the totalitarian premise that "everything is possible".

Arendt argues that ideologies purport to give an adequate explanation of the meaning of history and the universe:

> For an ideology differs from a simple opinion in that it claims to possess either the key to history, or the solution for all the "riddles of the universe," or the intimate knowledge of the hidden universal laws which are supposed to rule nature and man.16

Ideologies claim to comprehend the laws of history, and by virtue of this comprehension, ideological thinking becomes self-sufficient, emancipating one from the need to perceive reality. In this way, ideologies become instruments of control. Everything that men do has been preordained: there is no room left for freedom, spontaneity, or creativity.17 Ideologies also create their own method of demonstration, based on the inner consistency or logicality or deduction from a given premise, which compels one to act within an insulated reality. Within this insulated organization, no inconsistencies presented by reality and facticity are admitted. According to Arendt, ideologies follow their own "supersense", which makes no sense or is above the common sense with which we ordinarily perceive reality.

In Arendt's notion of "ideology", therefore, we have an idea of what she means when she says that totalitarianism distorts reality. For her, reality in the totalitarian regime is ordered in accordance with the ideology, even if this means liquidating large classes of people, for example, the Jews during Hitler's regime. One of the aspects of ideology is that large numbers of people can be deceived into denying reality and going along with the most atrocious sorts of crimes. For Arendt, Eichmann is a perfect example of a man who was able to work within the Nazi ideology without realizing how he was harming innocent victims or destroying all that was best in the Western tradition. He was totally removed from reality, for he only knew how to operate successfully within the facade of the onion-like structure. He accepted the Nazi distortion of history through ideology and could only see meaning in life through ideology.

Again we find that Arendt condemns totalitarianism because it ruptures the human structures of reality. Although it is still not clear what reality is according to Arendt, politics is its shared ground. Therefore, the destruction of reality is an assault to both the public structure and personal structure of individuality and freedom. What is important here is that the notion of reality in Arendt is closely related to that of freedom.

In the same way that Arendt portrays the hostility toward freedom evidenced by ideology, she also portrays terror as hostile to freedom. Through the use of terror, totalitarianism intends "to make the world consistent, to prove that its respective suspersense has been right".18   In order to accomplish this and subordinate reality to ideological proposition, totalitarianism is prepared to use terror to transform nature and human nature. In totalitarianism, terror becomes a necessary means of reducing man to a function of those natural processes that admit predictability.   Terror acknowledges only the beginning and the end of the natural process, the individual's physical birth and death; otherwise, the individual is simply reconstructed to serve the greater whole.   Only the movement as a whole, proceeding in accordance with the ideological supersense, is allowed to progress. In this way, terror is not only directed at the destruction of human beings who may think independently and mutually contest the fictitious basis of ideological supersense; it is basically an attempt to destroy the very bases of human creativity. It eliminates spontaneity and the will to act.   For what the principle of freedom gives to individual action, the idea of terror gives to totalitarian regimes--its application marks the destruction of any ability to act in human affairs.

The apparent arbitrariness of terror has as a purpose to subjugate the individual even though, like the principle of freedom, it cannot always know the consequences of its endeavour:

> This consistent arbitrariness negates human freedom more efficiently than any tyranny ever could. One had at least to be an enemy of tyranny in order to be punished by it.
>   Freedom of opinion was not abolished for those who were brave enough to risk their necks. Theoretically, the choice of opposition remains in totalitarian regimes too; but such freedom is almost invalidated if committing a voluntary act only assures a "punishment" that everyone else may have to bear anyway.19

Furthermore, terror creates a "novel form of government" that is opposed to Arendt's idea of freedom. For her, as previously mentioned, freedom is achieved in action, and yet that public forum--or "public space of appearance", as Arendt called it--which is necessary as an arena for action, is systematically eliminated through totalitarian terror. Totalitarian terror breaks down the possibility of speech and cooperation, responses that signify an order stabilized by law and encourage action by means of certain inspirational principles.

The system of terror eliminates human plurality by fabricating a form of government that makes "it possible for the force of nature or of history to race freely through mankind, unhindered by any spontaneous human action".20

Arendt claims that totalitarian terror creates a form of government that is worse even than tyranny. She says that under tyranny there is still some interpersonal speech and cooperation, even if it must often go underground, and that there is enough of a world for common sense calculations of interest to be made and acted upon to some degree. But the terror of totalitarianism jeopardizes even these political remnants as never before. She argues:

> By pressing men against each other, total terror destroys the space between them; compared to the condition within its iron band, even the desert of tyranny, insofar as it is still some kind of space, appears like a guarantee of freedom.21

Under totalitarian terror, men are deprived not only of public speech and action but also of human dignity or even utility. They are reduced to a single, unthinking mass of individuals who just conform to anything that happens. Terror moves men to unreflective obedience. Whether by act, suspicion, or, ultimately, arbitrary selection, all individuals deemed as impeding the law and movement of the process are removed.22 Under totalitarian terror, therefore, freedom is replaced by the grip of total domination. Totalitarianism as a system of total domination subverts the ground of freedom by attempting to kill the capacity for action and its source.

Concentration Camps

The full implications of fictitious world of ideology and terror became manifest in the concentration camps, which Arendt designates "the true central institution of totalitarianism's organizational power".23 Only in the society of the concentration camp is total domination possible:

> It develops that the society of the dying established in the camps is the only form of society in which it is possible to dominate man entirely.24

Arendt regards the concentration camp as the apogee of totalitarianism.

Arendt points out, however, that despite the systematic efforts of the Nazis to use the concentration camps as an instrument of terror, terror actually reached its apex in Soviet Russia. While in both the Nazi concentration camps and the Russian system to rule the Kulaks terror was used as an instrument to rule people, terror reached its ultimate height in the hands of the Soviets because of its apparent arbitrary use. For the Soviets, "arbitrariness of terror is not even limited by racial differentiation, while old class categories have long since been discarded, so that anybody in Russia may suddenly become a victim of the police terror".25

Nazism still offered the illustration of terror as an ideological technique. Arendt's distinction between the Nazi concentration camps and the Soviet labor camps indicates that her concept of totalitarianism refers most properly to Nazism:

> Concentration camps can very aptly be divided into three types corresponding to three basic Western conceptions of a life after death: Hades, Purgatory, and Hell. To Hades correspond those relatively mild forms, once popular even in non-totalitarian countries....Purgatory is represented by the Soviet Union's labor camps, where neglect is combined with chaotic forced labor. Hell in the most literal sense was embodied by those types of camp perfected by the Nazis, in which the whole life was thoroughly and systematically organized with a view to the greatest possible torment.26

For Arendt, the concentration camps served more than the obvious function of systematic extermination. This system was a "type" of non-freedom and non-worldliness.

Arendt finds no parallels to the life of the concentration camps, even though the experience of the camps is not totally outside our human experience. We are aware of similar things from our perverse and malignant fantasies. Nevertheless, it is not easy to realize that this phantom world has materialized "into a world which is complete with all sensual data of reality but lacks that structure of consequence and responsibility without which reality remains for us a mass of incomprehensible data".27 Even the reporting of the facts about the concentration camps does seem to bring them out of the realm of the "fantastic", except for potentially totalitarian people:

> If the propaganda of truth fails to convince the average Philistine precisely because it is too monstrous, it is positively dangerous to those who know from their own

imaginings that they themselves are capable of doing such things and are therefore perfectly willing to believe in the reality of what they have seen.28

Arendt emphasizes that concentration camps were purposeless and useless except from the perspective of totalitarianism. From that perspective it was only in the concentration camps that the radical possibility of totalitarianism could be fully tested:

> The camps are meant not only to exterminate people and degrade human beings, but also serve the ghastly experiment of eliminating, under scientifically controlled conditions, spontaneity itself as an expression of human behavior.29

The destruction in the camps was so successful that people began to view themselves as objects, not persons. Arendt delineates this success as a calculated destruction of the individual's juridical, moral, and physical being. Individuals were so atomized in those camps that resistance for them became morally meaningless and politically pointless.

> Totalitarian terror achieved its most terrible triumph when it succeeded in cutting the moral person off from the individualist escape and in making the decisions of conscience absolutely questionable and equivocal. When a man is faced with the alternative of betraying and thus murdering his friends or of sending his wife and children, for whom he is in every sense responsible, to their deaths; when even suicide would mean the immediate murder of his own family--how is he to decide? The alternative is no longer between good and evil, but between murder and murder.30

In fact, Arendt claims that the Nazis, through conditions in the camps, succeeded in destroying individual personality to the extent that most of the victims had so far lost the possibility of action that very few of them ever made any attempt to resist death. Both victims, because of their lack of freedom, and executioners, because of their enslavement to the fiction, were stripped of all the traits that contribute to willful persons, stripped of the entire worldly context that could confirm one as a responsible actor:

> The extermination camps--where everything was an incident beyond the control of the victims as well as the oppressors, where those who were oppressors today were

106

to become victims tomorrow--created a monstrous
equality without fraternity and without humanity, an
equality in which dogs and cats could have easily
partaken, and in which we see as in a mirror the horrid
image of superfluousness.31

Thus, action was nullified, and with it the pathos of anonymity
developed. For Arendt, the camps were the fundamental characteristics of totalitarianism: the destruction of individual freedom to act,
the disdain of reality, the elimination of the space of appearance, and
the ultimate submission to a will that could not even be identified.
However, Terence Des Pres presents some evidence against this
depiction of the concentration camps.32 Arendt's omission of any
vestige of human freedom in her analysis of totalitarianism is also
striking because she has the evidence of at least one eyewitness
account that indicates the presence of human freedom even within the
concentration camp. She is aware of small acts of resistence in the
Buchenwald underground, acts in which the prisoners were sometimes
aided by a symphathetic Nazi. Arendt might have omitted this
evidence of human freedom within the concentration camp for the
greater purpose of showing how totalitarianism was unprecedented. To
show how different totalitarianism was from other forms of govenment
she had to construct an ideal type that neglected many significant
"details".

It is only later that Arendt considers more seriously the
evidence of human freedom within the totalitarian system. She admits
that only the extraordinary person, at great risk to himself, retains
limited freedom in such a state. She states:

Freedom of opinion was not abolished for those who were
brave enough to risk their necks. Theoretically, the
choice of opposition remains in totalitarian regimes too;
but such freedom is almost invalidated if committing a
voluntary act only assures a "punishment" that everyone
else may have to bear anyway.33

Arendt insists that even this limited freedom would be
impossible since through indoctrination and terror individual personality
is destroyed; resistence, as we have seen, becomes meaningless. The
problem here is that Arendt, after insisting that the Nazis succeeded
in destroying individual personality to the extent that most prisoners
had lost the possibility of action, then claims that the possibility of
action was never totally destroyed. We shall later see that she
maintains that the Jewish leaders and the victims still had choices and
were responsible for their actions during the Nazi domination.

Totalitarianism and Modernity

Even though Arendt claims that there are no parallels to the life of the concentration camps, she regards that life as a new basis for judging the events of our time:

> Thus the fear of concentration camps and the resulting insights into the nature of total domination might serve to invalidate all obsolete political differentiations from right to left and to introduce beside and above them the politically most important yardstick for judging events in our time, namely whether they serve total domination or not.34

In Arendt's view, the characteristics that are boldly portrayed in the concentration camps, like the contempt for reality, the lack of freedom and enslavement to fiction, reflect the experience of the masses in our time. For us this state of affairs is brought by loneliness. She writes:

> Loneliness, the common ground for terror, the essence of totalitarian government, and for ideology or logicality, the preparation of its executioners and victims, is closely connected with uprootedness and superfluousness which have been the curse of modern masses since the beginning of the industrial revolution and have become acute with the rise of imperialism at the end of the last century and the breakdown of political institutions and social traditions in our own time.35

In the modern world the space of appearance between men is subverted and turned into a world that is neither real nor recognizable. The individual, forced into a world of isolation, can only think according to the standards or premises that are established for him.

Arendt strongly asserts that under totalitarianism and present day mass society the individual is submerged in the vast anonymous process of life itself. He no longer acts; he simply behaves:

> The last stage of the laboring society, the society of jobholders, demands of its members a sheer automatic functioning, as though individual life had actually been submerged in the overall life process of the species and the only active decision still required of the individual to let go, so to speak, to abandon his individuality, the still individually sensed pain and trouble of living, and

acquiesce in a dazed "tranquilized", functional type of behavior. The trouble with modern theories of behaviorism is not that they are wrong, but that they could become true, that they actually are the best possible conceptualization of certain obvious trends in modern society. It is quite conceivable that the modern age, which began with such an unprecedented and promising outburst of human activity, may end in the deadliest, most sterile passivity history has ever known.36

Arendt condemns the terrible simplifications of ideological sloganeering and modern industrialized society for threatening the freedom of human spirit. Man remains man, with the capacity for responsible action instead of automatic "behaving". One can behave efficiently within a certain system-thinking and yet fail to act responsibly.

She also claims that the modern masses, like the masses under totalitarian regimes, "do not believe in anything visible, in the reality of their own experience; they do not trust their eyes and ears but only their imaginations, which may be caught by anything that is at once universal and consistent in itself".37 Modern man is just interested in a system and coherence. He thus fails to distinguish between distinctness and uniformity. The reality is therefore pushed to one side.

The loss of contact with reality is also the result of the decline of the public realm. This implies the loss of freedom. Modern man's entire alienation from the world is the result of the modern concomitant dissolution of coherence in the life of the species, the abolition of identity in the life of the individual, and the attrition of man's basic ability to think, an ability that is the essence of his nature. Finally, Arendt points our that the efforts of the modern technology and science to "explain all things--the same premise as in totalitarian ideology--are dangers to our freedom". She suggests that the modern world can experience freedom only in and through revolutionary action.

Though Arendt does not claim that the modern age culminates necessarily in the totalitarian experience, and though the latter cannot be explained by the elements of the modern age, the inadequacies of the modern age offer insight as to why freedom cannot be found in any system that allows the destruction of the public realm as totalitarianism does. Arendt insists that "the success of totalitarianism is identical with a much more radical liquidation of freedom as a political and as a human reality than anything we have ever witnessed before".38

Critics

Despite Arendt's insistence that the "success of totalitarianism is identical with the destruction of freedom as a political reality", several writers have noted that her notion of totalitarianism and political action are not wholly dissimilar. Others find her notion of totalitarianism so inconsistent that it fails to support her claim that totalitarianism is identical with a radical liquidation of freedom. Now we have to establish whether totalitarianism, as Arendt sees it, really destroys political freedom, and whether her analysis of it reveals her notion of freedom.

George Kateb says that there is a "seeming resemblance between Arendt's conception of totalitarianism and her conception of political action".39 He observes that the Nazis and the Stalinists behaved like the members of the polis in ancient Greece. They did not use purges and violence against each other. They used speech and made an audience for each other--"if not public, then not private or social either".40 He also claims that since "they did not act out of crass motives; they did not see their action as a means to some delimited goals", their activity had some little connection to ideal political action.41 Therefore, in Kateb's view, the ideal political action and totalitarianism bear some likeness to each other.

Along the same lines, Mary J. Leddy also proposes that the polis and the concentration camps "are alike in that both are forms of human freedom".42 She concedes, however, that in the case of the polis, human freedom creates political freedom:

> In the case of the concentration camp, human freedom destroys political freedom, and even human freedom. The eruption of human freedom in history may initiate either the new political form of the council system or the new political form of totalitarianism.43

The main argument here is that, if freedom is originality as Arendt emphasizes, this capacity may or may not be actualized in political freedom. This is supported by Arendt herself in her assertion that

> the periods of being free have always been relatively short in the history of mankind...what usually remains intact in the epochs of petrification and foreordained doom is the capacity of freedom itself.44

TOTALITARIANISM

In her essay "Understanding and Politics", Arendt consistently affirms that totalitarianism is originality. So, like any originality, it is the basis of the possibility of new and/or unprecedented political forms. For her, totalitarianism constitutes an unprecedented event because it introduces elements foreign to "all our traditions" of thought and judgments. In her reply to Voegelin she says:

> What is unprecedented in totalitarianism is not primarily its ideological content, but the event of totalitarian domination itself. This can be seen clearly if we have to admit that the deeds of its considered policies have exploded our traditional categories of political thought (totalitarian domination is unlike all forms of tyranny and despotism we know of) and the standards of our moral judgment (totalirarian crimes are very inadequately described as "murder" and totalitarian criminals can hardly be punished as "murderers").45

Voegelin does not agree with Arendt that totalitarianism was not even anticipated. He thinks that it was the direct result of the modern denial of classical transcendentalism. For him it represented no more than another departure from the classical politics. However, he agrees with Arendt on our major point of concern, that is, on the fact that totalitarian domination totally obliterated freedom.

For Richard Bernstein, "it is the same capacity in man, the capacity to act and initiate, that gave rise to not only the Greek polis but also the nightmare of Twentieth-century totalitarianism".46 Freedom, novelty and the capacity to begin are the essential elements of action itself. Bernstein detects that totalitarianism and political action are not wholly dissimilar because they share the elements that are most essential to both activities.

O'Sullivan fervently argues that totalitarianism does not create a fictitious world as a result of its onion-structure because even the free democratic community has the same structure:

> Reference to the onion structure of such regimes as the device which ensures their insular, unreal existence does not help since the various "layers" within the onion, from the moderate front organizations through to the élite cadres at the centre, are to be found in any democratic community which faces the problem of getting in the vote....It is not the onion structure but tight centralized control based upon the leader principle which distinguishes the totalitarian system of government from the structure

of liberal democratic regimes. Arendt's notion that totalitarianism creates a world which is in some sense fictitious seems indeed to be something of a red herring.47

It may be true that the onion structure that Arendt attributes to the totalitarian regimes is also found in the democratic community, but Arendt definitely insists that such a structure distorts reality in the totalitarian regime.

Margaret Canovan categorically claims that Arendt's work on totalitarianism is marred by a "serious inconsistency".48   Other commentators, however, share Ernst Vollrath's view that "every attempt to show some discontinuities in her work is inherently doomed".49 They claim that the polemical attacks on her work on totalitarianism fail to do justice to her as a philosopher. Michael Denney sums up their view thus:

> The Origins of Totalitarianism will probably stand as her greatest work because it is--however pell-mell--an act of astonishing intellectual courage and moral responsibility, an act not of a professional working in her field but of a person answering back the great hammer-blows of Fortune. For this act of intellectual courage she was amply rewarded, for it opened all the many avenues her thought was later to take. For us, in quieter though no less ominous times, it should serve as a reminder of what intellectual activity is all about.50

I think her critics have a point. It is a fact that Arendt's views on totalitarianism are at times not clear. After stressing how impossible it is to have freedom in the totalitarian regime she seems to be contradicting herself by saying that there is still some freedom in the totalitarian regime. This becomes evident when she deals with the case of Eichmann in which she makes an effort to present the evidence of human freedom within a totalitarian state. She asserts that during their extermination the Jews, rather than participate in their own destruction, "still had a certain limited freedom of decision of action".51

Arendt strongly argues that even under totalitarianism people are never mere irresponsible functionaries.52   They are still human beings who should be asked individually, "Did you, such-and-such, an individual with name, date, and place of birth, identifiable and therefore not expendable, commit the crime you stand accused of, and why did you do it?" She claims that answers such as, "If I had not done it, somebody else could and would have" or "It was not I as a person who did it, I had neither the will nor the power to do anything out of my own initiative, I was a mere cog expendable, everybody in my place would have done it", should be dismissed as non-sensical excuses. According to Arendt, individuals under totalitarianism are responsible for their actions. The responsible individual is one who did the thing in question, or at least whose action or omission made a substantial causal contribution to it.

It is true that there are certain actions no individual can perform in isolation. Actions like revolution can only be done by an organized group, or even by random collections of individuals, that is, individuals who have come together at a particular place and time not for any common purpose but simply for the pursuit of their own ends. Arendt seems unaware that in such cases, a group and only a group is responsible for organizing itself properly so as to be capable of taking the required action. In such cases an individual can rightly declare, "I did not do it alone".

Participation or non-participation in a system is the core of Arendt's argument. She remarks:

> Non-participation taken as a legal standard for right and wrong poses considerable problems precisely with respect to the question of responsibility. For the truth of the matter is that only those who withdrew from public life altogether, who refused political responsibility of any sort, could avoid becoming implicated in crimes; that is, could avoid legal and moral responsibility.53

Participants get involved sometimes because of the power of the ideological propaganda that hides the truth from them. But sooner or later, often later, they realize the horror of the regime they have created. Sometimes they participate not as convinced adherents of the regime but simply as politically neutral people. Sometimes they participate with an intention to prevent the worst from happening, since there is always a possibility for those who are inside to mitigate things and help at least some people. The members of this last group can declare: "We gave the devil his due without selling our souls to him, whereas those who did nothing shirked all responsibility and thought only of themselves, of the salvation of their previous souls."

Arendt is right. One can always choose either to participate or to retire into private life. It is irresponsible to refuse to choose altogether. Even those who choose to participate because they think that participation would be a lesser evil should be aware that while it

113

may be plausible to think they are cooperating with an evil system in order to prevent the worse from happening, the evil that takes place is within their responsibility. They should also realize that sometimes nothing worse than the evil they allow could possibly happen.

Arendt's contention on this issue of cooperation is that in a totalitarian regime any organization or individual who compromises with the system becomes immediately ineffectual in opposing it and usually ends up helping it. She claims that if one takes the first step in cooperating with the totalitarian system, one is soon caught in a web that tightens with each step of cooperation until it becomes impossible to break free. To prove this, she raises a very uncomfortable and sensitive question on the role of the Jewish functionaries during the "Final Solution":

> The Final solution...needed the active cooperation of all Ministries and of the whole Civil Service.54

> Mere compliance would never have been enough to smooth out all the enormous difficulties of an operation that was soon to cover the whole of Nazi-occupied and Nazi-allied Europe or to soothe the consciences of the operators....55

The cooperation of the civilian population as well as other governments was necessary. In 1944 Eichmann went to Hungary to arrange for the deportation of the Jews to the extermination camps, and his worst fears concerned the possible resistance of the Hungarians with which he would have been unable to cope, because he lacked manpower and also knowledge of local conditions. These fears proved quite unfounded.56 But the German military officers in Western occupied countries were "always reluctant to cooprate and to lend their troops to round up and seize Jews".57 The very sad fact is that the "Final Solution" also needed the cooperation and assistance of its victims. For the most part it received even that. Some Jews and non-Jews did refuse to cooperate and did resist; their actions saved many lives, often their own. That does not, however, remove the fact of widespread cooperation. Arendt calls this collaboration "undoubtedly the darkest chapter in the whole dark story". It took different forms; she recounts:

> Wherever Jews lived there were recognized Jewish leaders, and this leardership, almost without exception, cooperated in one way or another, for one purpose or another, with the Nazis. The whole truth was that if the Jewish people had really been unorganized and leaderless there would have been chaos and plenty of misery, but the total

number of victims would hardly have been between four and half and six million people.58

According to Arendt, individual participants should be asked a direct question: "Why did you cooperate in the destruction of your own people?" Even the dead, if dead men could tell tales, could rightly be asked: "Why did you allow yourselves to be slaughtered?" The common response to such questions is to point out the extreme difficulties of the situation that faced the victims, both the dangers of resistance and the numbed state of mind the Nazis had induced in their victims. The victims were also completely unprepared, and certainly untrained, for conducting resistance to such a regime and policy. Arendt takes these responses as arguments with which the participants justified themselves in their own eyes and in those of others.

It is now clear that Arendt's suggestion that the Jews should have resisted or gone "underground" rather than cooperate with a system that killed millions of them is contrary to her analysis of totalitarianism. In stressing the existence of individual responsibility and freedom even under totalitarianism, she ignores the fact that her very analysis of totalitarianism, as a perfect, powerful system seems to lead to an opposite conclusion, namely, that an individual can never be held responsible for anything that happens under a tight system. Individuals can only be held responsible for what happens under contingent systems.

Arendt agrees that there was no possibility of active resistance but that there existed the possibility of doing nothing. And in order to do nothing, one does not need to be a saint; one only needs to say: "I am just a simple Jew, and I have no desire to play any other role." She asserts that these people, rather than participate in their own extermination, still had a certain limited freedom of decision and of action:

> These people had still a certain, limited freedom of decision and of action. Just as the SS murderers also possessed, as we now know, a limited choice of alternatives. They could say: "I wish to be relieved of my murderous duties," and nothing happened to them.59

Arendt is here trying to make a distinction between freedom of decision or thought and freedom of action. According to her, the Jews still had a choice to do nothing, not because that would have brought them to a different fate, but because such a decision would have enhanced their human dignity. The non-participants, called irresponsible by the majority, were the only ones who dared judge by themselves. In Arendt's view, their conscience did not function in an automatic way. They decided that it was better to do nothing, not because better things would happen or happened, but because only on that condition could they go on living with themselves. They also chose to die when they were forced to participate because they were unwilling to live as murderers. As we shall see in the following chapter, she regards this habit of living with oneself, that is, of being engaged in the silent dialogue between one and oneself (which since Socrates and Plato we have usually called thinking), as the essential resort when one is faced with difficult situations in life. This is especially necessary under totalitarianism, where all traces of group solidarity, including family ties and memberships in various associations, are eliminated. Individuals should learn to live with themselves in such states where all measures are designed to prevent the growth of any stability and human togetherness. The line between doing nothing and rebellion is thin indeed.

Arendt's argument follows from her claim that totalitarian movements demand unconditional loyalty and obedience from their members. Those who participate in such movements often justify themselves on the moral grounds that they are just doing their duty and obeying superior orders. Arendt is aware that "every organization demands obedience to superiors as well as obedience to the laws of the land. Obedience is a virtue; without it no body politic and no other organization could survive."60 But since to accept passively an unjust system is to cooperate with that system and thereby to become a participant in its evil, when obedience serves a malevolent cause far from appearing as a virtue it is transformed into a heinous sin.

Arendt denies that there is such a thing as obedience in political and moral matters. It is a fundamental mode of thinking for a great many people that once they are locked into subordinate position in a structure of authority and are unable to defy the authority of the superior, they attribute all responsibility to him and pretend to take a position of obedience. In these matters, one who obeys actually supports the organization or the authority or the law that claims "obedience":

> Even in a strictly bureaucratic organization, with its fixed hierarchical order, it would make much more sense to look upon the functioning of the "cogs" and wheels in terms of overall support for a common enterprise than in our usual terms of obedience to superiors. If I obey the laws of the land, I actually support its constitution, as becomes glaringly obvious in the case of revolutionists or

116

rebels who disobey because they have withdrawn this tacit consent.61

So the question addressed to those who participate in any system and obey the orders of the superiors should never be why they obey but why they support. The non-participators in the totalitarian regime are those who refuse to support it by shunning the places of responsibility where such support, under the name of obedience, is required. But if we still understand totalitarianism on her terms, not only political resistance should be impossible but also every moral resistance. Otherwise we will have to say that, in Arendt's view, men are not politically free under totalitarianism but are still somehow humanly free. This would be a mistake because Arendt insists that political freedom is human freedom.

It is in fact not clear how Arendt can still talk of individual freedom while stressing that totalitarianism as a system of total domination subverts the ground of politics by seeking not to control and direct human activity but by attempting to kill the capacity for action at its source. Totalitarianism is organized around the "killing of man's individuality".62 It has the power to render moral opposition ambiguous and without significant result. Arendt holds that the impossibility of moral resistance applies not only to minority groups in totalitarian states, denied the rights of citizenship, but also to the nationals of such states. We have noted her contention that people can be made to carry out the most inhuman projects in the totalitarian regime when they are dehumanized and made to feel superfluous. Now she has to show us how an individual can be held responsible for what he does in a totalitarian state when we know that totalitarianism exists precisely whenever the state abrogates the rights of the individual and leaves him no freedom. Certainly, Arendt cannot come to this conclusion through her analysis of totalitarianism.

Arendt's analysis of totalitarianism presents some problems. The first is that her interest is not primarily historical. She focusses only on the metaphysical side of totalitarianism, that is, she describes it as "the truly radical nature of evil" or as "absolute evil" and thus detaches it from any specific historical context. This would still be all right had she not overstated the case by saying that she gives an historical account of the elements that crystallized totalitarianism.

As Margaret Canovan points out, Arendt's model exhibits features that were never fully realized in either Germany or Russia or any totalitarian state:

[F]or instance, it includes both the refinements of total

domination in the Nazi concentration camps and shows trials and false confessions of Stalinist party members.63

Nazism and Stalinism are assumed to be so alike as to be virtually identical. The only differences she repeatedly refers to are the bases of the ideological appeals--race and socialism--and the fact that Stalin had to create artificially the atomized society that had been prepared for Hitler by historical circumstances. Otherwise, Arendt fails to anticipate or allow for the possibility that it may be more useful to think in terms of more than one variant of totalitarianism. Her model cannot really be extended beyond Nazism. Even Nazism was never such a purposeful system.

Arendt's problem is to regard totalitarianism as a thing in itself, a concrete universal with a form and logic of its own. She takes it to be a whole, a system, the parts of which hang together and are manifested in both the Nazi and Stalinist regimes. But totalitarianism does not provide a consistent framework into which everything appears to fit and every explanation is given. It still has some inconsistent elements, and it leaves room for contingency and freedom. It is precisely because it is not a whole with parts hanging together that individuals are responsible for what they do in such a regime.

Arendt's interpretation of totalitarianism follows from the use she makes of the ideas of "ideology", "the mass" and "terror". An essential part of her thesis is the contention that "the totalitarian movement represented those masses that were no longer willing to live in any kind of structure, regardless of its nature".64 These masses, she writes, exist potentially "in every country and form the majority of those large numbers of neutral, politically indifferent people who never join a party and hardly ever go to the polls".65 The reality is that under Mussolini, Hitler and Stalin there were some formerly deprived sections of the population who could believe with some justification that their interests had at long last been served. Some men just accepted totalitarianism in return for security and in order to gain release from the burden of responsibility that freedom imposes. In fact, it is only in the years prior to 1930 that the Nazi party could be said to represent people with the purely irregular tendencies ascribed by Arendt to the masses. The middle class that joined the party in 1930 could not be described as "no longer wishing to live in any kind of structure". What it wanted was an escape from the insecurity brought by the economic crisis and the concomitant fear of proletarianization; its support for Nazism originated in real economic, social and political needs which, although they produced the material for party propaganda to manipulate, were not a purely blind hostility toward all social order. The working class, on the other hand, was predominantly Social Democratic, without any urge for "the glorifying myth is of the fatherland", and contented with "sober scepticism".66 It is very difficult to know who might or might not qualify for the superfluous, blind and dehumanized class of people that Arendt calls "the masses".

Another striking feature of Arendt's totalitarianism is the non-utilitarian character of terror. Unlike the terror of other systems, totalitarian terror is not understandable in terms of the utilitarian motives or self-interest of the rulers. It is explicable only as a means to the insane, anti-utilitarian and selfless "experimental inquiry into what is possible".67 Nevertheless, the sheer ubiquity of terror also distinguishes Arendt's conception of totalitarianism. The instruments of terror--the secret police and concentration camps- --assume paramount significance as her theory unfolds. The party, bureaucracy and other instruments of rule derive their importance and distinctiveness solely from the terroristic essence of totalitarianism.

Arendt correctly recognizes totalitarianism as a presence of general lawlessness, but her emphasis on the role of the party is too great. The party never succeeds to the degree of perfection she thinks it does applying terror and ideology. Arendt rightly recognizes the role of ideology, and she is right in regarding terror as used not only to frighten people into submission but also to isolate them, leave them enclosed by a wall of "loneliness". But terror and ideology never work as efficiently as she seems to imply. It has always been difficult to use terror and ideology. Terror and the purges must be internalized to the extent that the victim wills his own submission to the system, and in practice this never happens. Ideology is the means whereby the will of the rulers is made the will of the masses. But since according to Arendt ideology is a form of lie, it can never achieve the complete susceptibility of the populace to totalitarian manipulation and mobilization. It is not always true that the adherents of an ideology prefer the system to the facts. A totalitarian system is not one in which the populace is simply subdued and brainwashed. Arendt says that terror's iron hand compresses to mash all men into a mass. Deprived of public speech and action, people have only ideology to guide them in belief and behaviour. The very pressure of repression, however, is a measure of failure in a totalitarian system. I think it is only when all the people have been made to want what they have that the difference between a totalitarian and a despotic regime is fully manifest. In other words, the mass totalitarian regime is the one where the penetration of the regime into the soul of the individual is as complete as it can ever be. Her belief is that "totalitarian terror...is let loose when all organized

opposition has died down and the totalitarian ruler knows that he has
no longer need to be afraid".68 This really never happens.

Arendt leaves few loose ends; virtually everything is traceable to
the initial premise. Unfortunately, her deductions from this premise
lead to an extremely reductionist theory. In the process, the facts
and the great complexity of the reality she chooses to call
"totalitarian" are sacrificed to simplicity and consistency. The theory
that issues from this process does not approximate reality, even to the
degree required of an ideal type. In short, Arendt seems to succumb
to the pattern of thought she most decries--"the logicality of
ideological thinking".

This weakness can be attributed to the fact that Arendt's
notion of totalitarian regime is as idealized as that of the Greek polis.
However, it serves the purpose and reveals Arendt's notion of political
freedom. While for her the polis is an existential field in which
freedom was possible, totalitarianism stands in opposition as a symbol
of the death of freedom. In this way we slowly discover what
political freedom is according to Arendt and that it cannot be found
in the totalitarian regime.

Conclusion

We have so far seen that Arendt regards totalitarianism as a
paradigm of the destruction of freedom since, unlike the public sphere
in which freedom flourishes, it leaves no room for freedom. She
observes that the totalitarian form of government, unlike other forms
of government, is a systematic attempt to destroy the existential
field in which freedom is possible. Through its "essential and unique"
elements, the concentration camps, it destroys the space of appearance
in which every participant's words and deeds take place and are
remembered. In place of free exchange of opinions through persuasion
and debate it imposes ideologies that are enforced by manipulation and
violence. It destroys the meaningfulness of language and traditions
and, above all, of the person himself, both in his private and public
life. It enforces behavior of the people rather than permits individual
action and thus reduces men to corpse-like "cogs". In her view,
totalitarianism is also a systematic attempt to distort history and to
destroy the possibility of living on in memory after one is gone. It
creates the realm of oblivion in which no witnesses exist to remember
those who have disappeared and where there is no room for one to
appear before others. While the sphere of freedom arises in the
condition of human plurality and mutual respect of equals,
totalitarianism forces the isolation of human beings so that there be

neither community of equals in which there is collective action nor the respectful treatment of one person by another.

Since Arendt fails to distinguish between the aim and the achievement of totalitarianism when she pursues the above insights to their consequences, her elaboration veers toward regrettable flatness. In spite of the fact, however, that there is disparity between what Arendt states and the ascertained facts, her analysis of totalitarianism abounds with brilliant formulations and profound insights. She correctly remarks that politics is rooted in the human sense of reality while totalitarianism ruptures the human structures of reality. Politics is the shared ground of reality. Totalitarianism assaults the public structure of "normal reality" and the personal structure of individuality and freedom. The notion of reality in Arendt's thought is related to that of freedom. The notion of reality in Arendt's thought is related to that of freedom. Politics affirms and shapes freedom into independent reality. As we have seen, there is no politics without the fact of human freedom, and so freedom is impossible outside the order that politics establishes. Thus, the distortion of reality by totalitarianism is an elimination of freedom.

Certainly, Arendt cannot come to the conclusion that this style of regime eliminates freedom only through her analysis of totalitarianism. She comes to this conclusion through her notion of "thinking", which is the theme of the next chapter. The totalitarian regime is a form of organization that requires the suspension of reflective judgment by its members. But sometimes individuals in such organizations refuse to conform to the given rules and thus refuse to suspend their reflective judgment. Arendt insists that people lose their freedom when they refuse to think what they are doing, that is, when they surrender their own potentially active reason and unconsciously abdicate from reacting as human beings by making themselves mere tools of the state. Arendt's strongest point is not how totalitarianism affected all who had tied their lives to it--persecutors and victims- -but rather the force of individual human "thoughtlessness" and lack of judgment, which the totalitarian regime, more quickly than any other sort, may mold.

NOTES

1 "Understanding and Politics", Partisan Review 20 (1953), 379.
2 "Reply to Eric Voegelin's Review of The Origins of Totalitarianism", Review of Politics 15 (January 1953), 78.
3 Ibid., pp. 77-78.
4 Ibid., p. 83.
5 Between Past and Future, p. 99.
6 The Origins of Totalitarianism, p. 375.
7 Ibid.
8 On Revolution, p. 473.
9 The Human Condition, p. 176.
10 The Origins of Totalitarianism, p. 175.
11 Ibid., p. 477.
12 Ibid., pp. 85, 125.
13 Hans Morgenthau, "Hannah Arendt on Totalitarianism and Democracy", Social Research, 44, No. 1 (Spring 1977), 127.
14 The Origins of Totalitarianism, p. 156.
15 Ibid., p. 469.
16 Ibid., p. 159.
17 Ibid., pp. 462-67.
18 Ibid., p. 162.
19 Ibid., p. 433.
20 Ibid., p. 163.
21 Ibid., p. 466.
22 Ibid., pp. 121-22.
23 Ibid., p. 136.
24 Ibid., p. 454.
25 Ibid., p. 6.
26 Ibid., p. 445.
27 Ibid.
28 Ibid., p. 466.
29 Ibid., p. 438.
30 Ibid., p. 71.
31 Ibid.
32 Ibid., pp. 29-31.
33 Between Past and Future, p. 148.
34 Wayne Francis Allen, The Concept of Authority in the Thought of Hannah Diss. University of California J Riverside 1979, p.76.
35 Thinking, p. 38.
36 The Human Condition, pp. 294-95.
37 The Origins of Totalitarianism, p. 351.
38 Eric Voegelin, "The Origins of Totalitarianism", Review of Politics, 15 (January 1953), 68-85. Cf. particularly pp. 84-85.
39 George Kateb, "Freedom and Worldliness in the Thought of Hannah Arendt", political Theory, 5, No.2 (May 1977), 165.

40 Ibid., p. 166.

41 Ibid., p. 165.

42 Mary Joanna Leddy, "The Event of the Holocaust and the Philosophical Reflections of Hannah Arendt", Diss. University of Toronto 1980, p. 125.

43 Ibid.

44 Between Past and Future, p. 169.

45 "Reply to Eric Voegelin's Review of The Origins of Totalitarianism", p.80.

46 Richard Bernstein, "Hannah Arendt: The Ambiguities of Theory and Practice", in Political Theory and Praxis, ed. Terrance Ball (Minneapolis: University of Minnesota Press, 1977), p. 151.

47 O'Sullivan, "Politics, Totalitarianism, and Freedom: The Political Thought of Hannah Arendt", American Journal of Political Science, 22 (May 1978), 191.

48 Margaret Canovan, "The Contradictions of Hannah Arendt's Political Thought", Political Theory, 6 (February 1978), 5-6, 13, 20.

49 Ernst Vollrath, "Hannah Arendt and the Method of Political Thinking", Social Research, 44, No.1 (Spring 1977), 161.

50 Michael Denney, "The Privilege of Ourselves: Hannah Arendt on Judgment", in Hannah Arendt: The Recovery of the Public World, ed. Melvyn A. Hill (New York: St.Martin's Press, 1979), p. 270.

51 Hannah Arendt and Scholem Gershom, "Eichmann in Jerusalem", Encounter (January 1965), 53.

52 "Personal Responsibility Under Dictatorship", The Listener (August 6, 1964), p. 205.

53 Ibid., p. 186.

54 Eichmann in Jerusalem, p. 99.

55 Ibid., p. 102.

56 Ibid., p. 125.

57 Ibid., p. 135.

58 Ibid., p. 111.

59 Hannah Arendt and Scholem Gershom, "Eichmann in Jerusalem", Encounter (January 1965), 55.

60 "Personal Responsibility under Dictatorship", p. 205.

61 Ibid.

62 The Origins of Totalitarianism, p. 401.

63 Margaret Canovan, The Political Thought of Hannah Arendt (London: Aldine Press, 1974), pp. 38-39.

64 The Origins of Totalitarianism, p. 398.

65 Ibid., p. 311.

66 Karl Dietrich Bracher, The German Dictatorship (London, 1971), pp.158-59.

67 The Origins of Totalitarianism, pp. 436, 440.

68 Ibid., p. xiv.

CHAPTER V

PHILOSOPHICAL FREEDOM

In her works earlier than The Life of the Mind1 especially in her essay "What is Freedom?", Arendt opposes freedom of the will to political freedom; or as she puts it, "freedom as related to politics is not a phenomenon of the will".2 In these works she is very much concerned to establish that politics represents the most authentic expression of freedom, a type of freedom not to be confused with the inward freedom to which man may retreat and still call himself free even when he is outwardly restricted. This inward type of freedom, which was applauded by philosophers, is for Arendt "politically irrelevant".3 It is concerned with the simple "I-will", whereas political freedom is not concerned with the internal, the individual "who", but rather also with others, "one's peers", in a public realm where laws and other wills create boundaries.

Are philosophical freedom and political freedom as understood by Arendt two distinct variants of her notion of freedom, or simply two expressions of one and the same mood? Are they, so to speak, two sides of the same coin, or are they entirely different coins? What is the relation between inner freedom and public freedom? Arendt, it seems, is fully aware of their distinct generative sources when she contends that

> the phenomenon of freedom does not appear in the realm of thought at all, that neither freedom nor its opposite is experienced in the dialogue between men and myself in the course of which the great philosophic and metaphysical questions arise, and the great philosophic tradition...has distorted, instead of clarifying, the very idea of freedom such as it is given in human experience by transposing it from its original field, the realm of politics and human affairs in general, to an inward domain, the will, where it would be open to self-inspection.4

Yet she evidently recognizes their close relationship when she claims that without the philosophical and pre-philosophical activities of thinking, willing and judging, neither politics nor freedom are made real. She asserts that without the will no proper notion of freedom can come to light.

In this chapter I wish to suggest that although Arendt opposes philosophical freedom to political freedom, she definitely regards them as complementary. To achieve this I shall first demonstrate that in her view political freedom is not to be confused with the inward kind of freedom to which man may retreat and still call himself free even though its outward manifestation is restricted by external forces. Then I shall indicate how contrary to Rousseau, Arendt finds in political freedom not the chains of the will but freedom of action. Finally, I shall discuss her repudiation of philosophers' efforts to eliminate altogether the distinction between freedom and necessity by remolding our concept and practice of freedom in the image of necessity. She finds philosophers to be very much at home with the ideas of necessity and stability rather than those of freedom and contingency.

Inner Freedom

Philosophers from St. Augustine through seventeenth and eighteenth centuries thinkers like Hobbes and Spinoza have claimed that freedom exists outside the realm of politics. Arendt traces the birth of our present concept of freedom to St. Paul and says that this was given greater elaboration by Augustine. So for her it is just a Christian concept of freedom and decidedly non-political. It had no expression in either Greek or Roman experience. For Augustine philosophical freedom was founded within the individual in which the dialogue was established between "me and myself" and was, as a result, outside the intercourse of other men.

In fact, the appearance of the problem of freedom in Augustine's work was preceded by "the conscious attempt to divorce the notion of freedom from politics, to arrive at a formulation through which one may be a slave in the world and still be free".5 Arendt claims that the notion of freedom as an inner freedom, that is, as the property of "man's own self" independent of the world and other men, is already present in the philosophy of Epictetus, who was an emancipated slave. The experience underlying theories of inner freedom is the loss of a place or home in the world. For those who were excluded from the political realm, as was the case with all slaves, freedom consisted in the ability of the self to do what no one could stop him from doing. The slaves claimed that they could still experience an inward freedom, which is a permanent and real attribute of the self. This line of thinking has been promoted by modern thinkers like Bonhoeffer, who claim that one can still retain one's freedom even when in bondage to the outside world or under conditions of dictatorship and tyranny. It is also important to not that most schools of existentialism articulate an identical notion of freedom to inner freedom. Sartre and Heidegger are good examples of those who do not regard freedom as worldly or political phenomenon. In Arendt's view, however, inner freedom is not freedom at all since it

125

entirely any "interrelationship with the world":6 unworldly freedom contradicts the very principle and meaning of freedom.

This transposition of freedom from its "original field, the realm of politics and human affairs in general, to an inward domain, the will, where it would be open to self-inspection" for Arendt is a sheer distortion of the very idea of freedom. The reason for philosophy's distortion is likewise clear: the tradition of political philosophy "was founded explicitly in opposition to the polis and its citizenship".7 As we have seen earlier, freedom according to Arendt is "actually the reason that men live together in political organization".8 So the idea that experience of freedom is an inner one, an element of the dialogue between me and myself, indicates the loss of freedom as a worldly reality in the contemporary era. To Arendt this fosters the growth of worldlessness, which results from the failure to experience reality and failure of theoretical consciousness.

On the one hand, Arendt separates thought and action and insists that there is an unbridgeable dichotomy between the solitariness of thought and the communality of action. This dichotomy is crucial to her concept of freedom because she believes that freedom is to be found only in communal action in the public realm in what she refers to as "the space of appearance", where dialogue is among equals. It is not to be found in a private inward domain, where dialogue is only between "me and myself". On the other hand, she enlists thought in the confirmation of the free and unique appearance of person. She also blames Eichmann's behavior, that is, failure to act, on his thoughtlessness. Faced with what she considered to be Eichmann's unthinking nature, Arendt wonders whether there is something in the thinking activity that helps men to refrain from doing evil.9 Is there any connection between Arendt's notion of "thinking" and action that is essential for freedom? How then does she relate being with oneself to being with others?

Thiking

Arendt refers to thinking as "the soundless dialogue between me and myself".
She claims that this is Socrates' idea of the essence of thought.
Plato translated this idea into "conceptual language" and formulated the phrase "to legein pros eauton [a dialogue between me and myself]".10 She is not therefore claiming any originality in describing "thinking" in this way. She indeed refers to a passage of the Theaetetus in which Socrates describes the process of thinking as a "discourse that the mind carries on with itself about subject it is

considering". For Socrates, when the mind is thinking, it is simply talking to itself, asking questions and answering them, and saying yes or no. Arendt derives the further idea, that this type of dialogue is sounndless, from the Sophist where Eleatic says to Theaetetus: "Thinking and discourse are the same thing, except that what we call thinking is, precisely, the inward dialogue carried on by the mind with itself without spoken sound."11

Arendt accordingly infers that the notion of an inner dialogue, the mind's discourse with itself, connotes a "difference in oneness", a phenomenon that is actualized when the thinking self actualizes the dialogue of the self with the self: "It is this duality of myself and myself that makes thinking a true activity, in which I am both the one who asks and who answers."12 Such actualization of a duality within consciusness is not just self-consciousness or self-awareness. The duality of myself with myself allows me to be with myself and to converse with myself as in a dialogue.

To show that thinking is the two-in-one, Arendt again cites from one of Plato's works, Gorgias, where Socrates tells Callicles that it is best to be in harmony with oneself. He asserts:

> It would be better for me that my lyre or a chorus I directed should be out of tune and loud with discord, and that the multitude of men should disagree with me rather than the I, being one, should be out of harmony with myself and contradict me.13

An individual appears before others as one, but in thinking he is two in that he can talk, agree or disagree with himself. Should he disagree with himself, then he becomes an enemy to himself, and that makes it very difficult for him to live with himself. He has to change his point of view in order to be in harmony with himself. The inner dialogue is like a discourse in a court of law. The thinker is both the judge and the accused. He asks questions and gives the answers. As in every dialogue, the thinker is not lonely. He may appear solitary, but he is not without the company of himself. He is still alone, however, because there is no one from outside to help him, during the thinking process, to see straight or decide.

Arendt further claims that the dialogue one has with oneself is an indication that "man exists essentially in the plural". In fact, the dialogue one has in the public realm with one's peers is the continuation of the internal dialogue because according to Aristotle a friend is "another self". Arendt asserts:

> What Socrates discovered was that we can have
> intercourse with ourselves, as well as with others, and
> that the two kinds of intercourse are somehow
> interrelated. Aristotle, speaking about friendship,
> remarked: "The friend is another self"--meaning: you can
> carry on the dialogue of thought with him just as well as
> with yourself. This is still in the Socratic tradition,
> except that Socrates would have said: The self, too, is a
> kind of friend.14

While Arendt's intention here was to describe what friendship is, we can already see the relationship she notes between the inward dialogue in the private realm and the dialogue between equals or friends in the public realm. In this way freedom, which is experienced through the media of language and speech in the public realm, can be said to originate from the inner dialogue one has with oneself. The very activity of thinking encourages an awareness of freedom by undermining the givens of the self. It destroys the givens of one's sequestered self and lifts one from an acquiescence to the ongoing flow of life. Thinking prepares the self for the conditions of human plurality. It aids in the translation of the self into the form of appearance, which is the same as saying that one creates and confirms oneself in such a way that one is acknowledged by one's fellow spectators. It fosters an "enlarged mentality", a willingness to examine experience on a shared and interchangeable basis with other men.15

Arendt, however, accepts solitude as necessary for thought. She claims that when "a man indulges in sheer thinking, and no matter on what subject, he lives completely in the singular, that is, in complete solitude, as though not men but man inhabited the earth".16 She had already explained in The Origins of Totalitarianism that

> [i]n solitude...I am "by myself", together with myself, and
> therefore two-in-one. All thinking, strictly speaking, is
> done in solitude and it is a dialogue between me and
> myself.17

It is in solitude that the duality of the thinker is actualized, so whoever wants to become active in thinking should deliberately choose solitude. But in solitude man cannot appear before others. He misses the reality of seeing and being seen, and he escapes from the public realm into the privacy of the self.

We have seen that fellowship and discourse between men in the community belongs in the public realm where one appears and lives among one's peers. The public realm is the realm of freedom and action; these are never possible in the private sphere or in solitude because they require co-actors. There is, therefore, a separation between action and thinking that can be said to be a distinction between singularity and plurality. Plurality represents the basic condition of action, for in action men find themselves in concert with beings who are quite like them and yet distinguished from them on the very basic point of bodily appearance. In order to act one needs a public realm where one can be in company with one's peers, "hence in an existential situation that effectively prevents thinking".18

Here we find a paradox in Arendt's thought. On the one hand, she insists that thinking is a dialogue with the self, involving plurality of selves. On the other hand, she asserts that thinking cannot be an action since it is the most solitary occupation. This is further complicated by her assertion that thinking is an activity that surpasses action and other activities in intensity. Citing Cato she claims:

> Never is a man more active than when he does nothing, never is he less alone than when he is by himself (Numquam se plus agere quam nihil cum ageret, numquam minus solum esse quam cum solus esset).19

For Arendt, thinking is the essence of man: man is a thinking being, and the ability to think has always been with him.

But then if thinking, which is based on solitariness, is the essence of man, how can politics, which is public, be the essence or nature of man? How does "man exist essentially in the plural"? Arendt is actually very much troubled by the withdrawal of the thinker from the world of appearance. Despite her claim that without thinking one is not fully alive, Arendt is also aware that one who withdraws from the world into solitude, as thinking activity requires, is dead to the world. Somehow, in Arendt's view, the contemplative life (vita contemplativa) misses reality and leads beyond the human condition. Since she holds that the world as our physical home is also the sphere of political action, that is, the realm of freedom, she characterizes thinking as worldless and as such not essential for political freedom.

Philosophy has been concerned inter alia with the need for thought to withdraw from reality. As we have seen, thinking requires a retiring into the self, into an invisible realm beyond the view of other selves. It interrupts the intercourse with others and the world; as Arendt says, thinking is "out of order" and requires a cessation of "normal" activities. It has the power to lift the thinker from the world of reality or from the context of space and time into the worldless sphere. Arendt asserts that the thinking ego withdraws from the world of appearances into the land of invisibles, a land of the distant, the non-present in which

> it is rather as though the invisible had come forward, as though the innumerable entities making up the world of appearances....20

We still recall that Arendt suggests that the sense of reality can only be achieved by appearance in a world of similarly appearing spectators. But thinking does not appear in the world directly. It is worldless and its major contribution is the refinement of the inner world.

Arendt, however, thinks that thinking, although confined to the private or inner domain, is related to freedom and action, which are experienced in the public realm. She asserts that it transpires in the medium of speech, which prepares it for communicability and shareability with others who likewise think and speak. Through speech, thinking creates a metaphorical link between the inner self and appearance. Arendt asserts:

> Though with its accompanying conceptual language, since it occurs in and is spoken by a being at home in a world of appearances, stands in need of metaphors in order to bridge the gap between a world given to sense experience and a realm where no such immediate apprehension of evidence can ever exist.21

By this she insinuates that the metaphorical capacity resident in speech allows one to convey meaningfully to others "what goes on in one's mind", to convey one's own perspective on reality so that it can be appropriated by others.

For Arendt, speech enables thinking to disclose manifestly what seemed invisible and unassimilable to the appearing world. The satisfactory rendering of this disclosure requires the elements of thinking to be dependent on the realities of appearance, and it also requires the mind to unfreeze the meaning in what she calls the frozen analogies of language. In a worderful image she portrays Socrates as standing in the wind of thought, an "invisible element" whose "nature is to undo, to unfreeze...what language, the medium of thinking, has frozen into thought....22

She tries to make a connection between an individual's dialogue with himself and with others in order to show that thinking is occasioned when a certain kind of range of otherness is interiorized. She seems sometimes to be saying that if one does not make an appropriate response to others, one is not really thinking. This assumption is quite puzzling because at the outset of her argument, borrowing from the Gorgias, she sets the dialogue with oneself over against the dialogue with others or "the multitude". What Arendt is clear about is that one's thoughts, feelings, intimations and beliefs can be translated, through speech, into a form by which all other participants and spectators can use them as clues to decipher the meaning of one's action in the public realm. So thinking is as closely related to action as it is to speech because one's action "becomes relevant only through the spoken word in which he identifies himself as the actor, announcing what he does, has done, and intends to do".23

Arendt further connects thinking with action by claiming that "we must think what we are doing". She contends that if Eichmann had thought, he would not have done evil. She argues that what permitted him to do great evil was "not stupidity but thought-lessness".24 She asks:

> Could the activity of thinking as such, the habit of examining whatever comes to pass or to attract attention regardless of results and specific content, could this activity be among the conditions that make men abstain from evil or even actually "condition" them against it?25

Her observation of Eichmann's trial convinced her that Eichmann was banal and that his banality was revealed in his lack of thinking. This failure to think was shown through his repetition of trivial and empty truths. He simply refused to think, that is, to conduct an inner dialogue with himself about the meaning of what he did.

The effects of refusing to think are far-reaching. "Unthinking men are like sleepwalkers".26 In refusing to think for oneself one does not only come to speak in clichés or merely to parrot words, one also gives up one's potential for revealing who one is through action. Failure to think reduces one to a state of sheer behaving, that is, a state in which one does not perceive and assess the meaning and significance of what one is doing. Eichmann's failure "to think what he was doing", for example, put him at the mercy of others who judged what was proper for him to do. He took the desires and the orders of the party leadership as a substitute for his own judgment. In doing so he placed his judgment in an ever more passive state and thus approximated the ideal bureaucrat. Therefore, thinking obliterates the secure adherence to abstract rules and authoritarian pronouncements and liberates the faculty of judgment, which evaluates each new phenomenon as a reality with an integrity of its own. Thinking is required to divert the habit of obedience from thwarting the meaning of the novel and the unique.27

Finally, Arendt thinks that the very activity of thinking is related to freedom because this activity opens a space for freedom. Thinking halts the flow of life in order to allow for a beginning. In her article "Lying in Politics", she shows in practical instances how thinking is the source of freedom. In order for action to take place, Arendt says, thinking must first remove or destroy the physical limiting factors:

> Such change would be impossible if we could not mentally remove ourselves from where we physically are located and imagine that things might as well be different from what they actually are.28

Thinking lifts one from the inward domain to the realm of objectivity. It liberates the mind from the given, whether it be the given of experience or social reality. By examining every reality that appears to it, thinking breaks down the hold that the usual and words have over the mind. This is what Arendt calls "philosophizing", and she claims that "philosophizing sounds the appeal to my freedom and creates the space for unconditioned deeds that would invoke transcendence".29 For her, thinking obliterates the secure adherence to abstract rules and authoritarian regulations. It also opens the possibilities for something new to happen. Thus, thinking can be said to enhance the possibility of freedom by its liberation of men from the given particulars to the universals. Against the givenness of reality the thinker discovers his own finitude and limitations and above all his potentiality to begin anew and constitute history in a realm of freedom.

Thinking disrupts the continuity of the everyday and casts man back upon himself where he discovers his existence at a singular point of time. Thus, the freedom to begin anew and to represent the new become linked in Arendt's thought with the ability to take on that form of meaningfulness that can be redeemed from the ruins of historical time. This interrelation testifies again to the link between being and plurality, being and the spectatorship of fellow human beings, a relation of primary focus in our first chapter. Again we see that the notion of beginning anew depends on the force of one's appearance in the community of one's fellows.

Using Kafka's parable of the anonymous hero who is depicted as having two enemies, one pushing him from behind and the other driving him back from ahead, Arendt shows how the space opened for freedom and the "where" of thinking are actually phenomena linked to the emergence of temporality. Kafka's presence seems to encourage and perpetuate the struggle, yet he still dreams of gaining a perspective from which he could overlook and judge the entire spectacle. Like Kafka, the thinking ego pulls together and holds apart what belongs to the public and private domain. Thinking allows the private and the public to come together. It also links one's life and plurality, that is, the individual self and the spectatorship of fellow human beings. Through Kafka's parable, Arendt shows how freedom to begin anew and to represent the new become linked with the ability to rethink the past.

As we see, although Arendt firmly claims that inner freedom is "politically irrelevant" since it cuts off human plurality, at the same time she also links the "inward domain of consciousness" to human plurality. She connects thinking with the realm of freedom and claims that John Stuart Mill's presentation of inward freedom as an escape from plurality and a retreat to an inner self where no other has access was just an attempt to divorce freedom from politics. She maintains that the decline of political philosophy is its withdrawal to the inner domain of the mind and its retreat from the world in which men live. She argues that

> in spite of the great influence the concept of an inner, nonpolitical freedom has exerted upon the tradition of thought, it seems safe to say that man would know nothing of inner freedom if he had not first experienced a condition of being free as a worldly tangible reality.30

For her the mind is not a place for political freedom because it is a place excluded to others. It cannot be the foundation of political freedom.

Willing

In her essay "What is Freedom?", Arendt claims that action is free as long as it is under neither the guidance of the intellect nor the dictates of the will. In this essay she opposes freedom of the will to political freedom, which latter represents for her the most authentic expression of freedom. But in The Life of the Mind, she asserts that without the will no proper notion of freedom can come to light. What, in Arendt's view, is the relationship between freedom and the will? We shall answer this question by exploring Arendt's notion of the will and her analysis of the views of thinkers who have written about it.

The substance of Arendt's position is that the will is not the basis of political freedom even though it is the exploiter of contingency and the initiator of spontaneous, unpredictable, causally inexplicable actions. She regards the will as the "spring of action". The difficulty of such a position is quite apparent to her, as George Kateb remarks:

> She knows that the very notion of spontaneous action, of freedom as free will, is exceptionally problematic. But unless it is true, freedom is a lie.31

Arendt holds that the discovery of the faculty of will coincided with that of human "inwardness" in early Christianity. She asserts that the notion of the will began with St. Paul. By this she does not deny that there were some traces of it in the ancient Greek thought, especially in Aristotle's idea of proairesis, which contains his account of how men exercise their faculty of choice. But proairesis or liberum arbitrium, as the Romans called it, is not a faculty independent of reason, whereas the will is. Proairesis is the process of choosing means to an end; it is not the end itself. Therefore, freedom of will as set forth by Paul and later given greater elaboration by St. Augustine had no expression in either Greek or Roman experience. Such a freedom, if it meant anything to Greeks, could be found in bios theoretikos, or vita contemplativa, in which man could reason or withdraw from the world, hence out of the polis where political freedom could be experienced. It was only after the decay of the polis, when it was no longer necessary to look to politics for one's freedom, that freedom of the will was discovered.

Arendt does not mean that the mind acquires "new faculties in the course of history", but rather that the will was discovered as a result of some changes in the world, like the decline of the Greek political world. The will was also discovered because of some new perspectives, for example, the realization that an individual's freedom does not depend only on the elimination of external obstacles but also on inner conflict that prevents him from fulfilling whatever he wants. The inner conflict is experienced when one begins "to doubt the coincidence of the Thou-shalt and the I-can, when the question arises: are the things that concern only me within my power?"32

Since Arendt claims that the Greek polis is the paradigm of authentic freedom, the logical conclusion would be that the will has nothing to do with freedom. But she insists that without the will neither politics nor freedom are made real. Without the will one could not say that one could have not done something; and this is essential for free acts. The further examination of Arendt's concept of the will should help us realize how she links it with freedom.

As we have seen above, in the thinking process there is a dialogue within the self. The Greeks could not conceive that such a dialogue might result in a disagreement of self with self, which the willing faculty could resolve. St. Paul recognized the inner struggle between the I-will and I-can that arose when he wanted to fulfill the law but could not. This is how he expressed this duality in thought underlying man's will: "I do not what I want, but I do the very thing I hate."33 For Paul, who did not philosophize about his experiences, the discrepancy between the "I-will" and the "I-can or I-cannot" was a simple conflict between the spirit and the flesh. In trying to fulfill God's law, Paul found that something within him prevented him from doing so. Consequently, no matter how much he wished to obey the law, he would always end up in disobeying it unless he got divine help. But for Arendt the struggle Paul described was actually the will turned in upon itself, perpetually challenging itself, creating a "nil" or counter-will to every intended act.34

By its very nature the will gives rise to a counter-will that is not merely a negative I-will-not but an active nil. The fact that the will can respond by both willing and nilling shows that the will is free from itself within itself. It is free because it can choose either alternative and does not remain enslaved by its choice. It neither wills nor nils completely.

The will's choice is not the same as the Aristotelian proairesis, which is just a choice of means to best realize a given end. The will's choice involves choosing and creating the end itself. For Arendt this idea is based on St.Augustine's contention that man, being created in the image of God, is radically free. Like God the creator, man is capable of initiating something entirely new. Arendt relies on this Augustinian initium, which is related to the condition of natality, and on the Kantian "power of spontaneously beginning series of successive things or states".35 She discusses the will as the mental faculty corresponding to spontaneous freedom.

> The will is either an organ of free spontaneity that
> interrupts all causal chains of motivation that would bind
> it or it is nothing but an illusion.36

This is how Arendt regards the faculty of the will as both the "spring of action" and the principle of individuation, which endows man with the freedom to initiate without being coerced in any way by outside forces.

Arendt, following St. Augustine, is very disappointed with Aquinas because he gives the intellect primacy over the will:

> The Intellect, which, according to Thomas, is "a passive power", is assured of its primacy over the will not only because it "presents an object to the appetite," and hence is prior to it, but also because it survives the Will, which is extinguished, as it were, when the object has been attained.37

Aquinas opted for the primacy of the intellect over the will not only because it survives the will, but also because man's ultimate happiness is to know God by intellect, and this intellect ultimately ends in contemplation.

For Arendt it was Duns Scotus who put a balance on the notion of the will by admitting its primacy and its limitations. She acknowledges that the will is not omnipotent in actual effectiveness. It cannot change the world or human inclinations as such, but it is free to accept or reject the world as it is given. It can affirm or negate freely what has already come into existence, but it cannot revoke choice once it has been executed, or undo deeds. So the will's freedom is just a mental freedom guaranteeing the individual's independence both from other men and from the world itself. Its power lies in the fact that it cannot be coerced to will.

She concludes her work on the will with the discussion of Nietzsche, Heidegger and Jaspers. She feels that none of them places the will at the centre of the human faculties. For her this demonstrates her contention that thinkers or philosophers treat the will in biased way. She holds that even German idealism after Kant presents the will in an amiguous role. In German idealism the will is not considered as the faculty bestowing freedom of choice but is equated with the innermost secret of being itself. For her this represents a move from human being to personification, from the faculties of man to the activities of personified concept. The result of this shift is a world of disembodied spirits working behind men's backs, a world build out of nostalgia for another world.

The only philosopher she admires is St.Augustine, especially his assertions that man's beginning is a radical creation and that his will, his freedom and his being a veritable new beginning collectively make it possible for him to create himself anew.   She also retains considerable admiration for his elaboration of the will and the foundation of philosophical freedom.   Even then, however, she cannot accept his concept of the free will as the basis of political freedom because of the dualism set up by the will.   In Arendt's view the conflict within the will "to will and not to will at the same time" renders the will incapable of acting.   This conflict, therefore, is totally unfit for her theory of action and freedom.   The fact that the will can command and disobey itself, that is, the confrontation between the "I-will" and the "I-will not", does not create as much difficulty for action as the "I-will" and the "I-cannot", which totally paralyzes it.   According to St.Augustine

> [t]he will commands that there be a will, it commands not something else but itself....Were it entire, it would not even command itself to be because it would already be....Hence the will is both powerful and impotent, free and unfree.38

Anthony Kenny, in showing how will affects action, also realizes the dualism set up by the will. He asserts:

> The will that p may be manifested by bringing it about that p, by not bringing it about that not-p, by commanding that p, and by forbidding that not-p.39

The will thereby renders the self impotent by presenting the individual with the desire to act and the inability to act at the same time. Arendt could not ground her concept of political freedom in a faculty that lacked a "force" for action by its constant struggle to act and not to act.

Another reason why Arendt thinks that the will is not the basis of political freedom is because the will is closely related to coercion. But coercion and freedom are incompatible. The foundation for politics cannot be a dialectical process in which generation of power to act is blunted by an internal struggle with the self. The dialectical internal struggle results in the oppression of the self by the self. Therefore, any attempt to extend this internal struggle of the will into the public realm brings into this realm unpolitical consequences like the oppression of the self by others. Arendt argues:

> I can only hint at the fatal consequences for political theory of this equation of freedom with the human capacity to will; it was one of the causes why even today we almost automatically equate power with oppression or,

at least, with rule over others.40

This oppression can easily take place because the dialogue one has with oneself becomes, in a plural situation, a dialogue one has with others. Arendt refers to historical instances like what happened during the early days of the French Revolution when oppression of the self by the self with the oppression of the self by others. It is on this point that Arendt rejects Rousseau's "general will" and "absolute sovereignty".

Rousseau is an outstanding defender of the faculty of will in the realm of politics. For him the "general will" is achieved when each individual identifies his "real self" or "real will" with others' wills. He claimed that "a divided will would be inconceivable". Arendt finds that more often than not the instrument for achieving this ideal "free will writ large" is violence because if freedom is being in accord with general will, then in order to be free one may be forced by others to be free. For Arendt freedom is incompatible with violence, force and coercion. Persuasion, discourse and consensus in politics do not mean forcing others to agree with one's will. While it is possible that in a discourse a consensus might be reached without anyone oppressing others, Arendt finds that Rousseau's "general will" can only be achieved at the expense of the diversity of opinions inherent in the very condition of human plurality.

The notion of a "general will" is contrary to Arendt's whole view of the political realm. It is against the freedom exercised in discourse and communication in the public sphere. For Arendt politics is the coming together of divergent opinions that are formed and developed among peers. This does not mean that she advocates a uniformity of opinion, which would not be different from Rousseau's "general will"; rather, she argues that "no formation of opinion is ever possible where all opinions have become the same".41

Arendt takes the basic argument of Rousseau's quest after a "general will" as a confusion of freedom with sovereignty, "the ideal of a free will, independent from others and eventually prevailing against them",42 and hence politically dangerous. Thus, she rejects the will as the basis of freedom:

It leads either to a denial of human freedom--namely, if it is realized that whatever men may be, they are never sovereign--or to the insight that the freedom of one man, or group, or body politic can be purchased only at the price of the freedom, i.e., the sovereignty, of all others.43

Like the idea of free will, the notion of sovereignty is anti-political. It is opposed to Arendt's concept of politics as the realm of human plurality. It denies plurality itself. Arendt finds that sovereignty is maintained only when a group of people surrender their freedom and are governed by the "general will" or the ruler's will. This is why she stresses that "if men wish to be free, it is precisely sovereignty they must renounce".44

Arendt further emphasizes that in linking freedom with the will we leave the sphere of the genuinely political and enter the private realm. Moreover, the power of the will "as a distinct and separate human faculty" is in its ability to command. This power "is not a matter of freedom but a question of strength or weakness".45 As we have seen, strength is a mutely natural, anti-political, singular quality of the individual:

> [I]t is the property inherent in an object or person and belongs to its character, which may prove itself in relation to other things or persons, but is essentially independent of them.46

Arendt does not, however, minimize the importance of philosophical freedom nor claim that the will has no relevance to political freedom. She recognizes that the will helps to make the person who he is and helps in beginning something new. The will for her gives an individual a sense of acting in the world. It helps to fashion character. Unlike thinking, which simply isolates the self from the world, the will fashions the self, who is capable of all particular acts of volition. The will creates the character; hence it was considered as the principium individuationis. She believes that the will is the source of the self's character, and, borrowing from Augustine, she claims that it individuates men radically by removing them from the common world of their fellow men. It establishes one's singular identity and forms his distinctive character.

The will, then, helps one to distinguish oneself as a free individual, as a maker of certain actions. It also discloses to others "who" an individual is. It is, however, confined to the individual and is the realm of the philosophical freedom insofar as it arbitrates between this or that choice. It is "relevant only to people who live outside political community, as solitary individuals".47

The individuation brought by the will is the source of trouble for the notion of freedom. Arendt is aware that whenever an individual asserts himself against the "they" and develops his own projects for the future, the notion of freedom is put in jeopardy. This is because the political freedom, with its quality of the I-can rather than of the I-will, only takes place within a condition of plurality. In this way Arendt gives credit to the will for helping to make the person who he is but not for being the essence of freedom.

Furthermore, Arendt regards the will as the "organ of the future" and maintains that it is then "identical with the power of beginning something new". Part of freedom's essence lies in the future. It appears always in becoming and never in total being. So the will, unlike thinking, which is past-oriented, is able to break the "ought" of existence, the notion that what was had to be. With its projects for the future, the will challenges the belief in necessity. Since it cannot be past- and present-bound, it opens the possibilities for bringing into existence something new. At this point we can see why Arendt asserts that it is the "spring of action". Following Duns Scotus' thought she affirms:

> Action insofar as it is determined is guided by a future aim whose desirability the intellect has grasped before the will wills it, whereby the intellect calls upon the will since only the will can dictate action....48

This implies that the will is a precondition for the act, that it first dictates action.

With this notion of the will, it is less surprising that Arendt criticized those philosophers who were unwilling to pay the price of the arbitrariness of the will and denied its spontaneity. According to her, these philosophers preferred necessity and universality over contingency and particularity. They denied any possibility of a new or unprecedented action. Against them, she reaffirms the contingency of the will and holds that "we are doomed to be free", that is, we are radically free whether we are pleased with the spontaneity of freedom or detest its arbitrariness. Therefore, it is not possible to deal with the willing activity without touching on the problem of freedom. Freedom for Arendt remains something essentially worldly and public, experienced in the tangible world of political action even though its roots lie in the spontaneity, contingency and autonomy of the will.

The Faculty of Judgment

We have so far seen how Arendt relates two mental faculties, thinking and willing, to her notion of freedom. There are, however, still some perplexities and conflicts presented by her notion of thinking and willing. Thinking is concerned with generals, which

140

with generals, which cannot be localized; willing is concerned with particulars. Thinking deals with the necessary; willing, with the contingent. The question is whether something as contingent as the faculty of willing can ever provide a suitable basis for human freedom.

Arendt considers the faculty of judgment as the solution to the problem of affirming human freedom. She holds that judgment is the culmination of the three mental activities because, as Ronald Beiner suggests, it both maintains the contract with "the world of appearances" that is characteristic of "willing" and fulfills the quest for meaning that animates "thinking".49 It also links thinking and willing by "mysteriously combining the particular and the general".

In Arendt's view, judgment allows one to experience freedom in the contingency of the particular. It can determine what is right and wrong in a particular situation; hence, it is of direct use to action, as we shall see. Judgment as the "by-product of thinking" relates thinking to action. Thinking deals with universals, whereas action is concerned with particulars. Arendt brings this up when she states that judgment is the "faculty of thinking the particular; but to think is to generalize, hence it is the faculty of combining the particular and the general".50 This means that judging is an activity of subsuming particulars under a universal:

> Judgment is the mental process by which one projects oneself into a counterfactual situation of disinterested reflection in order to satisfy oneself and an imagined community of potential collocutors that a particular has been adequately appraised.51

A careful reading of Arendt's works discloses two different notions of the faculty of judgment. In her earlier works she links judment to "representative thinking" and opinion. She claims that it has a role to play in the public realm as a function of the "representative thinking" and "enlarged mentality" of political actors, exchanging opinions in public while engaged in common deliberation and action. Beiner correctly observes that, according to Arendt, "the political actor on his own cannot secure meaning; the actor needs a spectator. Hence the necessity of judgment."52

Arendt's idea of spectatorship calls attention to the plurality presupposed in judgment as opposed to the solitary nature of thought. Unlike thinking, which requires that one be together with oneself, and will, which requires that one be identical to oneself, judgment requires that one be together with one's peers. It is an escape from individualism or the private realm. Since judgment involves accepting the diversity of men, Arendt finds it to be "one if not the most important activity in which this sharing-the-world-with-others comes to pass".53   She therefore concludes that judgment is the central operating principle of the human condition and of any theory of politics, like freedom, that is to be adequate to that condition.   It is also "the most political of man's mental abilities", "one of the fundamental abilities of man as a political being", the political faculty par excellence.

But, on the other hand, Arendt regards judment as a sheer mental faculty pertaining only to the contemplative life in its retrospective operations.   She places it exclusively within the bounds of the life of the mind by defining it as a function of the will, that is, as the liberum arbitrium, the "arbitrating function" of the will.   At other times she regards it as the will itself.   In many places she treats it as a separate mental faculty, distinct from both intellect and will.   She changes her idea of judgment as "the representative thinking" of political agents and aligns it with thinking.   Judgment comes to be defined as reflection on the past, no longer as the deliberation of political actors on future action.   Therefore, Arendt first considers judging as a feature of political life, then as an independent mental activity.

To place in its proper context this uncertainty as to where judgment fits, it may be helpful to recall that Arendt's reflection on judgment developed from her reading Kant.   In her view, the faculty of judgment was discovered by Kant, although he did not hold an exclusive monopoly in this field.   One commentator also affirms that, with the exception of Kant, judgment received relatively little consideration in the Western world:

> Now the faculty of judgment has received relatively little
> attention in the Western philosophical tradition.   Neither
> in politics nor in morality has it been considered of
> paramount importance, usually being considered a minor,
> subordinate faculty.   Aside from Aristotle, Shaftesbury,
> some men of letters in the Enlightenment, an occasional
> jurist, and, of course, Kant, it has scarcely been
> noticed.54

Kant based his moral philosophy on taste.   As he developed his theory on taste, he realized that judgment gives a better explanation of the "topics he had originally thought belonged to the taste".   For Kant, judgment is not practical reason, as many think.   Judgment deals with the beautiful and the ugly, right and wrong, whereas practical reason deals with what to do or what not to do.   He also considered judgment as inherently social since our aesthetic judgments make reference to a common or shared world, to what appears in public to all judging subjects, and thus not merely to the private preferences of individuals. In matters of "taste" one never judges for oneself alone because the act of judging itself implies a commitment to communicate one's judgment. Judgment is, then, as Habermas asserts, "a first approach to a concept of communicative rationality which is built into speech and action itself".55 One is committed to seek acknowledgment from one's peers, to get them to acknowledge the reasonableness or rationality of one's judgment and thereby to confirm one's "tastes". In the act of judgment one tries to satisfy oneself and an imagined community of potential collocutors.

Since for Arendt politics is a matter of judging appearances, she easily sees an affinity between politics and aesthetics because both concern the world of appearances. It can be said that Kant provided the inspiration for Arendt's notion of judgment and influenced her turning to aesthetics for a model of political judgment. She herself affirms that "in the work of no other philosopher has the concept of appearance...played so decisive and central a role as in Kant".56

According to Arendt, judgment, as preparation for how one should appear in public, enables man to orient himself in the public realm, in the common world. It helps us to "confirm the world and ourselves" and to "make ourselves at home in the world".57 This happens because the faculty fo judgment can locate past events.
Its capacity for reflection upon the deeds of the past "makes satisfactory provision for meaning and thereby allows us potentially to affirm our condition".58 It is through the use of reflective judgment that one becomes the judging spectator or historian, the preserver of human stories:

> ...only the spectator occupies a position that enables him to see the whole play--as the philosopher is able to see the kosmos as a harmonious ordered whole. The actor, being part of the whole, must enact his part...he is bound to the particular that finds its ultimate meaning and the justification of its existence solely as a constituent of the whole.59

This worldly application of judgment has an influence on Arendt's notion of action and freedom because it brings into the public realm one who presumes to tell the story of reality and to pass judgment.

It is also by reflecting on the "miraculousness of human freedom as instantiated in a particular moment of the past that we are able to accept the world and existential reality, which would otherwise be without meaning, and still retain hope for a better world:

[W]ithout the possibility of retrospective judgment, we
might well be overcome by a sense of the meaninglessness
of the present and succumb to despair over the future.60

Judgment brings meaning into the world of things and gets our
bearings in it. Hence, our feelings of meaninglessness in the twentieth
century have been accompanied by atrophy of judgment. It is
judgment that reconciles time and worldliness. Arendt claims that
lack of judgment has reduced the world we presently inhabit to a
realm that offers no prospect for genuine action and therefore for
freedom.

Arendt connects judgment with action and asserts that the
source of the greatest evils of the present century in the political
realm is "the refusal to judge: lack of imagination, of having present
before your eyes and taking into account the others whom you must
represent".61 Whereas the will represents a drive towards a singular
expression in action, which would then constitute man as a beginning,
as a beginner of new processes, judgment shapes that expression into a
form by which it can move others. Men are only beginners by virtue
of their appeal to other human beings. The "I will" is accomplished
by an "I can" only in cooperation with others--judgment accomplishes
this mediation and makes possible an appreciation of men as free
actors, new beginners.

Arendt extends the mind's ability to judge what should or should
not appear in the public realm to deeds as well as to works. She
allows that both spectator and actor reside in the imagination of every
actor, enabling him to conform his appearance to what can be
appreciated by other spectators:

[W]ithout this critical, judging faculty the doer or maker
would be so isolated that he would not even be
perceived...[and] the very originality of the artist (or the
very novelty of the actor) depends on making himself
understood by those who are not artists (or actors).62

There must be some conformity to judgment and consequently of
action to the antecedent standards of the public realm. Thus,
judgment is central to the constitution of an act as a beginning among
men. It enables one to discern the form that one's appearance should
take to move others--to bring a new series of possibilities into the
world. One's appearance as an actor and therefore as the incipient
initiator of a new series of actions only transpires when one's
appearance conforms to and exemplifies these tacit standards of how
one should appear.

144

Arendt does not, however, claim that judgment informs one exactly how to act, which actions to engage in, or what to do in complexities of action; it only prepares one for an appearance that, properly mediated by the common media of linguistic and customary expression, will be "explicable" in the eyes and minds of other men. This is confirmed by her discussion of the nature of a free act of a new beginning. The free action is not undertaken or judged by considerations of motivation or of intended goals.

Arendt insists that judgment participates in the vita activa. She claims that the evils of the modern age, the evils of totalitarianism epitomized in Eichmann, are the results of modern man's "refusal to judge" and that judgment "may prevent catastrophes...in the rare moments when the chips are down".63 She finds fault with the bureaucratic, technocratic and depoliticized structures of modern life. For her they encourage indifference and increasingly render men less discriminating, less capable of critical thinking, and less inclined to assume responsibility. Since people can no longer rely on traditional standards of judgment and ultimate values, they should be more discriminating. But unfortunately the structures of the modern life do not give them a chance to judge for themselves. Hence the norms of political and moral civility have become acutely vulnerable. Without the faculty of judgment people easily surrender to the forces of evil. Political judgment provides men with a sense of hope by which to sustain them in action when confronted with tragic barriers. It is in this context that Kant's analysis of taste provides the inspiration for Arendt's notion of judgment.

It is clear that although at times Arendt emphasizes the contemplative dimension of judgment and places it within the ambit of the life of the mind, she nonetheless integrates it into the vita activa. She considers it to be the solution to the problem of affirming human freedom. It is through judgment that man is able to engage courageously in action and to seek the fame of historical remembrance and freedom as human possibilities following from the concept of appearing predicated on plurality. It is also through Arendt's notion of judgment that human beings are able to take their bearings and plan their actions in the confidence that they will be properly judged. Being in history entails the active judgment of spectators to whose acknowledgment one's acts are intentionally directed.

We have so far seen how Arendt describes philosophical freedom as distinct from political freedom yet not irrelevant to it. Even though at times it is difficult to connect philosophical freedom with political freedom, she conceives of political freedom as the summation of the philosophical wellspring. Since man's freedom as an individual endowed with the faculties of thinking, willing and judging is bound up with the freedom of other people, philosophical freedom is closely related to political freedom. Also, through the use of his mental faculties an individual reveals himself, creates his own reality, and ensures the freedom of others. Arendt simply rejects philosophers' efforts to eliminate the distinction between freedom and necessity.

Freedom and Necessity

Arendt finds that philosophers are much more comfortable with the ideas of necessity, inevitability and stability than with those of freedom and contingency. Following Hegel, for example, history was regarded as that necessary process in which man found a fortuitous security. Man's freedom was more and more identified with his insight into necessity. Whenever man challenged his subordination to the ultimate Being or any surrogate for Being, like necessity, his expression of freedom was identified with mere defiance or rebellion. It is precisely to break the bond between freedom and necessity and to restore freedom's capacity to confirm the free and unique appearances of persons that Arendt sets out to reject philosophers' effort to remold our concept and practice of freedom in the image of necessity.

It is not all philosophers, however, who prefer necessity over freedom. Some philosophers maintain that both necessity and freedom are true and that any appearance of conflict is deceptive. This position was advocated, among others, by Kant in whose work it depends on fiburcation of the universe into the world of "noumena" and the world of "phenomena". Hegel, Hobbes, Hume and Mill also attempted to reconcile necessity and freedom. The main idea behind this position is that if by "free" we mean "uncaused", then of course necessity would imply that nobody is ever a free agent. But since free action does not mean "uncaused" action, one's action may still be free even though they are just as much caused as any unfree action. One's actions are free even though anybody knowing one's general disposition and the state of one's body and mind at the preceding moment could have predicted them without difficulty.

Another group of philosophers holds that necessity is not compatible with freedom. Certain philosophers of this group, like Spinoza and Schopenhauer, may be cited as supporters of necessity while others, like Arendt and many modern existentialists, accept freedom and reject necessity. We shall now explore Arendt's rejection of necessity imposed by life, nature, the world and plurality.

146

In Chapter One we saw how labor serves as Arendt's symbol of "unfree" activity because it is bound to "necessity". It will be helpful to restate Arendt's delineation of the essence of labor:

Labor is the activity which corresponds to the biological process of the human body, whose spontaneous growth, metabolism, and eventual decay are bound to the vital necessities produced and fed into the life process by labor. The human condition of labor is life itself.64

Implicit in this statement is the premise that labor and life are necessary. Arendt means that the labor of the body is a primary necessity in that life can not proceed without its metabolism. Labor is given its necessity and its repetitive nature because it produces materials that can be readily consumed, and it enables the body to return to the arduous process of labor. Regardless of the sophistication of the human ways of laboring at the task of subsistence, the driving necessity of the life process remains. Men are not free.

No matter how necessary labor may be for the maintenance of life, according to Arendt it can and must, to some extent, be mastered or escaped. Some men must even go to the extent of doing violence to others in order to escape the necessity inherent in labor and thereby to enjoy freedom. One has to liberate oneself from the necessity of life for the freedom of the world. Arendt also sees the danger of the social question's entrance into the political realm in terms of the biological necessity it introduces. She points out that biological activities belong to the private realm as opposed to those fully human activities through which men make history. The entrance of biological activities into the public realm bring with them the kind of irresistibility characteristic of all our life processes:

The most powerful necessity of which we are aware in self-introspection is the life process which permeates our bodies and keeps them in a constant state of change, whose movements are automatic, independent of our own activities, and irresistible--i.e., of an overwhelming urgency. The less we are doing ourselves, the less active we are, the more forcefully will this biological process assert itself, impose its inherent necessity upon us, and overawe us with the fateful automatism of sheer happening that underlies all human history.65

The emergence of necessity into the public realm overshadows all our other inclinations, all our other human possibilities. To Arendt, necessity is the exact opposite of the true political freedom of the polis, the true political freedom to which men can aspire.

Arendt rejects the modern world as a realm of freedom because its view is rooted in the realm of need and mastery: the modern world is devoted to the satisfaction of necessity and utility, insensitive to the much less concrete and tangible claims of worldliness. Survival is the ultimate aim, and human existence is nothing more than the cyclical recurrence of the species. From this point of view, labor is primary, not speech, action or freedom.66   Arendt holds that labor excludes speech and action, which are essential for human freedom, because it is "an activity in which man is neither together with the world, nor with other people, but alone with his body, facing the naked necessity to keep himself alive".67   Others appear not as others but as multiplied specimens of the same laboring process in which one is involved.

Arendt insists that scientists and philosophers prefer "necessity" over "contingency".   Sheldon Wolin captures Arendt's thought quite well:

> [A]nd just as labor once served as her symbol of "unfree" activity because bound to "necessity," so now she found among scientists and philosophers an ominous prediction for "necessity" rather than for "contingency" which, for her, was the presupposition of freedom.68

Marx was the last in a long line of modern thinkers to identify necessity and humanity in labor.   Other philosophers connect necessity with human nature.   Arendt is dissatisfied with traditional views of human nature (those of Plato, Cicero and others) because they identify human nature with general defining essences.   For her, general essences imply fixity and discount novelty.   General essences restrict individual freedom by implying that each individual should fit some preconceived model.

Arendt argues against the traditional view of human nature because it is also premised upon the belief that the conditions of human existence are fixed.   Like Sartre she says that these conditions are never fixed but rather are constantly changing.   Although she does not emphasize choice as do Sartre and many other existentialists, she agrees with them that men have no fixed universal nature because they are constantly re-making their nature through choices and actions. Arendt demonstrates that although people are conditioned beings, their conditions are not fixed for all time but rather are constantly changing; the world that people confront is constantly conditioning them, and people in turn are constantly conditioning the world:

Whatever touches or enters into a sustained relationship with human life immediately assumes the characters of a condition of human existence. This is why men, no matter what they do, are always conditioned beings. Whatever enters the human world of its own accord or is drawn into it by human effort becomes part of the human condition. The impact of the world's reality upon human existence is felt and received as a conditioning force. The objectivity of the world--its object or thing-character--and the human condition supplement each other; because human existence is conditioned existence, it would be impossible without things, and things would be a heap of unrelated articles, a non-world, if they were not the conditioners of human existence.69

Against the passive givenness of the world (necessity) she poses man's ability to create a world of his own. The Greeks recognized that one is born into a world that limits one in the antecedence of its order. Accordingly, the Greek actor was aware that he was dwelling within a closed universe, one in which his very aspirations to become distinctly human were inexorably tied. The Greek discovery of the tragic hero illuminates reality not on the basis of its exploration of the subjective interiority of the tragic soul but on its subordination to the darker and more powerful order of the world.

Much of modern philosophy has been concerned with the problem of whether man is a product of the world or its creator. Even Marx, who insists that man can, indeed must, change the world and that the World and Being are not merely given to man but are his product, gravitates into Hegelianism by arguing that freedom ultimately means an "understanding" of necessity. Along the same lines, Arendt claims that "man cannot be free if he does not know he is subject to necessity".70 Modern existential philosophy has also been preoccupied with a paradoxical tension between the givenness of the world and human freedom. The solution upon which they settle refrains from any attempt to change the world. This solution consists of an inner change in consciousness, which creates positive values to be lived in the realm of inwardness. The world is "now accepted--as unacceptable". It is accepted in lucid awareness of its faults, but accepted in a spirit of negation. Arendt is aware that for existentialists the world is not the repose of man in general but a home of the conquering hero. She refers to Nietzsche's amor fati, Kierkegaard's "Great Leap", Heidegger's "Resoluteness" and Camus' "Defiance" as attempts to create a condition that "consists in the homelessness of man in the World", and amounts to the abandonment to the world of an archetype. She points out that "/t/he hero's gesture has not accidentally become the pose of philosophy since Nietzsche; it requires heroism to live in the world as Kant left it."71

Arendt agrees that men are conditioned beings.72 The entire givenness and objectivity of the world serves as the conditioning force because human life would be impossible without worldly things. The world, however, is a world of existential significances among which men freely dwell. The freedom of this existential dwelling, according to Arendt, is made possible by reliance upon the common sense constitution of a stable reality at the rudimentary level of bodily communion with reality. The inhabitation of a human world signifies that men do not merely react to an environment or live according to prescribed interplay of instinctual demands, the living process, and the environment. The human world is overlaid with layers of existential significance, the results of human beliefs, intentions, acts and discourse that men can freely accept or reject. Human beings are not identified with their world, but they have a world; and they are able to take up and consider or put down and neglect features of this world, just as they are free to do with great human works.

This freedom, this open space of human endeavour and human significances, depends on the deeper world-achievements of the body. Since the body is not merely in the world like any other object, human beings are free to have and inhabit a world. This idea refers back to Arendt's claim that the body is conditioned but never wholly conditioned in its experience of the world. In Arendt's view, therefore, there is no fixed human condition.

Men partially create their conditions and partially receive them from the world. The stability and objectivity of the world allow men the freedom to consider reflectively significant relations within the world and to endow them with objectivity by viewing them from different "places" in an already affirmed world. It is also through the objectivity of the world that men relate to each other and reveal themselves to each other.

Arendt reacts against a view that since man is essentially a social animal he is not free from social demands. According to this view, mankind is compressed into the oneness of society, a community organized for the fulfillment of the necessities of life. This society fostered an equality, not of distinctly acting persons, but of conforming interchangeable functionaries. It nurtured a behavior that acquiesced in the anonymous administration of the community in accordance with the trends of economic forces and pressures. This compression of society promoted a levelling of action, precisely in order to render it translatable into the laws and statistics of a behavioristic science. The actual social structures, as well as the Western tradition, expect from man an automatic conformity to certain norms. They exclude free, thoughtful and spontaneous action.73 They "aim to reduce man as a whole, in all his activities, to the level of a conditioned and behaving animal".74

Arendt rereads the Western tradition in order to reject the conformity that inheres when the social realm is predominant and to recapture the logic underlying the conception of man as a distinctive actor. She asserts that whoever stresses only essential uniformities and conformities demanded of man as a social animal ignores the human condition of plurality and thus denies the freedom of individuals to be distinct. Speech and action are what enable each individual to manifest his uniqueness and resist his absorption into the processes of merely living. She demonstrates, against the traditional views of human nature that stress as essential only what men have in common (Plato, Cicero, Hume and Kant are representatives), that each individual is essentially unique. Hence, for Arendt, each individual has a particular essence, created and manifested through the individual's speech and action.

For Arendt, then, man is not only a social animal but above all a political animal. The political existence engenders deeper possibilities than mere social association. It is therefore understandable why Arendt considers the traditional views as one-sided, incomplete and only interested in necessity, not freedom. The emergence of necessity and automatism into the political realm tends to overshadow some human inclinations and possibilities. Necessity is the exact opposite of the true political freedom to which men can aspire.

It is important to note that Arendt does not deny human nature. She advances a view of human nature; or at least she presupposes a view of human nature. This is brought out in the fact that in prizing speech and action she makes a general value assertion about how people in general ought to live, though she does not in any explicit way employ the term "ought" in the prescriptive sense. The only difference between traditional philosophers and Arendt is that whereas traditional philosophers see man as having a fixed nature, Arendt holds that each individual by virtue of his freedom creates his own distinctive nature through speech and actions. In Arendt's view, the natural self is a necessitous, private and "worldless" creature.75 Necessity is the root of "worldlessness" because it eliminates people's interest in tangible property, as opposed to wealth. Politically the natural self is also a threat to the world and its worldliness because of his indifference to the space between men. This self treats all people as fellow predators in the battle with necessity; he has no use for the space of appearance. Arendt concludes that this natural relationship eliminates the physical and human space between men.

Finally, Arendt rejects the characterization of the historical process as necessary or irresistible. After Hegel history was celebrated as that necessary process in which human beings found a fortuitous security only through acquiescence. This notion of history resulted in the identification of man's freedom with his insight into necessity, or in the cases where this subordination was challenged, in an identification of freedom with mere defiance or rebellion. Action in history was regarded as "one supernatural body driven by one superhuman irresistible 'general will'".76 This experience of necessity engendered the notion of a fateful force behind the historical process that sanctioned or authorized human actions insofar as they contributed to the ends of the process.

For Arendt history does not overcome the contingency of action. It only reconciles one to reality by fashioning the sequence of happenings into a shape in which one can accept them as the consequences of human actions subject to the multivalent powers and deficiencies of human action. History just transforms the raw material of events into a coherent story, which, while not explaining as in a causal account, still makes sensible the reality that has transpired.

In conclusion, in her study of the human condition Arendt interprets the manner in which the media of man's appearance lead his existence to assume distinct conditions or forms of life. Life, nature, the world and plurality never condition men absolutely. They are necessary for political freedom because no concept of political freedom can be complete when it ignores the necessity that presses upon us from outside, the necessity that can be overcome where there is true political freedom:

> The necessity which prevents me from doing what I know and will may arise from the world, or from my body, or from an insufficiency of talents, gifts, and qualities which are bestowed upon man by birth and over which he has hardly more power than he has over other circumstances; all these factors, the psychological ones not excluded, condition the person from the outside as far as the I-will and the I-know, that is, the ego itself, are concerned; the power that meets these circumstances, that liberates, as it were, willing and knowing from their bondage to necessity, is the I-can. Only where the I-will and the

I-can coincide does freedom come to pass.77

Men value and cherish freedom when they constantly win it in the face of necessity. The presence of necessity spells the possibility of freedom as well. For Arendt, both necessity and freedom exist as distinct realities. She therefore rejects any effort to eliminate altogether the distinction between them.

Conclusion

We have so far seen how, in her attempt to distinguish philosophical freedom from political freedom in order to save the latter, Arendt conceptualizes political freedom as the apex of philosophical freedom. She distinguishes between the philosophical and pre-philosophical activities of thinking, willing and judging in order to preclude us from assuming them as philosophical preconditions for political freedom. Through the use of his mental faculties, an individual reveals who he is and thus creates his own reality and ensures the freedom of others. Finally, through the notion of necessity we see that Arendt's concepts of philosophical and political freedom are closely related.

We can therefore conclude that Arendt's exposition of freedom reveals that philosophical freedom and political freedom are not as compartmentalized as the titles suggest. They are interrelated. It is precisely this interdependence of politics and philosophy in Arendt's thought that seem to contradict what she asserts in her earlier treatment of freedom. She argues emphatically that one of the major characteristics marking the decline of political freedom is its withdrawal to the inner domain of the mind and retreat from the world of appearances. But we have just seen that it is with the mental faculties that philosophy and politics meet and work out their symbiosis. Arendt's notion of freedom is based on this symbiosis. In the next chapter we shall establish whether there is any continuity or reversal in her notion of freedom.

PHILOSOPHICAL FREEDOM

NOTES

1 Hannah Arendt, The Life of the Mind, Thinking/Willing, edited and with a postface by Mary McCarthy (New York: Harcourt Brace Jovanovich, 1978). Hereafter cited simply as Thinking and Willing.
2 Between Past and Future, p. 151.
3 Ibid., p. 146.
4 Ibid., p. 145.
5 Ibid., p. 147; and "Freedom and Politics: A Lecture", Chicago Review, 14(1960), 29.
6 Ibid., p. 146.
7 Ibid., p. 157.
8 Ibid.
9 Thinking, p. 5.
10 Plato's Theaetetus (190^c).
11 Quoted from the Theaetetus (190^a) and the Sophist (263^a) of Plato and referred to by Sherry Gray in "Hannah Arendt and the Solitariness of Thinking", Philosophy Today, 25(Summer, 1981), 121.
12 Thinking, p. 185.
13 Ibid., pp. 187 and 193.
14 Ibid., pp. 188-89.
15 Men in Dark Times, p. 79.
16 Ibid., p. 47.
17 The Origins of Totalitarianism, p. 476.
18 Thinking, p. 91.
19 Ibid., pp. 7-8, 123, 178 and 191.
20 Ibid., p. 87.
21 Ibid., p.32.
22 Ibid., p. 175.
23 The Human Condition, p. 179.
24 Thinking, p. 4.
25 Ibid., p. 5.
26 Ibid., p.191.
27 Ibid., p. 5.
28 Crises of the Republic, p. 5.
29 "What is Existenz Philosophy?", The Partisan Review, 8/1 (Winter, 1946), 55.
30 Between Past and Future, p. 151.
31 George Kateb, "Dismantling Philosophy", The American Scholar, 48 (Winter 1978), 124.
32 Willing, p. 63.
33 St. Paul in his letter to the Romans 7:15 as cited in Willing, p. 65.
34 Willing, p. 69.
35 Ibid., p. 6.
36 Thinking, p. 213.
37 Willing, p. 123.
38 Cited by Arendt in Between Past and Future, p. 161.

39 Anthony Kenny, Action, Emotion and Will (London: Routledge & Kegan Paul, 1963), pp. 234-35.
40 Between Past and Future, p. 162.
41 On Revolution, p. 228.
42 On Violence, p. 163.
43 Between Past and Future, p. 164.
44 Ibid., p. 165.
45 Ibid., p. 152.
46 On Violence, p. 143.
47 Willing, p. 199.
48 Ibid., p. 151.
49 Ronald Beiner, "Hannah Arendt on Judging: an Interpretive Essay", in Hannah Arendt's Lectures on Kant's Political Philosophy, ed. Ronald Beiner (Chicago: The University of Chicago Press, 1982), p. 144.
50 Willing, p. 271.
51 Beiner, P. 120.
52 Ibid., p. 145.
53 Between Past and Future, p. 221.
54 Michael Denneny, "The Privilege of Ourselves: Hannah Arendt on Judgment", in Hannah Arendt: The Recovery of the Public World, ed. Melvyn Hill (New York: St. Martin's Press, 1979), p. 254.
55 Jurgen Habermas, "On the German-Jewish Heritage", Telos, 44(1980), 130.
56 Thinking, p. 40.
57 Willing, pp. 104, 144.
58 Beiner, p. 154.
59 Thinking, pp. 93-94.
60 Beiner, p. 154.
61 "Basic Moral Propositions," seventeenth session of a course at the University of Chicago, (Hannah Arendt Papers, Library of Congress, Container 41), p. 024560.
62 Willing, p. 262.
63 Hannah Arendt: The Recovery of the Public World, p. 309.
64 The Human Condition, p. 96.
65 On Violence, p. 53.
66 The Human Condition, pp. 80-87.
67 Ibid., p. 212.
68 Sheldon Wolin, "Stopping to Think", New York Review of Books 25/16 (October, 1978), p. 19. Wolin draws upon Willing, pp. 32-33, for his reference.
69 The Human Condition, p. 9.
70 Ibid., pp. 52, 126, 135.
71 "What is Existenz Philosophy?" p. 41.
72 The Human Condition, p. 9.
73 Ibid., p. 37.
74 Ibid., p. 41.

75 Ibid., p. 233.
76 On Revolution, p. 54.
77 Between Past and Future, p. 160.

CHAPTER VI

CONTINUITY IN ARENDT'S THOUGHT

In the previous chapters we observed how freedom is the concept that unites Arendt's works. In her concept of freedom the political and philosophical elements of her work are joined. Each of her works reveals her concern with man's capacity for action and freedom. She firmly holds that man can realize himself as a free being only in the public sphere, where he appears before others.

Since the posthumous publication of Arendt's The Life of the Mind, the question of its relevance to her political theory has inevitably become a pressing one: does The Life of the Mind enhance in any significant and important way the theme of political freedom found in her earlier works? Does it elaborate on the same theme of political theory? Or, alternately, does it necessitate a serious re-evaluation of her political theory? The aim of this chapter is to answer these questions firstly by demonstrating that because of the apparent transition from the emphasis on the vita activa to the vita contemplativa, some scholars' answer to these questions is negative: they regard The Life of the Mind as unequivocally marginal and irrelevant to her political theory found in her earlier works. Secondly, I will show that through the "tensions", "turning operations" or "contradictions" in her political theory, her notion of freedom as the phenomenon of politics remains unchanged throughout her works. Although throughout she is directing us towards a sense of political freedom different from our usual one, she does not reverse her claims about political freedom and inward philosophical freedom.

Apparent Shift in Arendt's Thought

Arendt asserts that the life of practice, the vita activa, is not the same as and is neither superior nor inferior to the life of the mind, the vita contemplativa. She begins by emphasizing the role and importance of the vita activa and later emphasizes that the vita contemplativa is essential for the full enjoyment of the vita activa. This is why she claims that she has no preference between the life of the mind and the life of practice. Martin Jay, however, observed:

> [A]lthough she claimed that she had no preference between the life of the mind, the vita contemplativa, and the life of practice, the vita activa, Hannah Arendt significantly devoted virtually all of her intellectual gifts to an exploration of the latter realm.1

From her biography of Rahel Varnhagen, in which she described the harmful effects of being deprived of freedom, to the collection of essays constituting Crisis of the Republic, Arendt defined vita activa as a realm of freedom. Political freedom remained the principal motif of her thinking.

Although Arendt never claimed that philosophical freedom was irrelevant to political freedom, the sharp distinction she made between the vita activa and the vita contemplativa is a chief source for the view that in her last work she changed her mind about the relationship between political freedom and philosophical freedom. It is because of this distinction that her efforts to link both vita activa and vita contemplativa in her later writings appear to contradict her earlier assertions. But her attempt to show the interdependence of political and philosophical freedom marks her theory of freedom as both logically coherent and incomparable.

The distinction between the life of the mind and the life of practice already existed in Plato and Aristotle. For them vita contempltiva was definitely the superior way of life. Vita activa was not only subordinate to vita contemplativa, it was regarded as meaningless. It received some meaning and "restricted dignity" only when it served the needs and wants of vita contemplativa.2 Arendt maintains that vita contemplativa is separate and distinct from vita activa. She complains that the primacy of the vita contemplativa, either under Plato or in modern times, undermines the realm of politics and subverts the principle of freedom at the heart of the vita activa. But she attempts to reverse the situation of the assumed priority of life of the mind over that of action because of her conviction that vita activa represents the most authentic expression of freedom. For her vita contemplativa, because of its pursuit of truth and the associated capacities of reason and thought, tends to be concerned only with the domain of necessity.

Moreover, contemplation is a retreat to an inner self where no other person has access, whereas action presupposes human interaction. The realm of action or freedom is constituted by the plurality of men and their relationships. The solitary life of the mind cuts off human plurality and is inadequate in the political life. Arendt remains faithful to this position throughout her works. She does not deny the connection between thinking and acting; she always holds that there is a link between politics and morality, thinking and evil, conscience and goodness. But this connection does not make the faculties of mind part of the political domain. For Arendt the human faculties of thinking and willing presuppose withdrawal from the public realm, from the presence of other men. Thinking and willing are private mental capacities exercised in solitude. While thinking prepares for action and willing is the "spring of action", action, once begun, has very little use for either of them. Thus, Arendt maintains a contrast between philosophy, the sphere of theory or contemplation, and politics, the sphere of practice or action. She emphasizes that she wants to regard politics "with eyes unclouded by philosophy".

In The Life of the Mind, however, Arendt seems to ignore her conviction that the vita activa and the vita contemplativa represent different and distinct patterns of human life. While in her earlier writings she regarded vita activa as the only sphere of freedom, in The Life of the Mind political freedom seems to depend "upon the prior activities of willing ego".3 In her article "What is Freedom?", she opposed "the notion of the freedom of the will to political freedom" and argued that politics represented the most authentic expression of freedom; in The Life of the Mind, on the contrary, she states that "freedom of spontaneity is part and parcel of the human condition. Its mental organ is the will."

Some scholars agree that Arendt turned away from vita activa towards vita contemplativa. They accuse her of forsaking her emphasis on life in the world, vita activa, and favouring instead the life of the mind. They regard this change as a most paradoxical development in her thought. Even those who support her turning away from the life of the world in favour of the life of the mind as "an appropriate preparation for returning to the world with a viable politics" do not deny that as we go from the earlier to the later writings of Arendt there is an apparent change or transition from the vita activa towards the vita contemplativa.4

The most negative answer to the question whether Arendt's last work enhances in any significant and important manner our understanding of her notion as exposed in her earlier works is that it is irrelevant to her earlier notion of freedom. This view holds that Arendt does not just change her position in the last work but writes on a totally different issue. Even the theme of freedom, which now and then appears in The Life of the Mind, has no "significant bearing on her political theory".5 It is treated as something outside the public political realm, that is, as a purely philosophical concept. But this is definitely contrary to Arendt's notion of freedom because it suggests that her last work, unlike her earlier writings, which are primarily concerned with politics, is essentially philosophical. It is therefore taken to be different both in scope and content from Arendt's previous writings.

Some scholars claim that even Arendt's notion of judgment, which as we have seen links Arendt's earlier (political) works and later (philosophical) works, fails to establish such a link. Arendt described judgment as "the most political of men's mental activities".

In her earlier writings she regarded it as a part of the vita   activa, whereas in the last work she placed it exclusively within the life of the mind. There is indeed a tension, as Ronald Beiner also points out, between her early and late views concerning the relation between judgment and politics, or between the life of the mind and the world of appearances:

> On the one hand, she is tempted to integrate judgment into the vita activa, seeing it as a function of the representative thinking and enlarged mentality of political actors, exchanging opinions in public while engaged in common deliberation. On the other hand, she wants to emphasize the contemplative and disinterested dimension of judgment which operates retrospectively, like aesthetic judgment.6

Certain commentators further assert that Arendt's views on judging and judgment cannot be regarded as political because it is the spectator, not the actor, who judges after the act has taken place. One of them observes:

> Judging also entails detachment and distance from the scene of action. The person who judges cannot simultaneously be a participant. This expectation serves to deny the political actor the capacity to judge in the process of action, thus removing the faculty of judgment from the realm of politics.7

We have seen in the previous chapter that Arendt's notion of judgment is not irrelevant to her political theory. Even though she has two distinct conceptions of judgment, one political and the other contemplative, and is more inclined to the latter in her last writings, she abolished this tension by asserting that the exercise of judgment becomes practically efficacious in "times of crisis or emergency". She does not totally exclude any reference to the vita activa within the revised concept of judgment. For the moment it suffices to point out why it is generally agreed that as we go from the earlier to the later writings of Arendt, there is apparent change on her notion of freedom.

It now remains to show that her notion of freedom, as the phenomenon of politics, is unchanged throughout her works.

Continuity in Arendt's Notion of Freedom

The apparent transition from the emphasis on the vita activa to the vita contemplativa does not signify that Arendt changes her notion of freedom as a political action. It only shows that there is a link between these two forms of life and that political action is not mindless. Vita activa cannot be totally divorced from vita contemplativa as traditional philosophy held. Arendt's later insistence on the importance of the life of the mind is a reaction against the modern tradition, which tries to subordinate it to vita activa. This was the opposite mistake to that committed by traditional philosophy, which subordinated vita activa to vita contemplativa. Arendt claims that the repudiation of vita contemplativa first became evident in the thought of Hobbes who "denounced all past philosophy as nonsense".8 Hegel and Marx continued this trend by locating truth not in any transcendental realm but in the midst of human affairs. In short, Arendt claims that the general interest of modern thinkers was "the force of the life process itself, to which all men and all human activities were equally submitted and whose only aim, if it had an aim at all, was the survival of the animal species man".9

In Arendt's view, this attitude towards vita contemplativa not only reduced the vita contemplativa to an "altogether meaningless" activity but also marred the vita activa and blurred the distinction between man and animal. Arendt stresses the importance of both forms of life in order to rectify the situation. She also insists on the existence of the link between the two, since one makes sense only in terms of the other.10 To Arendt this link is quite important since, as one commentator points out, "to sever the link between the two is to dispense with transcendental claims in the realms of both morality and politics. To do so is to rob human existence of its meaning, which is exactly what happened in the modern tradition."11

Arendt sometimes stresses vita activa and at other times vita contemplativa, but such shifts just show, as we shall now see, that for her freedom depends on the distinction and interplay between the vita activa and the vita contemplativa.

Arendt blames the loss of freedom in the modern world on "the much more tangible loss of a privately owned share in the modern world".12 By this she does not mean the loss of private property but the lack of a space for personal thinking and thought in politics. Thus, the importance of the public realm does not depend on the absence of the private life. "A life spent entirely in public, in the presence of others, becomes, as we would say, shallow."13 For Arendt, both private and public spheres are essential for political freedom. The problem arises when one of these spheres is allowed to impose its principles and characteristic concerns upon the other.

Arendt regards the point of liberation and enjoyment in private life as being to allow the individual to enjoy authentic freedom among others. She expresses this view in both her earlier and later writings. The inner freedom that she so much talks about in her last work is an elaboration and extension of her earlier analysis of freedom. The inner freedom creates the person, the character, the "who" an individual is. This individual enjoys political freedom when he appears before others in the public realm.

(i) Appearing before others

For Aristotle, on whom Arendt so frequently draws, administration of justice was the reason people appeared before their peers in the public realm and were "more or less willing to share in the burden...of public affairs".14 People came together in the polis in order to promote the common interest. They came together to deliberate about right and wrong, morality and virtue, and also about economic privilege and social power.

For Arendt, on the contrary, citizens appear before their peers in the public realm just to disclose themselves and to distinguish themselves constantly by proving that they are the best of all.15 People appear before others in the public realm because of their "passion for distinction...a desire to be seen, heard, talked of, approved and respected", a passion whose "virtue" is the "desire to excel another", and whose vice is "ambition", aiming "at power as a means of distinction".16 The polis, the sphere of appearances, Arendt says, "had a twofold function" for the Greeks: it was "supposed to multiply the occasions to win 'immortal fame,' that is, to multiply the chances for everybody to distinguish himself"; and, second, it was supposed to "offer a remedy for the futility of action and speech, to make it more likely that greatness would be permanently remembered."17 Therefore, Arendt's notion of "appearing before others" is characterized by the citizens anxiety and egoistical striving. "Apprearing before others" becomes trivial vanity.

Of course, Arendt's main concern was to protect the public realm and political freedom from the economic and social conditions in which they have something at stake. She wanted to depict the public realm as a sphere that is valuable in itself, not degraded into a mere means to some lesser end. Arendt relied on de Tocqueville's idea that "who asks of freedom anything beyond itself is born to be a slave". Nevertheless, her way of trying to protect and revive the public realm succeeds only in making its real value incomprehensible to us who are used to regarding the political realm as the sphere in which, among other things, justice and fair distribution of economic wealth are established.

Arendt also insists, contrary to our observation that people usually reveal themselves in the privacy of their families or in the intimacy of their friends, that only the public realm is reserved for disclosing who one is. For her, any self-disclosure before the r-estricted audience of family and friends can provide only "a limited reality" because

> appearance--something that is being seen and heard by others as well as by ourselves--constitutes reality. Compared with the reality which comes from being seen and heard, even the greatest forces of intimate life...lead an uncertain, shadowy kind of existence.18

The public realm offers plurality of perspectives and a permanence of remembrance unavailable in privacy.

For Arendt, the main condition for freedom is the presence of the "space of appearance", the space of public interaction. Freedom exists only where persons, by action and speech, participate in this realm of appearance. Just as this space is constituted by the participating persons and disappears without them, freedom flourishes where this space is preserved.

Arendt's notion of freedom means that one participates in the public sphere of life. It is important to realize that this type of participation implies the existence of both inner and political freedom. Her idea of freedom as participation discloses how both inner and public freedom compliment one another. Arendt believes that full development of the person requires participation in both public and private activities. This development involves the passions and the intellect of the individual person and his public concerns.

The self-disclosure of the "who" is accomplished by the economy of the mind, as articulated in Arendt's notions of thinking, willing and judging. Participation in the public realm means that an individual, endowed with the mental capacities of thinking, willing and judging, decides that it is the best thing to appear before others by expressing his opinions and demonstrating his actions so that they in turn can judge what kind of a man he is and "also allow him to develop his capacities" and needs as he wishes. I would like to cite at length Erving Goffman's view on this issue:

> I have said that when an individual appears before others...sometimes the individual will act in a thoroughly calculating manner, expressing himself in a given way solely in order to give the kind of impression to others

162

that is likely to evoke from them a specific response he is concerned to obtain. Sometimes the individual will be calculating in his activity but be relatively unaware that this is the case. Sometimes he will intentionally and consciously express himself in a particular way, but chiefly because the traditions of his group or social status require this kind of expression and not because of any particular response (other than vague acceptance or approval) that is likely to be evoked from those impressed by the expression. Sometimes the traditions of an individual's role will lead him to give a well-designed impression of a particular kind and yet he may be neither consciously nor unconsciously disposed to create such an impression. The others, in their turn, may be suitably impressed by the individual's effort to convey something, or may misunderstand the situation and come to conclusions that are warranted neither by the individual's intent nor by the facts....19

Goffman is well aware that in practical everyday life people sometimes do not appear in the public as they are but in the way they choose to appear. This means that the given elements with which one is endowed at birth and in one's existence are usually moderated by what one thinks is fit to be seen or not seen. This choice of what should be seen determines which words, deeds, and public situations will receive one's attention for participation. By this capacity to indicate how they wish to be seen, individuals can project an identity that is unique and individual.

Arendt also tells us why a participant cannot just appear before others as he is and why it is important that the mind transforms the incohate self into a personality prepared for entry into the world. For all practical purposes we know that it is better for an individual to be prepared for appearance in the public realm. Let us explore a bit how, according to Arendt, the "economy of the mind" serves to prepare men for their appearance in the public realm, which is necessary for freedom. Why does Arendt think that freedom is lodged in the relation to others of the individual and his mental faculties?

(ii) The connection between the role of intellect and the role of public

The intellect enables an individual to decide what kind of individual he is to be in the public world:

> When I make a decision I am not merely reacting to whatever quality may be given to me; I am making an act of deliberate choice among the various potentialities of conduct with which the world has presented me. Out of such acts arises what we call character or personality....20

Arendt's analysis of thinking, willing and judging sets forth the structure of how the intellect transforms and prepares one for entry into a space of appearance.

Earlier, when dealing with "thinking", we realized that the thinking ego is not a passive receiver of experiences of reality. The thinker reflects on the "givens," questions them, reconstructs them in the imagination, and endows them with coherence and objectivity by linguistic and metaphorical means. In this way he liberates himself from mere acquiescence in the experiences and conventions of the everyday. Thus, the thinker is free to explore the living experiences that help make sense of the world. In short, thinking liberates the person from a generality of expression and allows him to live his life as he sees fit. In this way we can say that thinking prepares the way for actions. It also reflects upon the act and the situation. Through the act of thinking the thinker not only relates to himself in a dialogue between him and himself, he also relates to others.

Furthermore, even though Arendt simply asserts freedom of will without arguing for it, she finds that it actually structures the self in its predispositions to appear. We have said that for Arendt the will is a principle contributing to the individuation of men. But what really links the will to that which appears is the fact that men do things they could have left undone. This means that their freedom of action is connected with their wish to do whatever they want. The will designs new projects that will appear in the world in the future and also determines what shape men's personal appearance will take. The will draws the "who" into the world of appearance. Arendt emphasizes this fact when she says:

> Volition is the inner capacity by which men decide about "whom" they are going to be, in what shape they wish to show themselves in the world of appearance.21

Arendt links the will and freedom not just because the will prepares an individual for appearance in the public realm but also because freedom is a phenomenon of the public world--an openness towards new acts, like deliberately joining the revolution--and the will has a capacity to discern those acts that would initiate a new series in the world that would encourage the participation of others. Furthermore, the will renders the actor a personal author--one who freely acts without being determined by his acts.

If the person acts freely, for Arendt it is also the case that he acts willfully, which means that his acts are empowered by the personal source of his existence. A person acts willfully when his acts receive the blessing of his will. But Arendt is also aware like Paul that a person may will what he does not do. One may will to act and yet not be able to bring the full support of his person to begin the act. Therefore, according to Arendt, a person is not only evaluated on the basis of what he accomplished but also on whether he really meant or willed what he did with "all his heart and soul and mind".

It is essential also to realize that this notion of the will is related to the question of personal freedom. Again without giving any argument for freedom but just restating her assumption of it, Arendt claims that evaluation of one's person and one's meaning in accordance with whether one really meant or willed what he did makes sense only if one's person is conceived as having the freedom to act anew -- to act in ways undermined by one's past and present. In the same way, one's existence as a freely and willfully acting person demands that one's existence itself be considered a radically new beginning. Therefore, one's "who" is not revealed merely by what one does or begins or enacts in the public realm; it depends, rather, on whether a person's acts are willfully and freely undertaken.

Arendt then introduces judgment as the arbiter of what should or should not appear in the public realm. For her, judgment fits one into a community. Without this faculty, human appearance in the public realm resembles an insanity, a stubborn fixation on what is one's own even to the point of its loss of reality.22 The actor's appearance must be guided by the understanding of the premise of the public realm -- the realm is that which can be understood by its spectators. Through the use of judgment an actor conforms his appearance to what can be appreciated by other participants:

> [W]ithout this critical, judging faculty the doer or maker would be so isolated that he would not even be perceived -- the very originality of the artist (or the very novelty of the actor) depends on making himself understood by those who are not artists (or actors).23

According to Arendt it is not possible to understand the private "who"

165

if he is not manifest in some communicable fashion. It is one's judgment that aids one to appear as one should. For Arendt one's judgment bears on the possibility of one's appearance. We shall later see why Arendt seems here to be suggesting, contrary to what she said earlier, that the public self may reveal the private self.

What we have seen so far is how each of these mental activities, as portrayed by Arendt, prepares the self for what she calls presentation in appearance. Each prepares the person for an exchange of the inner for the outer, the private for the public. Thinking also "prepares us ever anew to meet whatever we must meet in our daily lives".24 The economy of the mind prepares one for an appearance in the public realm where political freedom can be enjoyed. Freedom requires appearance as the necessary precondition of its existence. By its very nature freedom occurs inter homines and requires publicity and appearance. Any philosophical tradition that is deeply suspicious of the world of appearance and reduces human plurality to singularity, as traditional political philosophy did, cannot appreciate Arendt's notion of freedom. Wherever there is no realm of appearance, there is no freedom. Arendt's later works support the earlier ones in showing that appearance is essential for freedom, since freedom cannot fully manifest itself where the space of appearance is absent or where men are excluded from it. While in her earlier writing she demonstrates how a public arena open to participation provides for the disclosure of the self, in her later writings she is concerned with how the disclosure of self can be achieved through the use of mental capacities. Both public and private spheres are vehicles for man's self-expression, which is essential for one's freedom.

Arendt also believes, like Cato, that political actions or "great deeds are not done by strength or speed or physique, they are the products of thought and character and judgment".25 So for Arendt one has to be both mentally and physically prepared to enter the public realm and to enjoy political freedom. This idea is in keeping with plea that we should "think what we are doing".26 The need to think is a uniquely human need to reflect on what one has done or will do.
It is important to bring before one's mind and critically assess all that one does or contemplates doing. For both Arendt and Socrates, who gave an account of the importance of living an examined life, thinking does not produce the maxims; it merely advises. One is still free to choose to follow the advice. In conformity with this idea, Arendt claims that "the principle by which we act and the criteria by which we judge and conduct our lives depend ultimately on the life of the mind".27

On the other hand, Arendt rejects the idea of thinking as a total withdrawal from the realm of appearances. When thinking is regarded as an activity that has no connection with acting, as is the case in the moden world, Arendt points out that "there is not clearer or more radical opposition than that between thinking and doing". She separates the activities of thinking, willing and judging from acting only when their autonomy is in danger of being overlooked. In that situation she attempts to show that mental activities are essentially private in nature and that, at least inwardly, they remove the person from life in the world. Rather than praising them too highly and thus "jeorpardize her entire enterprise of restoring the idea of freedom and worldliness", as Kateb phrases it,28 she demonstrates that there is an unbridgable dichotomy between the solidariness of thought and the communality of action. Arendt regards this dichotomy, the one between the individuality of the will and the freedom in a community, and the one between the detachment of judging and the involvement of participation as emphasizing that freedom is to be found in communal action in "the space of appearances". The failure to recognize this fact leads to the uncoordinated pursuit of private and selfish interests. Such pursuit turns away from the commnunity within which both political action and political freedom are found.

When Arendt later goes on to explore the relevance of the mental faculties for political action, it is not with the intention of destroying their autonomy or what she said about them earlier. Her reflections on these faculties is part of the large effort she makes to demonstrate the primacy of political freedom over the autonomy of the mental faculties. She neither denies the existence of philosophical freedom nor minimizes the role of the mental faculties in bridging the gap between radical reflection and the communality of human action. She recognizes that while the mind is no place for political freedom since it is by definition a private realm, it is nonetheless essential for without it, or because of its importance, neither politics nor freedom are made real. What she rejects is the idea that freedom can be fully enjoyed outside the realm of politics. She thinks that seventeenth and eighteenth century thinkers who regarded freedom as an exclusive feature of the interior world of the self and not the relation of the self with others, who situated freedom outside politics and not within it, were mistaken.

(iii) Seventeenth and eighteenth century view of freedom as pre-political

Arendt finds that the attention to the seventeeth and eighteenth century political philosophers, especially the French thinkers, was captured by socio-economic problems of their time and that as a result they were interested in civil liberties, which like free speech and association are pre-conditions for freedom as participation. She blames them for situating freedom outside politics and not within it.

Arendt is specifically critical of Rousseau and the French revolutionists because they promoted the intrusion of poverty and necessity into the political sphere, the ascendancy of the general will as the arbiter of political existence, and the emergence of violence as its executor. According to Arendt all these factors led to a denial of political freedom or to a claim that freedom of one group depends upon the oppression of another. These were attempts to divorce the notion of freedom from politics and the destruction of authentic freedom. Accordingly, Arendt rejects Rousseau's notion of "general will," arguing that "the ideal of a free will, independent from others and eventually prevailing against them", results from the mistake of identifying the "will" with freedom. The idea of general will leads either to a denial of political freedom or to a claim that freedom of one group depends upon the oppression of another. This is a destruction of authentic freedom.

Arendt was also highly critical of the French Revolution because it manifested the eruption of the life process of society into politics. That is, it became the movement of the poor and needy masses, who urged the economic alleviation of their poverty and the satisfaction of their biological necessities. The motivation of this revolution resided in a human desire for a stable political world in which one could act freely and be acknowledged in one's distinction. However, the appearance of the masses and the necessities of the life process inspired Arendt to interpret both the French Revolution and modern revolutions as based on the inner bodily sensations of life's necessary demands:

> The most powerful necessity of which we are aware in self-introspection is the life process which permeates our bodies and keeps them in a constant state of a change whose movements are automatic, independent of our own activities, and irresistible -- i.e., of an overwhelming urgency. The less we are doing ourselves, the less active we are, the more forceful will this biological process assert itself, impose its inherent necessity upon us, and overawe us with the fateful automatism of sheer happening that underlies all human history.29

The French Revolution was not a birth of a realm of public freedom. It was just a participation of individuals in an overwhelming movement of history, which would proceed with or without one's action. It was a mere force behind the historical process, sanctioning or authorizing human actions insofar as they contributed to the ends of the process. The intrusion of the life process into the political realm not only introduced the masses and the previously invisible many into light; it entirely transformed the conception of the political realm.

In the same manner that Arendt rejects Rousseau's "general will" she rejects the implication of the French Revolution and modern revolutions that a general will drives the course of revolution. This implication abrogates the foundation and preservation of revolution in a stable common human world. During the French Revolution participation in the political realm was premised on solidarity with this general will of the masses and their aspirations. In this subordination of the natural laws of the masses and their biological necessities, the revolution neglected its primary commitment to establish a political realm to preserve distinctly human action.

In Arendt's view, the natural goodness of people and the identification of all particular wills with self-interest mean that the political realm should be constituted by the totality of the people's will. She explains:

> The shift from the republic to the people meant that the enduring unity of the future political body was guaranteed not in the worldly institutions which this people had in common, but in the will of the people themselves.30

Arendt asserts that admittance into this will is predicated on a selfless subordination of the self to the dictates of the general will of the people.

What united Rousseau, the French revolutionaries, and all later revolutionaries influenced by the French revolution was that compassion constituted a principle in which sensitivity for the sufferings of others extirpated the experience of one's soul. By this internal gratification one could acquiesce in the selfless magic of compassion that "opened the heart...to the sufferings of others whereby it established and confirmed the 'natural' bond between men which only the rich had lost".31 Arendt believes that politics should be purged of compassion because it fails to found a long-lasting constitution for freedom; in fact, it leads inexorably to the end of the brief life of freedom, of the councils. Compassion and conformity to the general will as principles of the political realm inspired instability and the boundless self-consumption of the revolution, which prefigured the more extreme

169

logic of totalitarian terror.

Finally, accompanying compassion as the political principle, violence became an intrinsic element of the political realm. From the initial intimations that a new order, a new beginning, was imminent, the revolutionaries had imagined this new foundation as a tearing down and building up of the world. Although Machiavelli first intuited the necessity of violence in this building, the homo faber mentality reinforced his insight that a replacement of the natural world order would require the institution of a realm fabricated by man.32 As an activity, fabrication itself depends upon a violent reshaping of its material; however, the premises of this violent understanding of fabrication really took hold when the activity of homo faber was no longer subordinated to the dictates of the contemplative order but the cleansing process of the general will.

The seventeenth and eighteenth century thinkers' image of political man is, in short, of man acting in compassion with the masses by means of violence, subordinated to the general will and the necessities of life. Little remains of this portrait in Arendt's belief that the seventeenth and eighteenth century notion of politics originated in a desire for an articulated political space of freedom in which men could act and gain immortal fame.

General Problems with Arendt's Analysis

Arendt's analysis of political man raises a few problems. Firstly, Arendt claims that it is the mind that transforms and prepares one for entry into the "space of appearance". But what is this mind that is there before the self? Is there any self behind the self? Secondly, on one hand Arendt suggests that the public self may not reveal the private self, while on the other hand she claims that it is not possible to understand the private "who" if he is not manifested in some communicable fashion. Since the private self seems to be first formed and then projected into the public realm, does Arendt's analysis make the private self primary? Finally, in politics, where does play-acting end and genuineness begin? Does it?

Arendt knows that the distinction between the inner and outer realities of man is not a new phenomenon. Our tradition of philosophy originated in precisely that: the distinction between body and soul. Plato remains the supreme example of the philosophers who distinguished the mind from the body. He divided the soul into three "parts": the rational "part", the spirited or courageous "part", and the appetitive "part". These parts are analogous to a charioteer with two horses pulling in opposite directions; one horse is represented as the spirited part of the soul, which tends upward toward heaven, the other as the appetitive part, which tends downward. The charioteer, the coordinator of the two horses, is represented as the rational part of the soul, keeping control over the bad horse. Of the three parts, Plato obviously holds the rational to be the noblest, for it is what gives order to the drives of appetite and spirit and it can guide and motivate action. Moreover, the rational part has power to grasp the ideas, including the idea of the good, along with other moral ideas. From this follows the conception of man as a rational animal. In this view the relation of mind to body is designated by the relation between the rational "part" and the appetitive "part". The mind is related to the body as a hand in a glove.

The important thing is that in all the views on the union of mind and body, the relation of one's soul to one's body is unlike one's relation to any other worldly object. The physical appearance of one's body is not a merely adventitious access to the world, which is significant in that it makes possible the initiation of new processes. One's body is never merely a means to physical appearance. For example, the confirmation accorded to my body in my articulate uptaking of "I" signifies my acceptance and accreditation of my body as the source of all my meaningful action and utterance. My soul's relation to my body is of an uncommon, unworldly character; it is constituted by my soul's unshareable dwelling within it. Accordingly, whereas to the world my appearance occurs in a body, for me my appearance and the appearance of the world comes to be with my body. Therefore, my bodily appearance constitutes a radical act of beginning and is implicitly confirmed as such by my use of "I" as a personal act forthwith, not as a physical act that later leads to a personal presentation in the world. So, body and soul are united in one substance, the "self". This is why Arendt urges that each individual is essentially unique. Hence, each individual is to act in diverse and spontaneous ways to manifest this uniqueness.

It is therefore understandable why Arendt considers any view that identifies the personal with only the inner realm of subjectivity as one-sided and incomplete. Modern man was driven to this inner realm by the collapse of the given world and his body's stable place within it through the discoveries and techniques of modern science. Unfortunately, this retreat to an inner realm did not suffice to protect the integrity of the person. Empiricism explained away the presence of any unique personal reality resident in the unworldly confines of consciousness or a soul, and the political movements of the West effaced the image of man as a distinct actor. Arendt herself examined the inner realm of subjectivity and found it devoid of the reliability and stability requisite for the assertion of a unique personal identity. She is not arguing here that each person does indeed have a "subjective interior self" with whom he is in more intimate contact and which can be given a reflecting objective expression "outside" in the world. Rather, she is contending that the public reality of the person's self-achievement both mitigates the intangibility and elusiveness of the "who" and yet simultaneously preserves the sense that each "who" is a unique and inexchangeable person. In this way there is no inner self before the outer self; but both the inner and the outer self jointly work for the presentation of the self before others. This personal appearance occurs in the performance of the action, where who one is stands forth in one's full presence.

Indeed, the transfiguration of human appearance into the self-presentation of the "who" is accomplished by the economy of the mind, as articulated in Arendt's later works on thinking, willing and judging. Arendt intimates that it is judgment that achieves this transformation, and as we have already seen, judgment is intrinsically linked to the common sense of the public realm. But when Arendt says that the economy of the mind and judgment serves to prepare men for an appearance in the public realm, she does not imply that the mind is there before the self. The mind as a whole only enables the person to introduce an element of deliberate choice into the shape his appearance will assume in the public world. The given elements with which one is endowed at birth and in one's formative private existence can be moderated by what one thinks is fit to be seen. The mind is simply one's capacity to indicate how one wishes to be seen. Arendt holds that this capacity for deliberation enables each person to assess his identity as a givenness transfigured by choice. By the time the mind deliberates how one should appear before others, the self is pretty much formed. Arendt does not go overboard with the Kantian/Sartrean capacity (freedom) of one to create oneself and one's world. The mind only liberates the already formed self from a mere acquiescence in the experiences and conventions of the everyday.

So Arendt's analysis does not make the private self primary. In her eyes, the undisputed priority of the private, psychological self in modern thought is only the obverse of modernity's hostility to politics and the world. The modern age marks the fall of public man and the rise of the psychological self to the position of honor in the public mind. Arendt argues that philosophical abstractions of the experience of the psychological self contributed to the predominance of the inner realm over appearing and the definition of man in terms of his cognitive theoretical capacities. In the modern age, the psychological self has assumed the character of Being with the consequence that the world and all reality are reduced to the interior processes of consciousness. In short, the philosophy of the modern age, despite the manifest enlargement of man's powers of acting, is founded on the premise that the world appears as an object for a lucid, self-conscious subject. Arendt attacks the theoretical and egocentric bases of this tradition by claiming that the reality of the world is experienced only by participation in a common world with other appearing actors and spectators. The primary experience of the world is not theoretical, not in the classical sense of contemplation nor the Cartesian sense of aggressive introspective reduction. Human experience need not be afflicted by philosophical world-alienation, for both thinking and cognitive inquiry presuppose the intuitions of reality discovered in one's acting experience in the common world of appearing. In the same way, the primary experience of the world is not egocentric. The reality of oneself and the world emerges only with the affirmation and common acknowledgment of other human actors and spectators. The reality of objectivity of the world cannot be accredited by a theoretical examination of the transcendent structures of the inner being or the thinking ego; this reality is already given in the common sense bequeathed to one by an embodied participation in a communal reality. Arendt's rejection of the claims of the inner self thus prepares the way for a broader survey of the human condition and its construction of reality in its acting capacities.

The twist she gives to the classical polarity of the active and the contemplate life, of the practical and the theoretical, supports her emphasis that political freedom is prior to the inwardly philosophical freedom with which it has so often been confused. She consistently argues against the tradition that established the primacy of the philosophical freedom and its stress on the withdrawal to the inner domain of the mind over that of the political freedom. She stresses that,

> in spite of the great influence the concept of an inner, non-political freedom has exerted upon the tradition of thought, it seems safe to say that man would know nothing of inner freedom if he had not first experienced a condition of being free as a worldly tangible reality.33

Arendt's talk of the importance of the contemplative life for practical affairs and return to the views of Aristotle, such as an appreciation of various mental phenomena and as awareness of the difference between thinking and acting, does not assert the primacy of the mental freedom over that of political freedom. It only shows that for Arendt the human mind is not an escape from freedom but its articulator, while politics is its field of expression. Freedom depends on human thought, as Allen also observes:

> For Arendt, thought is the primum mobile, it is the prime
> mover, not only for political action, but for the very
> activity which elevates man from the primal needs of
> necessity to the arena of the bios politikos. For man is
> not merely man, he is thinking of man.34

Thus, for Arendt, both the inner domain of the mind and the world of
appearance are essential for the individual's full enjoyment of freedom.
Arendt insists on this apparent fact, in order to remove freedom from
the exclusive province of Kant's "professional thinkers". She is
reacting against a tradition that only stressed the inner freedom and
excluded any form of freedom in the space of appearance. For her,
freedom is found where the vita contemplativa joins the vita activa and
where the political realm transcends the private realm.

Her viewpoint is plausible in a world where theorizing is held to
be in total control over action. In such a situation every activity is
taken to be the end-product of a theory, and those who have no
theoretical knowledge of politics are usually excluded from the public
realm. Arendt tries to fight against a world in which "Absolute Mind
reigns supreme". Her solution is not the politics of mindlessness but
of reflection grounded in experience, participation, sharing and
deliberation. Theorizing must be kept strictly separated from action,
and at the same time their compatibility must be maintained.

Finally, since a political actor appears before others as he
wishes to be seen and remembered, we can ask whether there is
genuineness in the political realm. Arendt presents political actors as
a posturing group of men clamoring for attention and wanting to be
reassured that they are valuable, even real, and that they will ever be
remembered after they have vanished from the scene. She also admits
that the modes of appearance possible in this changing world are
steeped in semblance and illusion.

Although Arendt admits that all appearance transpires in the
medium of seeming, she nonetheless differentiates between inauthentic
semblances that can be corrected and authentic semblances that are
inherent in the earthly conditions for appearance:

> Semblance is inherent in a world ruled by the twofold law
> of appearing to a plurality of sensitive creatures, each
> equipped with the faculties of perception. Nothing that
> appears manifests itself to a single viewer capable of
> perceiving it under all its inherent aspects. The world

appears in the mode of it-seems-to-me, depending on
particular perspectives determined by location in the
world as well as by particular organs of perception. This
mode not only produces error which I can correct...it also
gives birth to true semblances...to deceptive appearance,
which I cannot correct like an error since they are
caused by my permanent location on the earth and remain
bound up with my own existence as one of the earth's
appearances.35

What Arendt means is that even authentic appearance of self-display is
performed in the integuments of semblance. No self-display renders
either a perfectly lucid or a transparent vision of the self, and no self
can create the conditions for such a disclosure. Authentic self-display
brings into being a disguise, in terms of which spectators acknowledge
one as discrete reality in the world. So the earthly conditions of
semblance demand an authentic self-display.

Science tries to understand reality and man's place in reality by
abstracting from the physiognomy of appearance and discerning the
laws of the microcosm and the macrocosm behind the features of
appearance. The aim of this effort is to read the secrets of Being
beyond sense perception, common sense, and the categories of
language. Science proceeds on the assumption that it can compel
responses from the deeper structures of Being, but it cannot say or
describe in normal language the constitution of this real world.36
Arendt discerns some relation to reality in the basic systems of
science.

Arendt also borrowed some ideas of appearance from Kant.
Kant was interested to offer clues of what is real. He explicitly
stated the separation of Being and Appearance in his doctrine of
noumenal and phenomenal realities. Arendt proposes that the model
for this relation between Being and Appearance must be found in
human experience itself. She discerns the inspiration for Kant's model
in the elusive experience of the thinking ego itself -- "in the
consciousness of myself in the sheer thinking activity...I am the thing
itself...although nothing of myself is therefore given for thought".37
We have seen that thinking and the process of consciousness insinuate
but never disclose their subject. The thinking ego is not even the
source of our intuition of reality. Arendt searches this source in the
irreducible nexus of the appearance of the world and the global bodily
presence. She suggests that

[r]eality in a world of appearances is first of all
characterized by "standing still and remaining" the same

long enough to become an <u>object</u> for acknowledgement
and recognition by a subject.<u>38</u>

How do subject and object reciprocally enlist each other in creating
the "standing still and remaining" of the real?

Arendt regards the mark of the real to be its "standing still
and remaining" because she excoriates the modern fascination with
introspection and states of conciousness as the loci of human reality.
It is also because she turns to one sense in particular as endowing a
stable aspect to the appearing world:

> It is characteristic of all theories that argue against the
> world giving capacities of the sense that they remove
> vision from its position as the highest and most noble of
> the senses and substitute touch or taste, which are indeed
> the most private senses...those in which the body
> primarily senses itself while perceiving an object.39

For her, sight can engender an objective attitude towards the real,
freeing the subject both from the transient appearances of the object
and from the immediacy of one's bodily experience.

Although admitting that all appearance must assume an aspect
of "seeming" because they appear to every individual in his own
subjectivity, Arendt discerns three factors that contribute to the
sensation of "realness": (1) the identity of an object for the five
differing senses; (2) the identity of context for each member of a
species; and (3) the identification of each object from the particular
perspective of each individual.40 Without getting into epistemological
justification of these points, Arendt proceeds to show how the real
self can be identified. Of course, her full elaboration of this claim
is in her delineation of personal action.

Arendt does not attribute "objective reality" only to tangible,
stable, physical entities; rather, objectivity is obtained by the mutual
confirmation of different fellows whose illuminations of different
aspects endow the object, which might be the other self, with a depth
and thickness that confirm it as real:

> [T]he reality of the public realm relies on the
> simultaneous presence of innumerable perspectives and
> aspects in which the common world presents itself and
> for which no common measurement or denominator can
> ever be devised....Being seen and being heard by others
> derive their significance from the fact that everybody

sees and hears from a different position....Only where things can be seen by many in a variety of aspects without changing their identity, so that those who are gathered around them know they see sameness in utter diversity, can wordly reality fully and reliably appear.41

In the way that physical durability of wordly objects represents the paradigmatic case of public existence because they "stand still" long enough to be confirmed, actions acknowledged by a community of spectators can reveal the real self. Personal action can reveal the true self because it can only be achieved by a being who lives within the cycle of life as impelled by the labor of his body and society, and within the world as constructed and upheld by his fellow men. In personal action Arendt finds the expression of an articulated appearance rich enough in public features to be accessible to the judgment of other men and their combined perpetuation of the distinct indices of the person. The logic of personal action culminates in an objective appearance evaluated on its own terms, rather than in the light of the given nature of the individual or the immediacy of his consciousness or intentions. On the notion of this logic of personal action Arendt bases her assertion that in this world being and appearing coincide and that men find their personal identities only in the world of fellow men.

We have seen that even works of art testify not only to the stability of a physical entity but also to the stability of the expressions of human hands and the human spirit. They reveal the artisan and the artist. Action, although it fashions no external tangible matter, calls attention to the entry of a human person who shapes his rather intangible identity by his chosen words and deeds. Since one's deeds can be clarified by one's words, one may pretend to be who he is not in the public realm; but this cannot last long because the freely chosen and enacted deeds are basic and inexchangeable data to the story that one is obliged to accept as one's own, to preserve, and to be able to retell.

Therefore, genuineness in the political realm is based on the public appearance, despite its flaws. It is the public appearance, through speech and action, that offers the possibility of a validation of the reality of the person, a reality endowed with a fullness and depth by the acknowledgment of other persons.

Conclusion

The earlier works of Hannah Arendt contain a sharp distinction between vita contemplativa and vita activa. They manifest her view that these were separate and distinct ways of life enjoined to different principles and impulses. Arendt tries to reverse the assumed priority of the life of the mind over that of action in all her works. She maintains that the human condition is constituted by the plurality of men and their relationships. The solitary life of the mind is not totally "out of order" in this condition, because there is a need to stop and think what we are doing in the public realm.

The life of the mind does not necessarily subvert the seminal impulse and the principle of freedom at the heart of the vita activa. Despite Arendt's sporadic lack of coherence and proper argument, the result of her tendency to link apparently disparate themes, the notion of vita activa and the theme of freedom are manifestly coherent in her works. I think her conviction that vita activa and vita contemplativa represent different and distinct patterns of human life is also affirmed by the relationship she later recasts between mind and politics through her use of the notion of judgment. She does not recast this relationship necessarily in favour of the mind and against freedom, action and politics. She does not assert the primacy of the mind over the realm of politics because that would undermine the latter as effectively as our philosophical tradition since Plato has done. What Arendt successfully does is to restore politics to its rightful duty in a world she believes has forgotten how to practise it.

CONTINUITY IN AREDNT'S THOUGHT

NOTES

1 Martin Jay, "Hannah Arendt: Opposing Views", Partisan Review, 45, No. 3(October 1978), 352.

2 The Human Condition, p. 16.

3 Jean Yarbrough and Peter Stern, Op. cit. p. 345.

4 J.S. Nelson, "Politics and Truth; Arendt's Problematic", American Journal of Political Science, 22 (May 1978), 293.

Public Self in the Thought of Hannah Arendt, Diss., University of Toronto 1983, p. 67.

6 Ronald Beiner, Hannah Arendt: Lectures on Kant's Political Philosophy (Chicago: The University of Chicago Press, 1982), p. 139.

7 Dossa, p. 69.

8 Between Past and Future, p. 56.

9 The Human Condition, pp. 293-94.

10 Between Past and Future, p. 30

11 Dossa, pp. 92-3.

12 The Human Condition, p. 257.

13 Ibid., p. 71.

14 Aristotle, Politics, trans. Benjamin Jowett, ed. Richard McKeon (New York: Random House, 1941), p. 142.

15 The Human Condition, p. 41.

16 On Revolution, pp. 115-16.

17 The Human Condition, p. 197.

18 Ibid., p. 50.

19 Erving Goffman, The Presentation of Self in Everyday Life (London: The Penguin Press, 1971), pp. 5-6.

20 Thinking, p. 37.

21 Ibid., p. 214.

22 Willing, p. 268.

23 Ibid., p. 262.

24 Elisabeth Young-Bruehl, Hannah Arendt: For the Love of the World (New Haven: Yale University Press, 1982), p. 452.

25 Cited by Young-Bruehl, p. 457.

26 The Human Condition, p. 5.

27 Thinking, p. 71.

28 George Kateb, "Freedom and Worldliness in the Thought of Hannah Arendt", Political Theory, 5, No.2 (May 1977), p. 171.

29 On Revolution, p. 53.

30 Ibid., p. 71.

31 Ibid.

32 Ibid., pp. 29-31.

33 Between Past and Future, p. 148.

34 Wayne Francis Allen, The Concept of Authority in the Thought of Hannah Arendt, Diss., University of California at Riverside 1979, p. 76.

35 Thinking, p. 38.

179

36 Between Past and Future, p. 265.
37 Thinking, p. 42.
38 Ibid., pp. 45-46.
39 The Human Condition, p. 114.
40 Thinking, p. 50.
41 The Human Condition, p. 57.

CONCLUSION

I have tried to reformulate Arendt's notion of freedom. It should be obvious now why freedom is a central concept of her political theory. She has developed her concepts of public and private freedom into a symbiosis through which freedom is no longer what destroys politics but what gives it meaning through time. I have also tried to elucidate the cohesion in her work by examining the interrelationship of the vita contemplativa and the vita activa in Arendt's analysis as well as her unique theoretical formulations. Contrary to the view that there is no unity in Arendt's thought because her earlier works focus on public freedom and are historically bound to the early Greeks while her later works, emphasizing private freedom, are based on the darkest period of the twentieth century, I believe that Arendt's unusual notion of freedom acts as a nexus between her earlier and later works.

What Arendt does is to restore the primacy of political freedom over that of philosophical freedom without repudiating the latter. Her project originates in and endeavours to be faithful to the language and experience of common human discourse. She is convinced that the primary organization of human reality has been recapitulated under the abstruse metaphysical claims of the philosophers and can be recaptured by diligent reflection; hence her understanding of the fundamental task of human reason and thinking as "to think what we are doing". This "thinking what we are doing", which occupied Arendt's thought throughout all her works, is central to her theory of politics. It involves drawing clear distinctions and categories to illuminate the fundamental concept of political freedom. The first one, of course, is the category of the vita activa, which she developed from the class of animal laborans, homo faber and men of action. The second one is that of the vita contemplativa, which she developed from the notions of thinking, willing and bios theoretikos. The real conjunction between these categories was for her located in the faculty of judgment.

We saw, however, that the use of these categories sometimes tends to becloud an understanding of political freedom, not because she is vague in presentation but because the categories themselves "hardly ever correspond to watertight compartments". In the same manner, Arendt has tried to clarify concepts central to politics and to bring new meaning to them by distinguishing among them. These concepts are even less watertight than the categories of the vita activa and vita contemplativa, not because she has been less materful at dealing with them but because they are concepts that, historically, have caused great confusion and disagreement. Arendt did not presume to offer new solutions or to repair singlehandedly the shattered tradition of Western thought. Neither was her rearticulation based upon a novel metaphysics or a novel conception of human nature.

She was preoccupied, rather, with discovering the original spirit that lurks within the conceptions she uses and the vita activa articulated throughout the Western tradition.

Furthermore, Arendt thought that the loss of distinction may coincide with the loss of freedom. As a consequence, she makes distinctions and further more subtle and cross-cutting distinctions in order to explain her notion of political freedom. She makes a distinction between "labor", activities that are tied to the meeting of biological needs and hence to necessity, and "work", that is, activities that produce enduring objects and an enduring world, in order to show that, unlike action, these activities do not reveal one's uniqueness in the public realm. She also distinguishes action from behavior, which she sees as habitual and non-governed and as characteristic of the society of laborers. Whereas action expresses individual distinctiveness, behavior supresses the distinctive aspects of the individual.

Arendt makes these distinctions in order to show that freedom is rooted in the condition of plurality. The actor, in contrast to the laborer, worker and behaviorist, enjoys the highest sort of freedom precisely because action is rooted in the condition of plurality. It is within the plural space of appearance that man's capacity to act, that is, his faculty of freedom, can be exercised. It is an action that combines harmoniously, as it did for the Greeks, the vita activa and the vita contemplativa. This means that even though vita contemplativa as contemplation has no bearing on the public realm and is sometimes even destructive of the political realm, it nevertheless has a claim on the vita activa generally because political action is not mindless and therefore cannot be entirely devoid of thought or mental capacity. The action to be political must, at least to a degree, be selfless and born of philosophical thought.

In her last work, Arendt spells out the nature and limits of the claims of the mind on politics. Her return to the life of the mind contains clues and strategies to guide us towards the world and political freedom proper. She makes another distinction between thinking and willing and other associated activities of the mind in order to show that although these faculties presuppose withdrawal from the world and are therefore not the preconditions for political freedom, they are nevertheless important in propelling action. They are the preliminary springs of all action. Thinking diverts the habit of obedience from thwarting the meaning of the novel. It opens the space in which human beings can begin anew and constitute a realm of freedom. It also encourages an awareness of freedom by preparing the self for the conditions of human plurality. It fosters an "enlarged mentality", a willingness to examine experience on a shared and

interchangeable basis with other men.   Willing is even much closer to
action.   The will is the spring of action, and as such, Arendt
maintains, it is not political but pre-political; because of its
importance, neither politics nor freedom would be real without it.

But it is with the faculty of judgment, "the most political of
men's mental abilities", that philosophy and politics meet and work
out their tentative and uneasy symbiosis.   For Arendt the public
faculty of judging, in which sharing-the-world-with-others comes to
pass, bridges the chasm between thinking and acting without
endangering the realm of freedom.   Judgment also bridges the gap
between vita activa and vita contemplativa because in her earlier
writings Arendt regards it as part of the vita activa, seeing it as a
function of the representative thinking and enlarged mentality of
political actors, exchanging opinions in public while engaged in common
deliberation.   In her last work she is able to place it exclusively
within the vita contemplativa.   This does not mean that Arendt
contradicts herself but only shows that her stressing the vita activa at
one time and the vita contemplativa at the other is an appropriate
way of analyzing the world of politics.   An apparent change or
transition from the vita activa toward the vita contemplativa that we
find as we move from her earlier to her later writings is only one way
of returning to the world with a viable politics.

The point that Arendt is making should now be obvious: that in
the final analysis the vita activa, politics and the public realm have
access to the vita contemplativa.   Political theory has to avail itself of
the vita contemplativa because it is obviously a species of thought and
thinking.   As such, vita contemplativa, understood as thought and
reason, never ceases to be binding upon the activity of political
theorizing.   Thus, Arendt intends neither to subordinate the vita activa
to the vita contemplativa, as it was in Plato and Aristotle where it
received its meaning and "restricted dignity" from the vita
contemplativa because it merely served the needs and wants of
contemplation; nor does she intend to eliminate the vita contemplativa
entirely from the range of ordinary political experience as in the
modern tradition, where it is not just subordinated to the vita activa
but is also consigned to the unscientific dustbin of the past.

According to the modern tradition, not only does the vita
contemplativa become an "altogether meaningless" activity, the vita
activa itself also suffers greatly because the traditionally lower
activities of labor and work emerge as higher than action.   Labor is
now regarded as the most important activity, the one that serves both
biological needs and human aspirations.   Arendt vehemently rejects the
modern thinkers' idea, especially Marx's, that labor's productivity is

the consummation and the raison d'être of human life. For her, labor and work neither loosen the rigidity of life by generating a climate in which action becomes a daily occurrence nor create spaces within which freedom finds a worldly home. Only those who have been liberated from the demands of work and labor can freely participate in politics.

From the preceding remarks it is clear that Arendt's thought is unusual and original. Politics as she understands it certainly departs from the recurrent activity of classical and modern thought. Her politics have no business -- at least not directly -- with the needs of the body. Socio-economic issues lie outside the province of politics proper. Socio-economic factors, which have become the ideal realm for political life in our own times, are regarded by Arendt as essentially pre-political. They spring from impulses antithetical to politics and are neither the cause, nor the effect, nor the purpose of politics. This means that the meaning of politics is not fixed or determined by socio-economic issues; rather, it is bound with the principle manifested in politics itself. This principle is freedom.

Arendt wants to remind the modern world that the essence of politics is the foundation of freedom and not the settlement of socio-economic problems. Although she is aware that today it is difficult to imagine economic transactions without government intervention at one level or another or find a government uninvolved in both economic and social matters, she believes the strictness of this division can help us understand the rationale behind the primacy of politics and safeguard its autonomy. She demonstrates how politics as performing art can be corrupted by these extraneous considerations.

Of course, the thorough destruction of politics reaches fruition in the movements of totalitarian regimes. Arendt's effort to reformulate the concept of freedom was ignited by the reality of totalitarianism. Relying on the Greek polis, the Rome foundation, the American Revolution and some modern councils, Arendt creates spaces in which men can find freedom. It is only through individual action and the effort to create the public realm that man can establish the anchors of human reckoning that can militate against the "thought-lessness" that is the force behind totalitarianism. Totalitarian regimes require the suspension of reflective judgment by their members. Totalitarianism also assaults the public structure of "normal reality" and the personal structures of individuality and freedom.

In her effort to find room for the individual, whose actions alone determine reality, Arendt returns to the tradition and situations in which the public realm was maintained. It is in the public realm that the speech of one becomes a discourse with others and where the action of one becomes participation with one's equals. Arendt's notion of participation, however, is different from the one to which we are accustomed. We have become used to seeing our modes of access to public life restricted by ever-increasing groups who claim to speak for us. We have modes of access available to us through representative government and the party system, with its never-ending series of interest groups. For Arendt, only the participation of the self, the revelation of one's thoughts through action and speech in concert with others, is what constitutes the public realm. Freedom, which is the reason for politics, can only be enjoyed by the individual in the company of men who act and speak together. The coming together of freemen creates a realm of opinions and discussion. This free play of oratory that results in decisions (and promise-keeping) cannot be tranferred or entitled to anyone else. Therefore, representation of political action is really not possible. Participation has to do with the freedom of the individual to act, to speak and to maintain the political realm -- the self-directed arena of freedom. For an individual to be represented by someone else in this freedom-recurring activity would mean an abdication of the self, an ultimate renunciation of who one is. Through the notion of freedom as participation, Arendt discloses how both inner and public spheres of life complement one another.

Arendt's later works were, therefore, focussed on how, through the use of his mental faculties, an individual reveals who he is and thus creates his own reality and ensures his freedom and that of others. Thinking prepares the self for deliberate self-appearance and establishes the order of history as the worldly appropriation of the meaning of the free action of individuals. In her effort to enlist thinking in the confirmation of the free and unique appearances of persons, Arendt concludes that thinking and the life of the mind can resolve the contradiction of the public world and the social structures that preclude the personal participation and appearance in the public realm.

The urgency of Arendt's reflections on the relationship between mental faculties and action stem from her two convictions: firstly, that a chronic thoughtlessness figured greatly in the decline of freedom in the modern age; and secondly, that the social conditions that had lent plausibility to the ideological claims and cunning of totalitarianism still persist. In the first case, her controversial analysis of Adolf Eichmann and the totalitarian mentality rests on the thesis that evil human actions thrive not upon demonic attributes of man but rather upon his complacent lapse into thoughtlessness. Thus, although thinking and the life of the mind were focussed upon by

CONCLUSION

Arendt only late in her public reflections, they chronologically precede her articulation of the vita activa. It is easier now to see why her notion of thinking and its import for the world of appearing human actor is logically connected with her articulation of human action. She recognizes the need to recast the relationship between mind and politics and hence to connect her later writings to her earlier ones.

In the second case, Arendt insists that in the modern age mankind is compressed into the oneness of society, a community organized for the fulfillment of the necessities of life. The modern society fosters an equality, not of distinctly thinking persons, but of conforming, interchangeable functionaries. It nurtures a behavior that acquiesces in the anonymous administration of the community in accordance with the trends of economic forces and pressures. Of course, this means that the modern social structures thwart the conception of man as actor whose distinctive appearance originates in thinking and the process of consciousness. (For Arendt, thinking and the process of consciousness insinuate but never disclose who the actor is.)

Arendt's concern is to recapture the logic underlying the conception of man as a distinctive but not isolated actor. She overcomes the seeming subjectivity of all appearing by integrating it in a worldly context. The model of this structure of objective appearance evokes the image of an illuminated space in the middle of which stands a clearly defined object being observed by surrounding spectators. The actor must conform his actions and disclosures to the conventions of judgment, which enable one to be recognized. One's appearance must achieve an adequately "objective" expression in word and deed, which can be understood and affirmed by fellow actors and affirmed by fellow actors and spectators. The reality or objectivity of oneself and the world emerges only with the affirmation and common acknowledgment of other human actors and spectators. Here Arendt again implicates the mind because thinking has to comprehend and round out the action in a form of preservation and the actor must also conform his actions and disclosures to the conventions of judgment that enable one to be recognized.

Through a redress of the balance between thinking and appearing reality, Arendt restores to each realm the integrity that is lost in the modern age. Since, for her, philosophers succumbed to the prejudice that reality is only a constituent of the will or the interiority of consciousness or the laws of the mind itself, Arendt proposes to ascertain the mind's relation to appearance as well as its possible contribution to human freedom. The full significance of these reconciliations of public appearance to the canons of the mind is elucidated in her work on <u>vita activa</u>.

It is clear that Arendt's work, over against any other analysis of political freedom, is unique. It is for the most part consistent and extremely comprehensive, though at the same time quite obscure. She gets to her notion of political freedom in a most indirect and complex manner. This concept is based on the Greek <u>polis</u>, has its foundation also in European existentialism, and is set against a backdrop of events and forces whose impact is still felt. Arendt's analysis of the notion of political freedom establishes an intimate connection between all her writings. This is one of the major results of this book.

In order to judge the greatness of Arendt's thought, we still have to delve further into the German existential phenomenology and ontology associated with Husserl, Heidegger and Jaspers. There is much room for further exploration to reveal how she moved out of the tradition that shaped her mind and came to rest upon Jaspers' communicative existential system in order to create her own original, independent position.

BIBLIOGRAPHY

This bibliography lists the most important of Arendt's essays not reprinted in her books. (For a comprehensive chronological bibliography of her essays, reviews and letters, consult Elisabeth Young-Bruehl's Hannah Arendt: For Love of the World, listed below, pp. 535-45). It also lists articles, books and dissertations most relevant to this thesis.

ARTICLES

Abel, Lionel. "Aesthetics of Evil: Hannah Arendt on Eichmann and the Jews".Partisan Review, 30 (Summer 1963), 211-30.

Arendt, Hannah. "Augustin und Protestantismus". Frankfurter Zeitung, 902 (12 April 1930).

--------. "Philosophie und Soziologie, Anlasslich Karl Mannheim, 'Ideologie und Utopie'". Die Gesellschaft (Berlin), VII (1930), 163-76. (Reprinted in Ideologie und Wissenssociologie. Darmstadt: Wissenchaftliche Buchgessellschaft, 1974).

--------. "Soren Kierkegaard". Frankfurter Zeitung (29 January 1932), 75-76.

--------. Berliner Salon" and "Brief Rahels an Pauline Wiesel". Deutscher Almanach fur das Jahr 1932 (Leipzig), 175-84 and 185-90.

--------. "Rahel Varnhagen. Zum 100. Todestag". Kolnische Zeitung, 131 (7 March 1933). (Reprinted in Judische Rundschau 28/29, 7 April 1933).

--------. "A Believer in European Unity". Review of Politics, IV/2 (April 1942), 245-47.

--------. "From the Dreyfus Affair to France Today". Jewish Social Studies, IV (July 1942), 195-240.

--------. "Portrait of a Period". The Menorah Journal, XXXI (Fall 1943), 307-14.

--------. Why the Crémieu Decree was Abrogated". Contemporary Jewish Record, VI/2 (April 1943), 115-23.

--------. "Approaches to the 'German Problem'". Partisan Review, XII/1 (Winter 1945), 93-106.

--------. "The Assets of Personality". Contemporary Jewish Record, VIII/2 (April 1945), 214-16.

--------. "The Seeds of a Fascist International". Jewish Frontier (June 1945), 12-16.

--------. "Dilthey as Philosopher and Historian". Partisan Review, XII/3 (Summer 1945), 404-406.

--------. "Christianity and Revolution". The Nation, (22 September 1945), 288-89.

--------. "Power Politics Triumphs". Commentary, 1 (December 1945), 3-30.

--------. "What is Existenz Philosophy?" The Partisan Review, XIII/1 (Winter 1946), 34-56.

--------. "French Existentialism". The Nation (23 February 1946), 226-28.

--------. "Imperialism: Road to Suicide". Commentary, 1 (February 1946), 27-35.

-------. "The Image of Hell". Commentary, II/3 (September 1946), 291-95.

--------. "No Longer and Not Yet". The Nation (14 September 1946), 300-302.

--------. "The Ivory Tower of Common Sense". The Nation (19 October 1946), 447-49.

---------. "The Hole of Oblivion". Jewish Frontier (July 1947), 23-26.

--------. "Beyond Personal Frustration: The Poetry of Bertolt Brecht". The Kenyon Review, X/2 (Spring 1948), 304-12.

--------. "Totalitarian Terror". The Review of Politics, XI/1 (January 1949), 112-15.

--------."The Rights of Man: What Are They?". Modern Review, III/1 (Summer 1949), 476-83.

--------. "Social Science Technique and the Study of Concentration Camps". Jewish Social Studies, XII/1 (1950), 49-64.

BIBLIOGRAPHY

--------. "The Aftermath of Nazi Rule: Report from Germany". Commentary, X (October 1950), 342-53.

--------. "Mob and the Elite". Partisan Review, XVII (November 1950), 808-19.

--------. "Totalitarian Movement". Twentieth Century, 149 (May 1951), 368-89.

--------. "The Imperialist Character". The Review of Politics, XII/3 (July 1950), 303-20.

--------. "Bei Hitler Zu Tisch". Der Monat, IV (October 1951), 85-90.

--------. "The History of the Great Crime". Commentary XIII (March 1952), 300-304.

--------. "Rejoinder to Eric Voegelin's Review of the Origins of Totalitarianism". Review of Politics, XV (January 1953), 76-85.

--------. "Understanding and Politics". Partisan Review, XX/4 (July-August 1953), 317-92.

--------. "Religion and Politics". Confluence, II/3 (September 1953), 105-26.

--------. "Understanding Communism". Partisan Review, XX/5 (September-October 1953), 580-83.

--------. "Reflections on Little Rock". Dissent, VI/1 (Winter 1959), 45-56.(Included in the same issue are criticisms by David Spitz and Melvin Tumin, in Dissent, VI/2 (Spring 1959), 179-81. Arendt replied to her critics; the article was reprinted in The Public Life: A Journal of Politics, IV/3 (May-June 1973), 92-97.

--------. "The Cold War and the West". Partisan Review, XXIX/1 (Winter 1962), 10-20.

--------. "Eichmann in Jerusalem". Encounter (January 1964), 51-56.

--------. "The Deputy: Guilt by Silence". The New York Herald Tribune Magazine (23 February 1964), 6-9.

--------. "Personal Responsibility under Dictatorship". The Listener (6 August 1964), 185-87 and 205.

BIBLIOGRAPHY

--------. "On the Human Condition". In The Evolving Society. Ed. Mary Hinton. New York: Institute of Cybernetical Research, 1966, 213-19.

--------. "Remarks on 'The Crisis Character of Modern Society'. Christianity and Crisis, XXIV/9 (30 May 1966), 112-14.

--------. "Martin Heidegger at 80". The New York Review of Books, XVII/6 (21 October 1971), 50-54.

--------. "Thinking and Moral Considerations: A Lecture". Social Research, XXXVIII/3 (Fall 1971), 417-46.

--------. "Karl Jaspers zum fundachtzigsten Geburtstage". In Erinnerugen an Karl Jaspers. Ed. H. Saner. Munich:Piper, 1974, pp.311-15.

--------. "Home to Roost". The New York Review of Books (26 June 1975), 3-6.

--------. "Public Rights and Private Interests". In Small Comforts for Hard Times: Humanists on Public Policy. Eds. Mooney and Stuber. New York: Columbia University Press, 1977.

Hannah Arendt also wrote a lot of material still being classified in the Library of Congress. I had access to:

--------. "Some Questions of Moral Philosophy". Library of Congress, 1965, Containers 40 and 41.

--------. "Kant's Political Philosophy". Library of Congress, Fall 1964, Container 41.

Bernard, F.M. "Infinity and Finality: Hannah Arendt on Politics and Truth". Canadian Journal of Social and Political Theory, 13 (September 1977), 29-57.

Beiner, Ronald. "Judging in a World of Appearance: A Commentary on Hannah Arendt's Unwritten Finale". History of Political Thought (1980), 17.34.

--------. "Hannah Arendt on Judging: An Interpretative Essay". In Hannah Arendt's Lectures on Kant's Political Philosophy. Ed. Ronald Beiner. Chicago: The University of Chicago Press, 1982.

Bell, Daniel. "The Alphabet of Justice". Partisan Review, XXX (Fall 1963), 417-29.

191

BIBLIOGRAPHY

Bernstein, Richard J. "Hannah Arendt: The Ambiguities of Theory and Practice". In Political Theory and Praxis: New Perspectives. Ed. Terence Ball. Minneapolis: University of Minnesota Press, 1977.

--------. "Hannah Arendt: Opinion and Judgment". A paper presented at the 1976 meeting of the American Political Science Association, Chicago, Illinois, September 2 - 5, 1976.

Blanshard, Brand. "Reflections on History". The New York Times Book Review (15 February 1959), 26.

Bondy, Francois. "On Misunderstanding Eichmann". Encounter (November 1961), 32-37

Botstein, Leon. "Hannah Arendt: The Jewish Question". The New Republic (21 October 1978), 32-37.

--------. "Hannah Arendt" Partisan Review, XLV/3 (1978), 368-80.

Cameron, James. "Bad Times". New York Review of Books (6 November 1969). Review of Arendt's BPF and MDT.

Canovan, Margaret. "The Contradictions of Hannah Arendt's Political Thought". Political Theory,6 (February 1978), 5-26.

Carne-Ross, D.S. "Classics and the Intellectual Community". Arion, 1 (Spring 1973 - new series), 7-66.

Cooper, Leroy A. "Hannah Arendt's Political Philosophy: An Interpretation". The Review of Politics, 38/2 (1976), 145-76.

Cranston, Maurice. "Ethics and Politics". Encounter (June 1972), 16-26.

--------. "Hannah Arendt". Encounter (March 1976), 54-56.

Dannhauser, Werner. "Hannah Arendt and the Jews". Commentary (January 1979), 70-72.

Dossa, Shiraz. "Human Status and Politics: Hannah Arendt on the Holocaust". Canadian Journal of Political Science, 2 (June 1980), 309-23.

--------. "Hannah Arendt on Eichmann". Review of Politics, 46/2 (April 1984), 163-82.

Elvitch, Bernard. "Hannah Arendt's Testimony". The Massachusetts

Review, 2 (Summer 1979), 369-76.

Ezorsky, Gertrude. "Hannah Arendt Against the Facts". New Politics, 2 (Fall 1963), 53-73.

Fruchter, Norman. "Arendt's Eichmann and Jewish Identity". In For a New America. Eds. James Weinstein and David W.Eakins. New York: Vintage, 1970.

Gerratana, Valentino. "Marx and Darwin". New Left Review, 82 (November-December 1973), 60-82.

Gray, Sherry. "Hannah Arendt and the Solidariness of Thinking". Philosophy Today, 25 (Summer 1981), 121-30.

Heather, G. P., and M.Stolz. "Hannah Arendt and the Problem of Critical Theory". Journal of Politics, 41 (February 1979), 2-22.

Hobsbawm, Eric. "On Revolution" (review). History and Theory, 4 (1965), 252-58.

Howe, Irving. "The New York and Hannah Arendt". Commentary, 4 (October 1963), 318-19.

Jay, Martin. "Hannah Arendt". Partisan Review, XLV/3 (1978), 348-68.

Kateb, George. "Freedom and Worldliness in the Thought of Hannah Arendt". Political Theory, 2 (May 1977), 141-82.

--------. "Dismantling Philosophy". The American Scholar (Winter 1978), 118-26.

Knauer, J.T. "Motive and Goal in Hannah Arendt's Concept of Political Action". American Political Science Review, 74 (September 1980), 721-33.

Laqueur, Walter. "Re-reading Hannah Arendt". Encounter (March 1979), 73-79.

Levin, Martin. "On Animal Laborans and Homo Politicus in Hannah Arendt". Political Theory, 7 (November 1979), 521-31.

Lowell, Robert. "On Hannah Arendt". New York Review of Books (13 May 1976), 6.

BIBLIOGRAPHY

McCarthy, Mary. "Saying Good-by to Hannah". New York Review of Books (22 January 1976), 8-11.

Macdonald, Dwight. "Arguments" (Eichmann issue). Partisan Review, 2 (Spring 1964), 262-69.

McKenna, George. "On Hannah Arendt". In The Legacy of German Refugee Intellectuals. Ed.Robert Boyers. New York: Schocken, 1972.

Nelson, John S. "Politics and Truth: Arendt's Problematic". American Journal of Political Science, 2 (May 1978), 271-301.

O'Sullivan, N.K. "Politics, Totalitarianism and Freedom". Political Studies, 21 (June 1973), 183-98.

Parekh, Bhiku. "Does Traditional Philosophy Rest on a Mistake?" Political Studies, 2 (June 1979), 294-300.

Parel, Anthony. "Machiavellian Origins of Modern Political Theory". Unpublished lecture delivered at Whitman College, April 1978.

Redfield, James M. "The Sense of Crisis". In New Views on the Nature of Man. Ed. J. R. Platt. Chicago: University Press, 1965.

Rubinoff, Lionel. "The Dialectic of Work and Labour in the Ontology of Man". Humanitas, 7 (Fall 1971), 147-76.

Schwartz, Benjamin. "The Religion of Politics". Dissent, 17 (March-April 1970), 144-61.

Shklar, Judith. "Hannah Arendt's Triumph". The New Republic (27 December 1975), 8-10.

Stillman, P.G. "Freedom as Participation: The Revolutionary Theories of Hegel and Arendt". American Behavioral Science, 20 (March 1977), 477-92.

Suchting, W.A. "Marx and Hannah Arendt's The Human Condition". Ethics, 73 (October 1962), 47-55.

Syrkin, Marie. "Hannah Arendt: The Clothes of the Empress". Dissent, 4 (Autumn 1963), 344-52.

Thomson, Kirk. "Constitutional Theory and Political Action". Journal of Politics, 31 (1969), 655-80.

Voegelin, Eric. "The Origins of Totalitarianism". The Review of Politics, XV/1 (January 1953), 68-76; Arendt's reply follows, 76-84.

Whitfield, Stephen J. "The Imagination of Disaster". Jewish Social Studies, 42 (Winter 1980), 1-20.

Wolin, Sheldon S. "Paradigms and Political Theories". In Politics and Experience: Essays Presented to Michael Oakeshott. Eds. P. King and B.C.Parekh. Cambridge, 1978.

--------. "Political Theory as a Vocation". American Political Science Review, 63 (December 1969), 1062-82.

--------. "Stopping to Think". New York Review of Books (26 October 1978), 16-21.

Yarbrough, Jean and Peter Stern. "Vita Activa and Vita Contemplativa: Reflections on Hannah Arendt's Political Thought in The Life of the Mind". The Review of Politics, 43/3 (July 1981), 323-54.

Young-Bruehl, Elisabeth. "Reflections on Hannah Arendt's The Life of the Mind". Political Theory, 10 (October 1982), 277-306.

There are also articles on Hannah Arendt compiled in the following issues:

"Hannah Arendt: L'exploration de la modernité, La Passion de la Démocratie". Esprit, 4/6 (Juin 1980), 3-124.

"Hannah Arendt: Memoril Issue". Social Research, 44/1 (Spring 1977), 3-190.

"Politics and the Social Contract on Hannah Arendt". Salmagundi, 60 (Summer 1983), i-139.

Reflections on Eichmann in Jerusalem". Partisan Review, 30 (1963), 211-30, 417-28; and Partisan Review 31 (1964), 82-94, 253-83.

BOOKS

Arendt, Hannah. Der Liebesbegriff bei Augustin. Berlin: J.Springer, 1929.

--------. Rahel Varnhagen: Lebensgeschichte einer deutschen Judin aus der Romantik. (Began in 1930, finished first eleven chapters in 1933, wrote the last two in 1938, published as Rahel Varnhagen: The Life of a Jewess. London: East and West Library, 1958. American edition: Rahel Varnhagen: The Life of a Jewish Woman. New York: Harcourt Brace Jovanovich, 1974.

————. Job's Dung Heap. Ed. Bernard Lazare. New York: Schocken Books, 1948.

————. Sechs Essays. Heidelberg: L. Schneider, 1948. (Reprinted in Die Verbogene Tradition: Acht Essays. Frunkfurt: Suhrkamp, 1976.

————. The Origin of Totalitarianism. New York: Harcourt, Brace & Co., 1951. Second enlarged edition: New York: The World Publishing Co., Meridian Books, 1958. Third edition with new prefaces: New York: Harcourt, Brace & World, 1966, 1968, 1973. German editions: Elemente und Ursprunge totaler Herrschaft, Frankfurt: Europaische Verlagsanstalt, 1955, 1958, 1961, 1961. (British title: The Burden of Our Time.)

————. Dichten und Erkennen: Essays. 2 vols. of Gesammelte Werke. Ed. Hermann Broch. Zurich: Rheinverlag, 1955. (Arendt's introduction, translated by Richard and Clara Winston, appeared in Men in Dark Times.)

————. Fragwurdige Traditionsbestande im politischen Denken der Gegenwart, Frankfurt: Europaische Verlagsanstalt, 1957. (Four essays, all included in Between Past and Future).

————. The Human Condition. Chicago: University of Chicago, 1958.

————. Between Past and Future. Enlarged ed. New York: Viking, 1968 (First edition 1961).

————. Eichmann in Jerusalem. Revised ed. New York: Viking, 1965. (Except for the postcript, this edition is identical to the first edition published in 1963.)

————. On Revolution. New York: Viking, 1963.

————. Men in Dark Times. New York: Harcourt, Brace & World, 1968.

————. On Violence. New York: Harvest, 1969.

--------. Crisis of the Republic. New York: Harvest, 1972.

--------. The Jew as Pariah. Edited and with an introduction by Ron H. Feldman. New York: Grove Press, 1978.

--------. The Life of the Mind. 2 vols. New York: Harcourt, Brace, Javanovich, 1978. Published posthumously and edited by Mary McCarthy.

--------. Lectures on Kant's Political Philosophy. Chicago: The University of Chicago Press, 1982. (Published posthumously, edited and with an interpretive essay by Ronald Beiner).

Aristotle. The Politics. Edited and translated by Ernest Barker. Oxford: Oxford University Press, 1946.

--------. The Nichomachean Ethics. Trans. Martin Ostwald. Indianapolis: Bobbs-Merrill,1962.

Augustine, Saint. Concerning the City of God against the Pagans. Translated by Henry Bettenson. Baltimore, Maryland: Penguin Books, 1972.

--------. The Confessions. Translated and with an introduction by John Ryan. New York: Doubleday, 1960.

Avineri, Shlomo. Hegel's Theory of the Modern State. Cambridge: Cambridge University Press, 1972.

--------. The Social and Political Thought of Karl Marx. Cambridge: Cambridge University Press, 1972.

Barker, Sir Ernest. The Political Thought of Plato and Aristotle. New York: Dover Publications Inc., 1959.

--------. Social Contract: Essays by Locke, Hume, and Rousseau. New York: Oxford University Press, 1962.

Bay, Christian. The Structure of Freedom. Palo Alto, California: Stanford University press, 1958.

Benjamin, Walter. Iluuminations. Ed. Hannah Arendt. New York: Harcourt, Brace and World, 1968.

Bentham, Jeremy. The Utilitarians. New York: Doubleday, 1973.

Bernstein, Richard J. Praxis and Action: Contemporary Philosophies of

BIBLIOGRAPHY

Human Activity. Philadelphia: University of Pennsylvania Press, 1971.

Bettelheim, Bruno. Surviving and Other Essays. New York: Vintage, 1980. (Includes "Eichmann: The System, the Victims" and "The Ignored Lesson of Anne Frank").

Burke, Edmund. Reflections of the Revolution in France. New York: Doubleday, 1973.

Canovan, Margaret. The Political Thought of Hannah Arendt. London: J.M. Dent, 1974.

Cropsey, Joseph. Political Philosophy and the Issues of Politics. Chicago: University of Chicago Press, 1977.

Davis, D.B. Was Jefferson an Authentic Enemy of Slavery? Oxford: Clarendon Press 1970.

Duns Scotus, J. Philosophical Writings. Edited and translated by Allen Wolter. Edinburgh, London, 1962.

Ehrenberg, Victor. The Greek State. New York: Barnes and Noble, 1960.

Fest, Joachim C. The Face of the Third Reich. Harmondsworth: Penguin, 1979.

Finley, M.I. The Ancient Greeks. Harmondsworth: Pelican, 1977.

--------. Aspects of Antiquity. Harmondsworth: Pelican, 1976.

Flatman, Richard E. Concepts in Social and Political Philosophy. New York: Macmillan Publishing Co., 1973.

Foster, Michael B. Masters of Political Thought. Boston: Houghton Mifflin, 1969.

Friedrich, Carl J., ed. Nomos. Vol. 4 of Liberty. New York: Atherton Press, 1962.

Gewirth, Alan. Political Philosophy. London: The Macmillan Company, Collier-Macmillan Ltd., 1965.

Gilson, Etienne. Jean Duns Scotus: Introduction a`ses Positions Fondamentales. Paris:Vrin, 1952.

BIBLIOGRAPHY

Goffman, Erving. The presentation of Self in Everyday life. London: Allan Lane, The Penguin Press, 1959.

Gomme, A. W. The Greek Attitude to Poetry and History. Berkeley and Los Angeles: University of Chicago Press, 1954.

Hampshire, Stuart. Thought and Action. New York: Viking Press, 1959.

Hare, R.M. Freedom and Reason. London: Oxford University Press, 1963.

Hegel, G.W.F. The Phenomenology of Mind. Trans. J.B. Baillie. Intro. by George Lichtheim. New York: Harper Colophon, 1967.

Heidegger, Martin. What is Called Thinking? Trans. Fred D. Wieck and J. Glenn Gray. New York: Harper, 1972.

--------. An Introduction to Metaphysics. Trans. Ralph Manheim. New York: Doubleday, 1961.

Hilberg, Raul. The Destruction of the European Jews. Chicago: Quadrangle, 1961.

Hill, Melvyn A., ed. Hannah Arendt: The Recovery of the Public World. New York: St. Martin's Press, 1979. (This collection includes some of the essays discussed in this study.)

Hobbes, Thomas. Leviathan. Ed. C. B. Macpherson. Harmondsworth: Penguin, 1968.

Hoffman, W. Michael. Kant's Theory of Freedom: A Metaphysical Inquiry. Washington, D.C.: University Press of America, Inc., 1979.

Howey, R. Heidegger and Jaspers on Nietzsche: A Critical Examination of Heidegger's and Jaspers' Interpretations of Nietzsche. The Hague: Martinus Nijhoff, 1973.

Jaspers, Karl. Plato and Augustine. Ed. Hannah Arendt. New York: Harcourt, Brace and World, 1962.

Jensen, Delamar, ed. Machiavelli. Boston: D.C. Heath and Co., 1960.

Jones, W.T. Morality and Freedom in the Philosophy of Immanuel Kant. London: Oxford University Press, 1940.

Kant, Immanuel. The Critique of Judgement. Trans. James Creed Meredith. Oxford: The Clarendon Press, 1973.

--------. Foundations of the Metaphysics of Morals. Trans. Lewis Beck. Indianapolis: Bobbs-Merrill, 1959.

Kaufmann, Walter. Basic Writings of Nietzsche. New York: Modern Library, 1968

--------. Tragedy and Philosophy. New York: Doubleday, 1969.

Kazin, Alfred. New York Jew. New York: Vintage, 1979.

Kitto, H.D.G. The Greeks. Harmondsworth: Penguin, 1957.

Kolko, Gabriel, Richard Falk and Robert Jay Lifton, eds. Crimes of War. New York: Vintage, 1971. (Includes Arendt's essay "On Responsibility for Evil".)

Laslett, Peter and W.G. Runciman, eds. In Philosophy, Politics and Society, Oxford: Basil Blackwell, 1967. (This collection includes Bernard Crick's essay "Freedom as Politics".)

Lichtheim, George. The Concept of Ideology. New York: Vintage, 1967.

Locke, John. Two Treatises of Government. Ed. Peter Laslett. New York: Mentor, 1963.

Machiavelli, Niccolo. The Prince and the Discourses. New York: Modern Library, 1950.

MacPherson, C. B. The Political Theory of Possessive Individualism. London: Oxford University Press, 1962.

Marx, Karl. A Contribution to the Critique of Political Economy. Ed. M. Dobb. Moscow: Progress, 1970.

--------. The German Ideology. Ed. R. Pascal. New York: International Publishers, 1947.

--------. Early Writings. Ed. T.B. Bottomore. New York: McGraw-Hill, 1964.

McCarthy, Mary. The Writing on the Wall and Other Literary Essays. New York: Harcourt, Brace and World, 1970. (This also includes her essay on the Eichmann controversy, "The Hue and Cry".)

Mill, John Stuart. Three Essays: On Liberty, Representative
    Government, The Subjection of Women. London: Oxford
    University Press, 1975.

Myres, John. The Political Ideals of the Greeks. London:Edward
    Arnold, 1927.

Nietzsche, Friedrich. Beyond Good and Evil. Translated and with an
    introduction by Marianne Cowen. Chicago: Henry Regnery Co.,
1955.

--------.The Complete Works of Friedrich Nietzsche. Ed. Oscar Levy,
Vol. II:Early Greek Philosophy, London: George Allen and
    Unwin Ltd., 1911.

--------. The Gay Science. Trans. Walter Kaufmann. New York:
    Random, 1974.

--------.On the Genealogy of Morals and Ecce Homo. Ed. W.
    Kaufmann. New York: Vintage, 1963.

--------. Twilight of the Idols and the Anti-Christ. Ed. R. J.
    Hollingsdale. Harmondsworth: Penguin, 1968.

Nyiszli, Miklos. Auschwitz. New York: Fawcett, 1960.

Oakeshott, Michael. On Human Conduct. Oxford: Clarendon Press,
    Oxford University Press, 1975.

Parekh, Bikhu C. Hannah Arendt and the Search for a New Political
    Philosophy. London: Macmillan, 1981.

Parel, A.J., ed. The Political Calculus. Toronto: University of Toronto
Press,1972.

Peters, Richard S. The Concept of Motivation. 2nd ed., London:
    Routledge and Kegan Paul, 1960.

Pitkin, Hanna Fenichel. The Concept of Representation. Berkley,
California: University of California Press, 1967.

Plato. The Collected Dialogues. Eds. E. Hamilton and H. Cairns.
    Princeton: Princeton University Press, 1961.

Pocock, J.G.A. The Machiavellian Movement. Princeton: Princeton
    University Press, 1975.

--------. Politics, Language and Time. New York: Atheneum, 1971.

Podhoretz, Norman. Doings and Undoings. New York: Noonday, 1964. (Includes his essay on Eichmann.)

Rawls, John. Theory of Justice. Cambridge, Massachusetts: Harvard University Press, 1970.

Robinson, Jacob. And the Crooked Shall be Made Straight: The Eichmann Trial, The Jewish Catastrophe, and Hannah Arendt's Narrative. Philadelphia: Jewish Publication Society, 1965.

Rosenberg, Harold. Act and the Actor. World Publishing, New York: World Publishing, 1970.

Rousseau, Jean-Jacques. Discourse on the Origins of Inequality. Edited and translated with an introduction by Roger and Judith Masters. New York: St. Martin's Press, 1964.

--------. Politics and the Arts. Ed. A. Bloom. New York: Cornell University Press, 1968.

--------. The Social Contract. Translated and with an introduction by Willmoore Kendall. Chicago: Henry Regnery Co., 1954.

Rubenstein, Richard L. The Cunning of History: The Holocaust and the American Future. New York: Harper Colophon, 1978.

Saner, Hans. Kant's Political Thought. Chicago: University of Chicago Press, 1967.

Sartre. Jean-Paul. Being and Nothingness. Trans. Hazel Barnes. New York: Washington Square Press, 1966.

--------. Search for a Method. Trans. Hazel Barnes. New York: Vintage, 1963.

Sharp. Gene. Social Power and Political Freedom. Boston: Porter Sargent Publishers, Inc., 1980.

Skinner, B.F. About Behaviorism. New York: Vintage, 1974.

--------. Beyond Freedom and Dignity. New York: Vintage, 1971.

Strauss, Leo. The political Philosophy of Hobbes. Chicago: Phoenix, 1963.

--------. Natural Right and History. Chicago: University of Chicago Press, 1953.

--------. Thoughts on Machiavelli. Seattle: University of Washington Press, 1958.

Streller, J. Jean-Paul Sartre, to Freedom Condemned. Translated and with an introduction by Wade Baskin. New York: Philosophical Library, 1960.

Taylor, A.E. Plato: The Man and his Work. London: Methuen, 1948.

Taylor, Charles. The Explanation of Behaviour. New York: Humanities Press, 1964.

Tocqueville, A. de. Democracy in America. Ed. J.P. Mayer. New York: Doubleday, 1969.

Tolle, Gordon J. Human Nature Under Fire: The Political Philosophy of Hannah Arendt. Washington D.C.: University Press of America, 1982.

Voegelin, Eric. The New Science of Politics. Chicago: University of Chicago Press, 1952.

Whitfield, Stephen J. Into the Dark: Hannah Arendt and Totalitarianism. Philadelphia: Temple University Press, 1980.

Woetzel, Robert. Philosophy of Freedom. New York: Oceana Publications, 1966.

Wolin, Sheldon S. Politics and Vision. Boston: Little, Brown and Co., 1960.

Young-Bruehl, Elisabeth. Freedom and Karl Jaspers' Philosophy. New Haven and London: Yale University Press, 1981.

--------. Hannah Arendt: For Love of the World. New Haven and London: Yale University Press, 1982.

Zimmern, Alfred. The Greeks' Commonwealth: Politics and Economics in Fifth Century Athens. London: Oxford University Press, 1931.

Zoll, Donald Atwell. Twentieth Century Political Philosophy. Englewood Cliffs, N.J.: Prentice-Hall, 1974.

BIBLIOGRAPHY

DISSERTATIONS (These are unpublished works on Hannah Arendt.)

Allen, Wayne Francis. "The Concept of Authority in the Thought of Hannah Arendt." Diss. University of California, Riverside, 1979.

Dossa, Shiraz Abdul Noormohaned. "The Public Realm and the Public Self in the Thought of Hannah Arendt." Diss. Unversity of Toronto, 1983.

Edwards, Scott E. "The Political Thought of Hannah Arendt: A Study in Thought and Action." Diss. Claremont Graduate School, 1964.

Hall, Mary Elisabeth. "The Meaning of Being Human in Selected Works of Hannah Arendt." Diss. University of Denver, 1977.

Hansen, Phillip Birger. "A Critical Philosophy and its Critical Limits: the Aesthetic Dimension of Hannah Arendt's Political Thought." Diss. University of Toronto, 1981.

Hinchman, Sandra Kuracina. "Hannah Arendt's Phenomenology of Politics." Diss. Cornell University, 1977.

Khan, Vera Suzanne. "Hannah Arendt: A Study in Anti-Utopia." Diss. University of Michigan, 1971.

Klein, Mary Katherine McKeon. "The Concept of Political Freedom in Hannah Arendt." Diss. Boston University Graduate School, 1973.

Knauer, James T. "Hannah Arendt and the Reassertion of the Political: Toward a New Democratic Theory." Diss. State University of New York at Binghampton, 1975.

Leddy, Mary Joanna. "The Event of the Holocaust and the Philosophical Reflections of Hannah Arendt." Diss. University of Toronto, 1980.

Martin, Richard Thomas. "Nietzsche and Arendt: On Public Action in Mass Society." Diss. Kent State University, 1977.

McClusky, John Evans. "A Dilemma of Existential Political Theory: An Analysis of Political Cohesion and Freedom in the Writings of Jean-Paul Sartre and Hannah Arendt." Diss. University of California, Berkeley, 1971.

McKenna, George N. "A Critic of Modernity: The Political Thought of Hannah Arendt." Diss. Fordham University, 1967.

BIBLIOGRAPHY

Meyerson, Robert Eric. "Hannah Arendt: Romantic in a Totalitarian Age 1928-1963." Diss. University of Minnesota, 1972.

Modschiedler, John Christian Emigholz. "Fundamental Thought and Political Action in the Works of Martin Heidegger and Hannah Arendt: Towards a Hermeneutic of Violence." Diss. The University of Chicago, 1980.

Olsen, Gary Raymond. "The Effort to Escape from Temporal Consciousness as Expressed in the Thought and Work of Herman Hesse, Hannah Arendt, and Karl Loewith." Diss. University of Arizona, 1973.

Roach, Timothy Shawn. "Appearance in History: Hannah Arendt's Metaphorical Logic of the Person." Diss. Duke University, 1981.

Skaperdas, Theodore. "Arendt's Concept of Politics" (M.A. Thesis). Diss. McGill University, 1972.

Washington, Johnny. "Hannah Arendt's Conception of the Political Realm." Diss. Stanford University, 1978.

Waterman, Robert Dunning, Jr. "Political Action: Dialogues with Hannah Arendt." Diss. University of California, Berkeley, 1978.

Young, jon Morgan. "The Concept of 'Worldlessness' in the Thought of Hannah Arendt." Diss. Florida State University, 1982.